Working in International Child Health

2nd Edition

Author

American Academy of Pediatrics
Section on International Child Health

Editors

Caroline Dueger, MD, MPH, FAAP
Cliff O'Callahan, MD, PhD, FAAP

American Academy of Pediatrics
141 Northwest Point Blvd
Elk Grove Village, IL 60007-1098

Library of Congress Control Number: 2008925449
ISBN-13: 978-1-58110-332-8
MA0476

13-1/0508
Last digit is the print number: 9 8 7 6 5 4 3 2 1

Editors

Caroline Dueger, MD, MPH, FAAP
Retired Pediatrician
Concord, NH

Cliff O'Callahan, MD, PhD, FAAP
Assistant Professor of Pediatrics
Middlesex Hospital/University of Connecticut
Middletown, CT

Contributing Editors

Bronwen Anders, MD, FAAP
Professor of Pediatrics
University of California–San Diego
San Diego, CA

Jonathan Spector, MD, MPH, FAAP
Assistant Professor of Pediatrics
University of Massachusetts Medical School
Worcester, MA

Kajal Khanna, MD
Fellow
University of California–San Francisco
San Francisco, CA

Table of Contents

Acknowledgments

Working in International Child Health was originally published in 2000. The 2008 edition is revised and printed with the permission of the original authors: Donna Staton, MD, editor; Christopher Harding, PhD; Anthony Berner, MD; John Edelsberg, MD; Marcus Harding, MD; and Susan Kalma, MD.

We gratefully acknowledge Walter Dueger, MD, for his photographs, which appear throughout the book.

Foreword

A Note From the American Academy of Pediatrics Section on International Child Health

We are proud to share this new edition with you and hope that you will not only enjoy using it, but find much of what you seek from such a book. We strive to continually update and improve on it, and can do this better with your help through feedback to wiichedit@aap. net. The Section on International Child Health (SOICH) Web site (www.aap.org/sections/ich) will have an area with updates that occur between editions.

The SOICH consists of members and affiliates from around the globe who are passionate about children's health in general, and especially the health of those in vulnerable conditions. Members are pediatricians who are fellows of the American Academy of Pediatrics (AAP) from North America as well as international members, while section affiliates are any professionals who take a serious interest in global children's health. We support the Millennium Development Goals through our goals and objectives.

The overarching SOICH goal reflects that of the AAP: We are committed to improving the health and well-being of the world's children. This will be accomplished by addressing the needs of children, families, and health workers through education, service, advocacy, and the facilitation of effective global partnerships. To accomplish this lofty goal, we concentrate our efforts in 4 strategic areas: education, service, advocacy, and partnerships/diplomacy. I invite you to learn more about the most current specific activities within each strategic area by going to our Web site. I would like to point out 2 of our programs in particular. One is our financial support of pediatric resident travel grants, which we believe is a critical investment in the experiential training of the next generation of global health workers. The other is our International Community Access to Child Health

(I-CATCH) program of grants for our pediatric colleagues, primarily in areas of great need, to initiate or expand on unique community endeavors.

I assume that in picking up this book you are interested in the health of children everywhere. Therefore, please consider also looking at our Web site for more resources. There you will find archives of our general and review newsletters. Please enjoy and be well.

Cliff O'Callahan, MD, PhD, FAAP

Introduction

Overview

This manual is a guide for anyone interested in working or volunteering in international child health. It is designed to provide information and advice not easily found in other sources. Most sections are written primarily for people from developed countries who want to become more involved in caring for children in poorer nations. Other sections are designed to benefit those already in the field. It begins with resources and recommendations on how to prepare for international health work. Details are included about helpful training, continuing medical education, certification and degree courses, books, newsletters, CD-ROMs, and Web sites. Separate areas also discuss finding and evaluating international assignments, your own health and safety, and acronyms and definitions of terms used in international child health. Although clinical treatment guidelines are not included, numerous references for this information are provided.

The Challenge

International child health deals with the health and well-being of all children. However, by their sheer number and disproportionately heavy burden of disease and social problems, the children of developing countries are often the focus. Thus this manual reflects a preferential concern for marginalized children, especially those in developing nations who comprise most of the children on earth. In spite of gains in certain areas, such as the global eradication of smallpox and sharp declines in a few other vaccine-preventable diseases such as polio, poor children around the world continue to suffer and die in unacceptably high numbers.

The World Health Organization estimates that nearly 10 million children younger than 5 years die each year, primarily from conditions that could be easily prevented or treated with existing resources. The greatest burden of mortality falls on the world's poorest populations, who suffer from environmental conditions that promote development of illness. These include unsafe water and sanitation systems, food insecurity, broad exposure to disease vectors such as insects, and limited access to basic preventive and curative health services. Seventy percent of childhood deaths in resource-limited settings result from just 5 diseases: pneumonia, diarrhea, measles, malaria, and malnutrition. Malnutrition deserves special mention; given its dramatic effects on multiple organ systems it is implicated as an underlying factor in close to half of all child deaths. Also of note is the disproportionately large burden of disease carried by the world's youngest children. Approximately 4 million deaths annually occur in infants during the first month of life, principally from birth asphyxia, sepsis, and complications related to prematurity. Fortunately, many interventions that target global childhood illness are not expensive or sophisticated. The challenge for the international community is timely, effective translation of resources from industrialized countries to parts of the world where they are most needed.

Who Cares for Children?

Most of the world's children will never see a pediatrician. Living in developing countries, they are cared for locally; their caregivers are most often community health workers, traditional healers, or nurses. Local resources are often supplemented by outside assistance from wealthy countries, but largely remain inadequate. This assistance can be technical, financial, or programmatic. Technical assistance comes largely from agencies like the World Health Organization or the United Nations Children's Fund (UNICEF), which recommend policies and give guidance in implementing them. Financial assistance may be through grants or in the form of favorable loans from institutions like the World Bank that lends about $2 billion annually for health. This expenditure represents an investment of less than 50 cents per person per year in developing countries. Programmatic assistance can take the form of vaccination campaigns coordinated between intergovernmental agencies like UNICEF and local ministries of health. When all outside financial assistance for health from wealthy nations is added up, it amounts to around $1 per year per person in the developing world. With this help added to local resources, children in the poorest nations can hope to receive only in the range of $5 to $20 per year worth of health services. Such meager care in the setting of inadequate parental education, lack of children's educational opportunities, civil conflict, governmental mismanagement, malnutrition, unclean water supplies, or tropical diseases greatly increases childhood morbidity and mortality. These children, at such high risk for vaccine-preventable diseases, do not even receive the same vaccinations children in wealthier nations can expect. Despite all this, significant progress has been made. Campaigns such as the Expanded Program on Immunizations and the use of oral rehydration therapy are sparing the lives of millions of children. Yet, the lives of several million additional children could be saved if existing vaccines were more widely used.

Why Assignments Abroad Can Be Difficult to Find

One of the paradoxes that becomes immediately apparent to almost anyone in the field is that although there are tremendous health needs in many developing countries, it is often difficult to find meaningful assignments working with children. Much of this difficulty relates to the lack of resources described previously. Relief organizations and local clinics and hospitals have very limited funds in comparison to the problems they face. They are regularly forced to make difficult resource allocation choices. Oftentimes, for example, the cost of airfare from the United States or Europe may exceed the annual salary paid to a local health employee. Thus they usually cannot afford to pay transport and housing even for volunteer health staff. Sometimes organizations hesitate to accept foreign or inexperienced health staff because they know that adapting to local conditions may be a slow or difficult process. Despite these obstacles, however, with a little effort one can find very rewarding assignments.

Challenges and Barriers to Health Work Abroad

Everyone who begins work in another country faces challenges such as lack of familiarity with local diseases, customs, and languages. Simply by virtue of their appearance, foreigners may be regarded with apprehension or mistrust by patients and other health staff. Adjusting to very hot climates or highly emotional situations (like refugee camps) can be a problem. For some, security issues and the inability to adapt to different living standards, customs, and food are also challenges. Frustrations sometimes arise because testing and treatment options are lacking, and referral and consultation options may be limited. The information in the following chapters is intended to help make meeting these challenges a little easier!

Chapter 1

Supporting International Health Efforts While at Home

Many people have personal, financial, career, or family constraints that prevent them from traveling abroad to work. Fortunately there are many ways that they can still contribute meaningfully from home to improve the lives of poor children abroad.

Here are some practical ways to help.

- Donate money and raise funds for worthwhile organizations. (For Web sites to help evaluate programs and organizations with respect to their goals and financial health, please see the list at the end of this chapter.)

- Participate in international child health educational activities (eg, through helping arrange resident and student electives and conferences, or by lecturing at and attending professional organizational meetings on international health).

- Donate supplies and equipment.

- Choose research subjects that have broad international implications rather than those that focus only on children in developed nations.

- Provide logistical support (Smaller organizations may need help securing and shipping supplies and equipment. You may be able to help with this.)

- Lend moral support to colleagues working on international child health issues. Offer to cover their practices if they are going abroad on a relief trip.

- Network with international colleagues for collaboration on projects or visitor exchange. Two new Internet-based networks, International Child Health Network (www.ichn.org/) and Global Medicine Network (www.globalmedicine.org/), can help you establish connections.

- Participate in advocacy or political campaigns that you think may benefit poor children abroad.

- Work with refugee children in the United States.

Donating Supplies and Equipment

Donated supplies and equipment are of great value to many health programs in under-resourced areas. The key is to be able to send only items that are truly needed. Useless materials only waste transportation costs and become a burden to the recipients. Communication with the people on-site or with other appropriate personnel is essential to proper planning. In general, worthwhile supply items include

- Bandages
- Items that can be re-sterilized, such as glass syringes or feeding tubes
- Hemoglobin color scale materials
- Medicines—but only those needed for the illnesses at hand, and not those outdated or within 6 months of expiration date
- Sterile needles
- Orthopedic plaster and reusable orthopedic splints
- Sutures
- Surgical tape
- Urine/blood test sticks

Worthwhile equipment is generally low-tech, durable, repairable, and in good condition. Examples include

- Autoclaves (basic models)
- Cast saws
- Centrifuges (hand-operated or basic electric models)
- Durable blood pressure equipment
- Electric generators
- Glass thermometers
- Laundering equipment

- Microscopes (good quality)
- Personal work items—stethoscopes, eyewear, face masks
- Reusable surgical or dental equipment (in good condition)
- X-ray machines (basic models)

Appropriate educational material and textbooks can be useful to medical relief projects. Unfortunately, most medical books are written in developed countries primarily for problems of developed countries. Most of the more appropriate material is published in Europe and is a little harder to find. See our Annotated Bibliography for Work in Developing Countries in Appendix A or visit Teaching-aids At Low Cost at www.talcuk.org/. Again, knowing which items to send usually requires direct communication with on-site personnel.

If you would like to help collect and donate items but aren't sure where to start, the American College of Surgeons Web site (www.operationgivingback.facs.org) lists organizations throughout the country that can help. Some of these are listed below.

Recovered Medical Equipment for the Developing World
3-TMP, 333 Cedar St
PO Box 208051
New Haven, CT 06520-8051
Phone: 203/737-5356
Fax: 203/785-5241
E-mail: remedy@yale.edu
Web: www.remedyinc.org

American Medical Resources Foundation
PO Box 3609
Brockton, MA 02304
Phone: 508/580-3301
Fax: 508/580-3306
E-mail: info@amrf.com
Web: www.amrf.com.amrf.com

Direct Relief International

27 S La Patera Lane
Santa Barbara, CA 93117
Phone: 805/964-4767
Fax: 805/681-4838
Web: www.directrelief.org

Child Family Health International

995 Market St, Suite 1104
San Francisco, CA 94103
Phone: 866/345-4674
Fax: 415/840-0486
E-mail: Info@cfhi.org
Web: www.cfhi.org

Partners in Health

641 Huntington Ave, 1st Floor
Boston, MA 02115
Phone: 617/432-3714 (donations)
Fax: 617/431-5300
E-mail: medicaldonations@pih.org
Web: www.pih.org

The following are Web sites that may be useful in evaluating organizations or nongovernmental organizations for potential donations:

Charity Navigator
www.charitynavigator.org
American Institute of Philanthropy
www.charitywatch.org
Independent Charities of America
www.independentcharities.org/index.asp
Better Business Bureau Wise Giving Alliance
www.give.org

Chapter 2

Getting Information About Opportunities

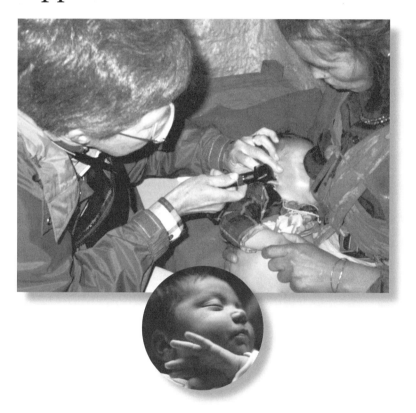

Get Leads by Word of Mouth

Almost everyone knows or has heard of someone in his or her area who has done some kind of international work. Sometimes you have just read about someone in a newspaper. If you don't have personal contacts, just ask around and you will surely find a few leads. You will find that most people are happy to share their experiences and give advice. Often they can introduce you to the proper contacts overseas and help pave the way for you to make a visit or to team up with an organization.

Getting in touch with doctors, nurses, health care workers, or other people from developing countries who are visiting or living in your area can also be productive. Often they can connect you with friends or relatives in other parts of the world that might interest you. Another good means of acquiring contacts is through acquaintances in the diplomatic service or through people working in relief and development agencies. A personal introduction from them can help open many doors. Regardless of which approach you use, don't be shy!

Scan Journals, Newspapers, Magazines

One of the best publications is *International Career Employment Weekly* published by the Carlyle Corporation (804/985-6444, www.internationaljobs.org).

InterAction, a consortium of health and development organizations, publishes *Monday Developments,* a biweekly newsletter that has an excellent section on available volunteer and paid positions. It is available by subscription by calling InterAction at 202/667-8227 or e-mailing publications@interaction.org.

Newspapers and magazines may carry stories with potential contact information, and periodically medical journals such as *Journal of the American Medical Association* (1999;282:413–418) and *American Journal of Tropical Medicine and Hygiene* publish directories of opportunities. *Diversion* magazine has a yearly edition devoted to medical volunteering.

Inquire at Medical Schools, Hospitals, and Public Health Schools

Departmental offices usually know which staff members are involved in overseas projects. Many academic medical institutions have faculty involved with programs such as Global Health Education Consortium (www.globalhealth-ec.org).

Inquire Through Religious Groups

Much of the US-based nongovernmental international health care is provided by faith-based organizations. Whether or not you belong to such an organization, chances are you can get some information about working on one of their projects. For example, *Connections,* a directory of lay volunteer positions, published by St Vincent Pallotti Center, is available by calling toll free at 877/865-5465 (www.pallotticenter.org, e-mail pallotti@pallotticenter.org). The Christian Medical & Dental Society (www.cmda.org) and the American Jewish World Service (www.ajws.org) also recruit medical volunteers.

Inquire in Person While Traveling Abroad

A very effective way of finding suitable positions can be to inquire in person while you are traveling. This strategy allows you to bypass some of the formalities that may be imposed by central offices, acquire firsthand knowledge of the people and facilities, and negotiate directly a mutually satisfactory work arrangement. The information you collect can also be shared with others. Even if a particular site is not right for you, it may be perfect for someone else. If you are overseas and are unclear where to start your search, simply introduce yourself to whatever health care facilities or churches you come across. They can often steer you to interesting sites and programs.

Inquire at Meetings/Courses Related to International Health

There are many international health–related courses and meetings conducted each year. Consider using these as opportunities to exchange information with colleagues who may know of sites or programs of interest. Medicus Mundi (www.healthtraining.org) has searchable international health–related course listings. ReliefWeb (www.reliefweb.int) also maintains extensive course information. International Health Exchange (IHE) and the London School of Hygiene and Tropical Medicine have numerous short and long courses. (See Selected International Health/Tropical Medicine Training Centers in Appendix E.) A more complete listing of international training programs in tropical medicine and health is available through the American Society of Tropical Medicine and Hygiene Web site at www.astmh.org.

Check With Professional Organizations

Become involved and aware of the activities of groups such as the American Academy of Pediatrics (AAP) Section on International Child Health (www.aap.org/sections/ich), the International Pediatric Association (www.ipa-world.org), or the Global Health Council (www.globalhealth.org). Many AAP chapters now have committees on international health, providing a local fellowship of residents and pediatricians to share experiences and resources.

Subscribe to Mailing Lists

Read nongovernmental organization newsletters; most groups will send you their newsletter with recruitment information.

Search Internet Lists of Opportunities

Two new Internet-based networks, International Child Health Network (www.ichn.org) and Global Medicine Network (www.globalmedicine.org) can make finding opportunities easier by allowing health and development workers to establish personal and professional contacts with others around the world.

Many international health organizations have Web sites that list their employment and volunteer opportunities.

The AAP Section on International Child Health maintains the searchable online Directory of International Service Opportunities for Pediatricians (www.aap.org/cgi-bin/overseas/aapartcl.cfm). It lists organizations that need volunteer pediatricians and other health personnel to work overseas.

The International Medical Volunteers Association is devoted exclusively to medical volunteerism. Its Web site (www.imva.org) is a clearinghouse of information including profiles and contact information for more than 150 medical volunteer–seeking groups. Potential volunteers can also personally register so that organizations can contact them for possible future assignments. The site also contains many links and advice for the first-time volunteer. E-mail them at info@imva.org.

Voluntary Service Overseas (www.vso.org.uk/doctors) also places volunteers. The organization works closely with the Royal College of Paediatrics and Child Health to facilitate a 12-month fellowship for pediatricians ST3, ST4, and up. Volunteers would have to be familiar with the British educational system because fellows teach and examine local students and residents.

The IHE in London (www.redr.org.uk) recruits health care workers (mostly from Europe) to work abroad (e-mail: info@ihe.org.uk).

Finally, a current listing of paid humanitarian job openings is posted by ReliefWeb at www.reliefweb.int/vacancies.

Chapter 3

Evaluating Potential
Assignments

Choosing opportunities carefully and making advanced preparations are well worth the effort. You may want to begin by assessing where you would like to work and for how long, and what special skills, including language, you have to contribute. Consider what kind of setting (rural/urban, clinic/hospital, war zone/refugee camp) would interest you. Think about whether you will go alone or with family or colleagues. Even reflect on whether religious missionary work is part of what you will be looking for. Then get in touch with organizations that interest you. The following considerations can help you evaluate your options.

Working Conditions

- Will your skills be well utilized? Is prior overseas experience required?
- How will local personnel be affected by your presence?
- What kind of training have the support staff and your colleagues had?
- What will be your work schedule?
- How many patients will you see each day?
- Will you have sufficient time off? Is "home-leave" available for those performing long-term service?
- What kinds of laboratory, diagnostic, referral, and consultation options are available?
- For students and residents, will this assignment qualify as a bona fide rotation? What type of supervision and teaching can you expect?
- Will there be enough interesting clinical material to make it worthwhile?

Facilities and Equipment

- At how many and at what kind of facilities will you be expected to work?

- How far are the sites from your living quarters?

- Who pays for and arranges transportation?

- What are the physical condition and upkeep of the buildings?

- Are electricity and uncontaminated water always available?

- What kind of equipment is available? Will it be familiar?

- Can you bring equipment that will work on local power sources?

- What happens when repairs are needed?

Licensing and Documentation

Valid US credentials are adequate for volunteer work in many but not all under-resourced countries.

- Is a passport, visa, or local work permit required?

- How long will it take to obtain the necessary licensing or documentation? What documents must you provide?

- If a special license is required, will your sponsoring organization assist with the paperwork?

Personal Health

An appointment with a travel clinic is usually all you need to obtain necessary advice, prescriptions, and vaccines.

- What immunizations are required or recommended for the region in which you will be serving?

- Are mosquito nets recommended for sleeping?

- Is malaria prophylaxis an issue?

- Will you have access to sanitation facilities and potable water?

Insurance

- Will your current US health, disability, and life insurance policies cover travel and service overseas?

- Does your sponsoring organization provide any coverage?

- What medical liability insurance (if any) is required or recommended? (See Chapter 7, page 51.)

Communication

What means are reliably available for you to communicate with your family and sponsoring organization back home: mail, telephone, cell phone, satellite phone, e-mail, fax, etc?

In Case of Trouble

- What kind of protection and assistance can you expect from governmental representatives and/or local authorities in the event of difficulties?

- Should you plan to register with your nation's consulate when you arrive?

- Have you left a detailed itinerary and other information (passport number, date and place of issuance, airline ticket numbers, credit card numbers, etc) with a resourceful individual back home?

Language

- What languages will you be expected to communicate in?

- In what language are medical records kept?

- If language training is required, who will pay for it?

- Will instruction take place before or after arrival?

- If it is not possible for you to learn the language, are there competent medical interpreters available where you will be working and living?

Culture

- Are you cognizant of and prepared for the customs and taboos of the culture where you will be practicing, which may differ greatly from the customs that you may be assuming are "universal"? In some countries, for example, it may be considered inappropriate to pat a child on the head, which is seen as the seat of the soul.

- Do any religious or cultural practices impinge on the practice of medicine (circumcision, dietary restrictions, concepts of modesty that may hamper physical examination)?

- Have you considered how you will react to culture shock, home-sickness, anti-Western sentiment, suspicion, and even ingratitude for your sacrifices?

Environment

- What range of weather conditions can you expect during your period of service? Inquire if any roads become impassable during the rainy season.

- Is there real danger from earthquakes, monsoons, or the like?

- What kind of insects and animals are you likely to encounter?

- What kind of clothing and equipment will you need to contend with these creatures (eg, mosquito netting, high boots)?

Living Conditions/Dependents

- Where will you live?

- Who will pay for room and board?

- How safe and feasible is it to bring your family along?

- Can you bring along a partner to whom you are not married?

- What will the food be like?

- Will you have sufficient privacy?

- Are electricity and uncontaminated water always available?

- How secure are your quarters?
- Are you personally willing to conform with local customs (such as refraining from alcohol) or specific dress codes?

With planning and a little research, one can avoid or improve assignments that might otherwise be unproductive, unrewarding, or overly demanding.

Chapter 4

Preparing for Work in Bon Chien, Haiti, or Banda Aceh, Indonesia—Sample Cases

To illustrate the importance of making ready, consider the following example and imagine how different things would be if these preparations were neglected.

You and your spouse have agreed to work for 2 months at a small mission hospital in the rural Haitian town of Bon Chien. One of you is a pediatrician; the other is a nurse. You will be bringing along your children, ages 4 and 7. You have never been to Haiti. The organization you joined up with sends you a packet of information, which provides an overview of the country, a brief description of the hospital, and instructions detailing where and when you will be met at the Port-au-Prince airport.

You want to prepare yourself and your family as well as possible, so you begin by going to a large bookstore. There you find that only 2 of the 10 guides to the Caribbean even cover Haiti. You buy the better of the two. Browsing through it you discover that most Haitians speak Kreyol rather than French as you had thought. The clerk orders you a small Kreyol language instruction book. The next day you call a foreign language specialty bookshop and obtain an English-Kreyol dictionary, some audiotapes, and even an English-Kreyol medical translator book.

Using Radio-locator.com and Web-radio.com, you search for Haitian Internet radio stations and quickly come across Radiovision 2000. As a bonus, its Web site offers hourly text updates/news bulletins of Haitian current affairs in French and English—a great way to get the pulse of the country.

You begin to wonder just what kinds of diseases you will be treating, so you send a letter to Dr Mudge, the hospital administrator, asking for more details. Not sure how long it will take to get a reply, you surf the Internet and find that the Pan American Health Organization has a fairly recent report on health conditions in Haiti. You learn that there are several diseases you have never seen. Also, as you suspected, tuberculosis is common, and you recall that you have treated very few cases. You therefore go to a nearby medical library and find some helpful chapters and articles. In addition, you decide to buy a copy of *Manson's Tropical Diseases* and the American Academy of Pediatrics *Red Book: Report of the Committee on Infectious Diseases* to take along as general references. You go online to WHOLINK, the World Health Organization's library, and print out several specific documents dealing directly with diagnosing and treating tuberculosis in children in developing countries.

Seeking still more information, you phone the American office of your sponsoring organization. Although they can't tell you just what kind of diagnostic equipment is available, they do give you the names of 2 people who recently were at the hospital for a short stay. Calling one of them, Carolyn, produces some important news. All 4 doctors on-site are called on to perform some basic ultrasounds and blood, stool, and urine microscopy when on night call. You will likely be obliged to do the same. Therefore, you take a 1-week ultrasound course and begin to brush up on your microscopy skills.

Having read a little about the political problems in Haiti, you ask about safety in the countryside. You learn that Bon Chien is both beautiful and secure. Political intrigue never troubled this idyllic coastal town even in the days of "Papa Doc" and his "Tonton Macouts."

Carolyn makes it clear that your children will be well taught at the mission school. However, the classes are in French. You decide that they will need to start learning it now. You realize that you too must brush up your high school French because that is the language used to communicate with the nurses.

To get better prepared, you hire Monsieur Jacques, a Haitian man who works at your hospital, to tutor you and your family twice a week in both Kreyol and French. From him you learn many things about Haitian culture and traditions. Your kids ask what kind of sports the Haitian children play. He responds that they like soccer, but that few rural kids can afford a ball. Although Monsieur Jacques was raised in the city, he is familiar with the rural people in Bon Chien. You learn something about their daily lives and their burdens of malnutrition and illiteracy. He speculates on their likely views of science and Western medicine. His voice becomes a little hushed when he speaks of Voodoo. You discuss how these practices and beliefs might affect the way you care for your patients.

A letter arrives from old Dr Mudge in Haiti. He is very happy that you are coming. He especially looks forward to having your spouse help in the dispensary and maternity ward. You both begin to wonder how the 7 midwives there will react. Somewhat daunted by the prospect of these new responsibilities, your spouse enrolls in a 4-week course in health care in developing countries at a local public health school. You wish that you could attend as well.

Carolyn tells you that the hospital is on a very tight budget and that most patients cannot afford to pay for the medicines they receive. You decide to collect donated medicines and supplies and get promises from your colleagues to do the same. You are very careful to get only the kinds of medicines that Carolyn says will be of use. You also ask the scrub nurses at your hospital to collect opened but unused suture material and other recyclable supplies. They promise to continue sending whatever they can.

A few months before your departure date, you and your family visit a local travel clinic to get the recommended vaccinations including oral typhoid, hepatitis A, and polio and tetanus boosters. You learn that all of you must take chloroquine weekly.

Over the final weeks before leaving, you collect and ship books and supplies you now know you will be needing. Realizing that there will be no television you decide to stock up on a few more children's books, an AM-FM shortwave radio that runs on batteries or hand crank, and snorkeling equipment. Since there is no electricity past 8 pm, you purchase rechargeable flashlights, four 12-volt fans, a battery charger, and an electrical inverter. With these items and car batteries you will purchase in Haiti, you plan to provide your family with a little nighttime lighting, relief from the heat, and radio service. As a final thought, you purchase a few gifts for your new colleagues and a half dozen inexpensive soccer balls, which you carefully deflate for shipping.

Another letter arrives from Dr Mudge. He is having great difficulty in finding a certain spare part for the diesel generator. Since you will be the next arrival, he asks that you try to bring the part. This turns out to be terribly important. Eight days before you get there, the generator conks out. Awaiting you (and the spare parts you are bringing), hospital life has become much more difficult. Without the electric pump to raise water to the storage tank, Bernard, an orderly, must toil 6 hours a day at a hand pump to meet the hospital's minimum water requirements. The autoclave, toilets, and sinks can function, but laundering must be performed in a river 3 km away. Kerosene lanterns (a significant fire hazard) are pressed into service, but they are too weak for surgical lighting, and too dangerous to use around oxygen. A pickup truck is rigged to power 3 automobile headlamps fashioned into a makeshift operating room light. Without regular electric power, laboratory testing is curtailed, and no x-rays can be performed. Small wonder that you are greeted so warmly when you arrive!

You and your husband applied online to International Medical Corps (IMC) to do overseas volunteer work 10 days after the Tsunami. You get an e-mail asking if you can be ready in 48 hours to go to Banda Aceh, Indonesia. They send a list of personal items needed. You have time to update vaccines, get travel documents together, and buy malaria prophylaxis pills, starting them right away. You pick up a few items from the list at REI and buy Pimsleur CDs on the Indonesian language. On the second day you get a list of medicines and supplies that they hope you can collect, since the needed larger shipments will not have arrived. This includes ketamine, bandages, anesthetics, and antibiotics. You call administrators from hospitals, pharmacies, and clinics where you have contacts, and donations are immediately forthcoming. You prepare to fill up a large duffle bag with these items. You have been assured by IMC that Malaysian Airlines will not be concerned with weight and will help to waive customs restrictions. Your diagnostic kit runs on batteries and you stock up. You know from other experiences that a memory stick can be useful to share pictures with colleagues and to download information from the United Nations epidemiological clearinghouse because it will get up and running before Internet is reestablished. You download the latest information on treatment of diseases (eg, malaria, measles) and any information on specific diseases in the area from the Centers for Disease Control and Prevention Web site. You download a couple of updated manuals, throw in some crayons, knowing that the back of these sheets can be used for art therapy for the children. You line up contact information for friends and family for occasional Internet communications. And you take off, expecting the unexpected.

Chapter 5

Preparing for Assignments in Under-Resourced Areas

If you will be working in an under-resourced area, your preparation will depend largely on where and for how long you are going, as well as on what you will be doing. Consider that international child health work varies in the following important ways.

Duration	weekend ↔ lifetime
Timing	intermittent ↔ continuous
	early in career ↔ mid-career ↔ late in career
Physical setting	rural/urban
	tropical/temperate
Work setting	mobile clinic ↔ year-round clinic ↔ hospital ↔ referral hospital
	refugee setting
	stable area ↔ area of conflict
	disaster ↔ chronically underserved ↔ well-resourced
Duties	clinical care ↔ teaching ↔ administration ↔ public health
Working	alone ↔ small organization ↔ large international group
	religious ↔ secular organization
Living	alone ↔ with family ↔ group housing

Thinking in these terms can help you choose assignments and focus your preparation efforts. **Probably the single most important step in preparing for an assignment is to find out specifically what you will be doing.** You can do this by talking to people who have recently been to your intended destination. Call, write, e-mail, or even visit ahead of time to get a clear idea of exactly what you will be asked to do. Ask about which diseases are encountered. Remember to take into account the time of year you will be going, since disease patterns frequently change with the season. Try to ensure that at least the minimum resources will be available to allow you to function in your medical capacity (some organizations, especially smaller ones, may have unrealistic expectations as to what you can do). With this information you can make more informed decisions about any training, books, instruments, or supplies you may need.

Many people who work abroad for a short time or the first time find it difficult to do much preparatory research, but even modest efforts are well worthwhile. Those choosing to commit to a career of service should ideally start to prepare as early as possible. It is, of course, desirable to study the languages of the part of the world where you will work. (See Language Preparation on page 36.) You may want to seek specific training in fields such as administration, accounting, public health, tropical medicine, education, and even anthropology. Although you may be a doctor, nurse, or pharmacist, you may be called on to perform administrative and planning functions. This sort of double duty is particularly common on long-term assignments. A little training beforehand can come in handy. Formal instruction in working well with others (especially with people from other cultures) is often extremely helpful. A working understanding of electricity, plumbing, construction, and mechanics can also prove invaluable.

You might also want to learn about the organization you will be working with. If you are going long term, it may be wise to choose to work with organizations that have a philosophy that is compatible with your own. You might also like to learn about other relief groups working in the same country because you may want to share equipment, cooperate on projects, or just get their advice. The catalogs produced by the Global Health Council (formerly NCIH) and Interaction (see page 140) contain descriptions of their affiliate organizations and tables listing where they work. Armed with this information you can call the home offices to learn more about the work they are doing overseas. They can also help you to get in contact with their in-country representatives.

The better you prepare, the more effective you will be and, hence, the more rewarding you will find your experience. Don't rely on anyone or any organization to provide you with all the information you will need. In short, do everything you can think of to prepare well for the assignment you choose. When you arrive, the learning will really begin. Ask for a briefing of the situation and your duties. The foundation you have laid will help get you up to speed much faster.

Training Resources

A wide range of continuing medical education, degree, and certificate short courses are available in many countries to prepare you for work in international health. The kinds and duration of training vary considerably. A brief list of international health and tropical medicine training schools is provided below. (See Selected International Health/Tropical Medicine Training Centers in Appendix E). Several more comprehensive listings of schools and courses are available on the Internet.

- The Humanitarian Assistance Training Inventory (HATI) (www.reliefweb.int)/) contains descriptions of training materials and activities offered by United Nations agencies, Red Cross/Red Crescent Movement, intergovernmental organizations, nongovernmental organizations, bilateral aid agencies, and academic and training institutions.

- Medicus Mundi's Health Training Web site (www.healthtraining.org) provides comprehensive information on training and further education opportunities in the fields of international health, public health and health system development, health economics and management, clinical tropical medicine, and related topics.

- TropEdEurope (www.troped.org) is the training and educational branch of TROPMEDEUROP—the association of the Institutes and Schools of Tropical Medicine in Europe. It consists of 18 institutions active in the field of international health mainly through training and research from 10 European countries.

Country and Culture Resources

You are likely to have trouble working well if you don't have at least a rudimentary understanding of the local culture. It will be easy to inadvertently confuse or even offend people if you are unaware of social norms. You have a much better chance of getting patients, families, and coworkers to follow your recommendations if they are based in an understanding of local realities. Although much of this knowledge can only be gained on-site, you can begin to lay the foundation before you go. Poke around the travel and language sections of bookstores and libraries. It is almost always worthwhile to buy a good, up-to-date guidebook to take along.

The reference librarian in your public library may be very helpful, pointing out references such as *Culturgrams* (short summaries by country containing important cultural tips) or book series like *Lands and Peoples* and *Countries of the World,* which give further background. Consult your library's *Reader's Guide to Periodical Literature* or indexes of newspapers to find recent articles about your destination. Get a feel for periodicals in your destination country by previewing them through www.thepaperboy.com, which usually has several from each nation to choose from and connects you to Babelfish (www.babelfish.com) to translate.

Intercultural Press (www.interculturalpress.com) offers a wealth of books, videos, and games about living overseas and cross-cultural communications. Request their free monthly catalog.

Internet news services such as the BBC (www.bbc.co.uk) and Reuters (www.reuters.com) can help you get a better idea of the current social and political conditions. Online bookstores like Amazon.com (www.amazon.com) and Barnes and Noble (www.bn.com) have many relevant books. Oxfam (www.oxfam.org.uk/resources) sells excellent country reports. The US Library of Congress (http://lcweb2.loc.gov/frd/cs) and the US Agency for International Development (www.usaid.gov/locations) have excellent online country background publications. The Pan American Health Organization (www.paho.org) has online reports on health conditions in individual countries in the Americas. ReliefWeb (www.reliefweb.int) has recent information about major humanitarian crisis events.

Get a feel for sociopolitical conditions by tuning to local radio stations through the Internet or on shortwave radio. Radio-Locator (www.radio-locator.com) points you toward online stations. Developed at the Massachusetts Institute of Technology, it has probably the world's most extensive listing of world radio stations and formats. Also try Radio-Stations.net (www.radio-stations.net).

Health Information Resources

Once you have a clear idea of what you will be doing, brush up on relevant infectious diseases, tropical medicine, or public health subjects. The annotated bibliography included in this manual and online bookstores like Amazon.com and Barnes and Noble can get you started on books and newsletters.

The Wellcome Trust's highly acclaimed *Topics in International Health* series of interactive CD-ROMs is now available through CABI publishing (www.cabi.org). Each CD-ROM covers a topic such as diarrheal diseases, malaria, nutrition, tuberculosis, etc.

A huge amount of information is now available online including disease information, specific e-mail lists, online discussion areas, and distance training. For example, one can learn to read malaria smears on the Web courtesy of the Royal Perth Hospital in Australia (www.rph.wa.gov.au/malaria.html). You can also use free medical literature databases like the National Library of Medicine's PubMed (www.ncbi.nlm.nih.gov/sites/entrez?db=pubmed) to find up-to-date medical articles. Remember that you may not have access to this kind of information after you arrive. Copies of recent publications may be appreciated by your in-country colleagues.

Language Preparation

English, French, and Spanish are the 3 principal languages of international health. Be thankful you already know English; it is the most widely spoken language in the world, outside of China, and is an official language in approximately 85 nations and territories. French and Spanish are the most frequently studied languages in the United States, and thus you may already have some knowledge of one of them.

If you plan to work in a Spanish- or French-speaking country, it will be worth your while to study the relevant language. Classes in these 2 languages are widely available at colleges, language schools, and night schools. In addition, many hospitals sponsor courses in medical Spanish.

The best way to learn a new language is to enroll in an immersion program in a country where the language is spoken. You can get information about such programs from a local university language department or from www.linguaserviceworldwide.com. With audio, video, and computer-based programs widely available, self-study of new languages is easier than ever. Since you will primarily use these languages for conversation, you should concentrate on listening and speaking; if possible, arrange sessions with a native speaker. Language tapes and CDs are available in most large bookstores and libraries. Those developed by Berlitz, Pimsleur, and the US Department of State are generally well regarded. The *Learn in Your Car* audiotape and CD foreign language series (www.pentonoverseas.com) was designed with the traveler in mind.

Commercial television programs in both French and Spanish are shown in many urban areas of the United States and may be helpful since the dialogue is usually clear. Movies have less clear soundtracks, as a rule, and less dialogue per minute. Two college language instructional video programs developed over the past several years may be helpful: *French in Action* and *Destinos* (a Spanish-language program). You can purchase both from Annenberg Media (www.learner.org). Part I for each series includes 26 half-hour videos, a workbook, a study guide, and audiocassettes and costs $299. Part II includes 26 videos plus supplementary materials and costs $299 for *French in Action* and $255 for *Destinos*. The Web site has ordering information on these and other languages, such as German and Japanese.

If this seems too expensive, you may be able to find these programs at a local public library, or you may wish to try one of the interactive home computer–based language programs. There are many products, especially for French and Spanish students, that are fun and user-friendly, and that allow you to hear yourself as you practice. CD-ROMs with elementary language lessons can be found for less than $15 in discount bins at office supply, computer, and other stores.

When you work with audiotapes, it is important to repeat aloud the words, phrases, and sentences that you have heard. If you don't have the assistance of a teacher to help you with pronunciation, record and listen to yourself. In addition to audiotapes, another valuable tool in learning a language is vocabulary cards. You can make your own or buy commercially prepared sets. Cards that have pictures rather than English words on the flip side will assist you to think in the new language. Applause Learning Resources (www.applauselearning.com) sells sets of 100 vocabulary cards in Spanish or French for $8.95. They also offer films, DVDs, and audiotapes. If you want to read medically oriented materials in Spanish, many publications are available from the Pan American Health Organization. The World Health Organization publishes almost all of its literature in both English and French. *The Control of Communicable Diseases Manual,* published by the American Public Health Association, is available in Spanish and French editions. Finally, David Werner's *Where There Is No Doctor,* the classic guide for community health workers in developing countries, has been translated into more than 40 languages, from Arabic to Vietnamese.

Contact the Hesperian Foundation (www.hesperian.org) for the latest on health guides that have been translated into other languages. Sixteen of their health guides are now available free online.

Because of the ever-increasing number of Spanish-speaking patients seen at many US medical facilities, there exists a large variety of teaching materials for health care professionals who want to learn basic medical Spanish. Two inexpensive and useful paperbacks are *¿Que pasó? An English-Spanish Guide for Medical Personnel* by Kantrowicz, Mondragon, and Coleman, University of New Mexico Press ($6.95, available from the American Medical Student Association, 703/620-6600) and *Spanish for Health Care Professionals* by William C. Harvey, Barron's Educational Services, 1994 ($11.95). The American Academy of Pediatrics publishes *Spanish for Pediatric Medicine,* a handy spiral-bound book nicely formatted with phrases useful for well checkups for various ages as well as for sick and emergency visits.

DiLoreno-Kearon and Kearon have designed a 12-audiocassette course called *Medical Spanish* ($195). The book alone for this course is available for $20.50. Schoenhof's Foreign Books (www.schoenhofs.com) and similar foreign language specialty bookstores carry most of the medical Spanish materials mentioned here as well as several other texts and medical dictionaries. If you do not have sufficient time to study Spanish comprehensively, one of the previously mentioned specialized medical Spanish books is a must. Even if you decide to study the language in depth, these books will provide useful vocabulary and phrases often not covered in traditional Spanish courses.

Finally, cable television presents viewers with increasing choices in Spanish-language programming. Mexican-produced time-limited soap operas called *telenovelas* are geared toward world markets and are often easy to understand. English-language discussion forums and chat rooms like www.telenovelas-internet.com can help bring

English speakers up to speed and are an entertaining way to get a daily dose of colloquial Spanish.

The Cadillac of English-French dictionaries is W. Gladstone's *English-French Dictionary of Medical and Paramedical Terms* compiled in 1996 ($140), while *Pocket Medical French* by Russell Dollinger, 1995 (JDV Publishing, 800/788-0064), goes for a more affordable $9.95. In addition, Schoenhof's Foreign Books carries several medical dictionaries entirely in French at reasonable prices. For those working in Haiti, the *Haitian Kreyol (Creole)-English Pocket Medical Translator* is available from the International Medical Volunteers Association (508/435-7377, e-mail: info@imva.org). International Medical Volunteers also publishes a *Portuguese-Cape Verdean-English Pocket Medical Translator,* covering standard Portuguese, Brazilian Portuguese, and Cape Verdean dialects.

If you plan on working in a country where English, Spanish, or French is not widely spoken, we strongly urge you to study the relevant language, although Arabic, Chinese, the Indian languages, and the languages of Southeast Asia will be much more difficult to learn than Spanish or French. Even if you only learn the basics, your efforts to communicate in the local language will be greatly appreciated by the people with whom you are working. Language courses of interest may be offered in your area.

What if you're faced with a more exotic language like Moroccan Arabic, Farsi, or Tagalog? Penton Overseas has teamed up with Lonely Planet to create TravelTalk 3-in-1 Survival Kits with audio-cassettes, phrasebooks, and dictionaries (www.pentonoverseas. com). Also, Schoenhof's Foreign Books (www.schoenhofs.com) has materials for learning more than 270 languages, and Audio Forum (www.audioforum.com) sells cassette courses in 103 languages, and a smaller number in video and CD-ROM formats. Both Audio Forum and Penton Overseas also produce language courses geared toward children.

Also see Country and Culture Resources on page 34 for ways to locate online radio stations, a useful way to hear a language as it is actually spoken in your destination country.

Final Advice Before Going Abroad to Work

Try to closely study the culture where you will be working before you begin. Anticipate and plan for cultural biases regarding science, gender, medicine, and religion. For example, male physicians are sometimes forbidden to examine female patients in some Muslim countries. Sharpen your listening and observational skills to pick up on local protocol, greeting patterns, and hierarchy. Don't assume that gestures are an international kind of sign language. What you intend as innocent miming may be perceived as offensive, insulting, or otherwise provocative. Midpoint Trade Books, Inc. (New York) publishes *The Simple Guide to Customs and Etiquette in...* series, concise books on more than 35 countries and religions ($8.95–$9.95). For information and ordering, call 800/742-6139.

Think of yourself as a goodwill ambassador. Like it or not, you will also probably be regarded on some level as a representative of your country. Maintain a cooperative team spirit. If you aren't able to get along, you may adversely affect the morale of the whole team. Be as flexible as possible in everything: your schedule, the duration of service, personal comforts, etc. Keep sponsors happy so that they will invite you or others back. Maintain the mind-set that you are expending your time not only to help, but to benefit from the experience yourself. Make a real effort to keep yourself healthy on your trip. Staying healthy will allow you to work better and you won't have regrets later.

Have realistic expectations about how much you can accomplish and how local people may or may not show their gratitude. Try not to promise or imply more than you or your organization can deliver. Be prepared in case some of your in-country colleagues have different work ethics than you. Make an effort to teach whatever you can while you are there. In this way the benefits of your service will outlast your visit.

Schedule extra time at the end of your trip before you return to work to unwind and digest your experience. Extra time can also provide an often-needed cushion in the event of travel delays. Be prepared for "reentry" culture shock. You may feel that life back home is extravagant and wasteful. Two helpful resources on reentry can be read online on The Center for Global Education Web site (www. studentsabroad.com/reentrycultureshock.html) and the University of Maryland International Programs Web site (www.international. umd.edu/studyabroad/626).

Chapter 6

What to Take With You

Each trip you take helps you refine your skills at selecting and packing what you take. Many factors will influence this process: the climate to which you travel, the illnesses you expect to encounter, the kind of work you expect to be doing (eg, treating war victims in Sierra Leone vs street children in Brazil), the length of your assignment, and your personal preferences. Obviously, avoid taking items that may be prohibited or that are likely to raise eyebrows at customs. For example, several countries have restrictions on radios and require a license for their legal possession. Alcohol, literature on certain topics, sexually oriented material, even money above a certain amount may all be forbidden. Items packed in cardboard cartons often seem to attract the attention of customs officials. A good travel guidebook can alert you to which items are prohibited.

It may help to take along an official-looking letter that explains any supplies or equipment you may be carrying. Take nothing irreplaceable or very fragile. The best-laid plans can change, and that hour-long plane-hop may turn into a week in the back of a truck.

Items You May Want to Hand Carry

Verify airline regulations about items that may be packed in carry-on luggage.

- Body safe (eg, money belt or leg safe [which looks like an Ace bandage and is worn just above the knee])
- Cash: some local currency; small US bills are also often very useful
- Documents (passport, visas, yellow World Health Organization health certificate, tickets), extra passport pictures
- Essential toilet articles and a change of clothes, if possible
- Medication (perhaps with an extra prescription)—leave in original bottle and bring the prescription

- Portable burglar alarm (can be fitted to a hotel room door or into a suitcase or purse)

- Spare eyeglasses/contact lenses, sunglasses, eyeglass strap

- Small bottle of water (buy after passing security)—and a spoon

- Telephone card, phone/address book

- Traveler's checks, credit cards

- Travel guide and phrase book

- Umbrella or poncho

Other Items (for checked baggage) *(Note: Some may be available locally.)*

- Candle and matches in waterproof container (eg, film canister)

- Fitness and leisure items (eg, snorkel and mask, soccer ball, harmonica, binoculars, reading material)

- Flashlight (ordinary, rechargeable, hand-powered, and/or headlamp style)

- Gifts from home

- Laundry detergent, disinfectant spray

- Light pot for boiling water

- Medical reference books—to help with unfamiliar diseases, physical diagnosis

- Medical or surgical supplies that you believe may not be available

- Mosquito net (if likely to be needed) with pushpins, nails, and string for hanging; mosquito coils, insect sprays, and repellants

- Personal medical kit, which may include
  1. Ace bandage
  2. Activated charcoal (especially if children are coming along)
  3. Analgesic/antipyretics
  4. Antacids
  5. Anti-inflammatories (pills and cream)
  6. Anti-diarrheals

    7. Antibiotics (pills, ointment, ophthalmic)

    8. Antihistamines, nasal decongestant

    9. Antifungals (cream/powder)

  10. Antimalarials (prophylaxis and treatment)

  11. Bandages/Band-Aids

  12. Contact lens supplies

  13. Motion sickness medication

  14. Oral rehydration salts

  15. Pepto-bismol

  16. Sterile needles and syringes

  17. Additional prescription medicines

  18. Tweezers

  19. Thermometer, tape

  20. VoSol or Cortisporin otic

- Plastic bags of various size

- Radio (if not restricted by law): small, portable, shortwave, perhaps crank-powered

- Sewing kit and basic tool set

- Solar shower (where sun is plentiful, but hot showers are not)

- Strong string and a few clothespins—for drying clothes, closing curtains, etc

- Swiss army knife

- Toilet articles (including sunscreen)

- Tupperware-type containers with tight lids for food storage (because insects and/or humidity, not to mention vermin, may be a problem)

- Water filter (Katadyn or Pur brands are popular)

Clothing

In many cultures, even in deepest poverty, appearances are more important than in our frequently casual-sloppy North America. Professionals should take their cues from local counterparts. You will need clothing for whatever seasons you will be experiencing (eg, sturdy, comfortable sandals for hot climates; rubber boots for rainy ones; warm winter boots for snowy spots; and so on). In much of Africa, all clothing and linens dried outdoors are ironed to destroy fly eggs, the cause of cutaneous myiasis. Unless prohibited by local customs (eg, women in some Muslim countries), your basic wardrobe should include long-sleeved shirts and long pants to protect against both sun and mosquitoes. Insect repellent clothing under the trade name of Buzz Off and others is available at ExOfficio (www.exofficio.com) and L.L. Bean (www.llbean.com). Clothing can also be sprayed with permethrin to repel insects. Shade-giving hats are important in the tropics.

Personal Items for Clinical Work

- Boxes or ziplock bags of baby wipes—used for cleaning hands and equipment (ear speculum, stethoscope) where water is scarce
- Extra disposable gloves, masks, and eye protection
- A gown, apron, or lab coat
- Examination equipment (with spare parts)—stethoscope, oto-ophthalmoscope set (preferably powered by disposable batteries), metal ear curette, metal cotton wool applicator (to fashion cotton swabs); inexpensive oto/ophtho field kit is available from CFM Technologies (www.cfmtechnologies.com)

Household Goods

For longer-term stays abroad, some useful appliances to have are fans (electric and 12 V), a small blender, an iron, a clamp-on light, and perhaps even a sewing machine. The electricity in many countries is 220 V; thus you will need a transformer if you bring any

American (120 V) appliances. Alternatively, you might want to purchase appliances en route (eg, in Europe so that they are made for 220-V current). Remember that plug styles also vary throughout the world; so even if your equipment is of the proper voltage, you may still need to use an adapter to plug in equipment.

Items that run on 12 V (eg, fans, lights, inverters) are great for places where a little battery power, such as from automobile-style batteries, is available when other electrical sources are off.

Chapter 7

Keeping Healthy While on Assignment

Introduction

You, your patients, and your colleagues will suffer if you become ill. Before leaving home, you should take a few simple steps to help protect your health. Many assignments have been ruined by an unexpected, possibly preventable, illness. Medical problems encountered by travelers can range from a simple sunburn to a life-threatening case of drug-resistant malaria. One should start several weeks, if not a few months, in advance to ensure enough time to do the necessary research, and to be certain that all appropriate vaccinations are up to date.

This chapter will discuss vaccinations (which may be legally required or recommended by authorities such as the World Health Organization [WHO]), communicable diseases that travelers may be exposed to, environmental factors influencing health, and several other related topics. Health conditions around the world frequently change, and for the most current recommendations about specific countries or illnesses, the reader is encouraged to consult a qualified travel clinic, WHO publications, or American Health Consultants *Travel Medicine Advisor,* and to contact the embassy of the country to which one is planning to travel. An excellent source is the Centers for Disease Control and Prevention's information-rich Web site (www.cdc.gov/travel), which gives country-by-country health recommendations.

Vaccinations

Yellow fever is the only disease for which vaccination may legally be required for international travel (though some countries may ignore the relevant international agreements and require others). This viral disease is endemic in certain areas of Africa and South America (roughly 15 degrees North and South of the equator) and is fatal in more than half of cases in nonimmune adults. The vaccine is very effective and is well tolerated. Even if not specifically required for entry into a particular country, persons who will be traveling in endemic zones, particularly outside of major urban centers, are strongly encouraged to receive this vaccine.

An International Certificate of Vaccination must be obtained from an officially designated vaccine center (a list is published by the WHO) and is valid for 10 years, beginning 10 days after vaccination. Most larger public health departments and travel clinics provide the vaccine and proper documentation.

Smallpox has been eradicated, and vaccination is no longer necessary. Some countries have required proof of immunization against cholera in the past, but this should no longer be the case. There is currently no safe and effective vaccine against cholera.

Perhaps the most important vaccinations for the international traveler are those for hepatitis A and hepatitis B. Hepatitis A can also be prevented by the use of immune globulin, although its protection is temporary. All health care workers should be certain of their immunity to hepatitis B.

Vaccinations that are considered routine in the United States and other developed countries are also highly recommended before foreign travel. Measles, mumps, rubella, poliomyelitis, tetanus, diphtheria, and pertussis are all common in various parts of the world and can be prevented by safe and effective vaccines. The traveler's vaccination history should be reviewed and any deficiencies corrected before leaving home.

Rabies is much more common in other parts of the world than in the United States. Those who will be working with animals, staying in highly endemic areas, or isolated from medical care should consider pre-exposure vaccination. If exposed to rabies, the pre-immunized individual still requires postexposure vaccination, but does not require immune globulin, which is often unavailable.

Other vaccinations recommended by the WHO for travelers to endemic areas include typhoid, bacille Calmette-Guérin (though rarely given in the United States; contraindicated in the presence of symptomatic human immunodeficiency virus [HIV] infection), meningococcus, influenza (for elderly or otherwise high-risk persons), and Japanese encephalitis.

Malaria and Other Insect-Borne Illnesses

Avoidance of insect bites, particularly mosquitoes, is very important. Malaria is one of the world's greatest health problems, and the list of arthropod-borne illnesses also includes yellow fever, dengue fever, filariasis, viral encephalitides, leishmaniasis, African trypanosomiasis, onchocerciasis, typhus, Lyme disease, Rocky Mountain spotted fever, relapsing fever, tungiasis, and plague.

Drug prophylaxis against malaria is not 100% effective. The first step in preventing malaria is preventing or at least minimizing mosquito bites. Dusk and dawn are the times at which mosquito bites are most common. Staying indoors and wearing long-sleeved, dark-colored clothing can reduce exposure. The use of deet (N,N-diethyl-m-toluamide) or dimethylphthalate-containing insecticides on the skin is also recommended. Buildings with tight doors, windows, and screens help to keep mosquitoes out, but mosquito netting over the bed may also be needed. After entering the net to sleep, you should inspect it from the inside to make sure that all edges are tightly tucked in, there are no holes, and there are no mosquitoes inside with you. Spraying the netting with permethrin or deltamethrin, or using mosquito coils or other insecticides, is also useful.

Travelers should check with a reliable source before their trip to establish whether malaria is endemic in the area of travel. Some points to remember include the following:

1. There is no prophylactic regimen that is 100% effective. If you travel to a malarious area, no matter what you do, you might get malaria.

2. Malaria can be a serious disease, with a case-fatality rate of about 1% (for *Plasmodium falciparum),* higher for pregnant women and children.

3. All prophylactic regimens can be associated with side effects.

4. Depending on what drug is used, prophylaxis must begin 1 to 7 days before travel, must be taken exactly as directed without fail, and must be continued for 1 to 4 weeks after leaving the area.

5. Malaria is much more likely to be fatal if it is diagnosed and treated late in the course. Early diagnosis is therefore essential. Fever occurring any time from 1 week after arrival to 2 months (or even longer) after return home potentially represents malaria, particularly in children.

6. Travelers who will be in remote areas with no readily accessible health care should bring their own "standby" treatment, to be started if the symptoms of malaria occur. This is not a substitute for seeking care, particularly for children, but is a temporary measure while further care is pursued as rapidly as possible.

7. Since prophylactic drugs can cause side effects, they should only be taken if the traveler is actually at risk of catching malaria. Some urban areas in otherwise endemic countries may be malaria-free. An individual's general health, other medical problems, drug allergies, concomitant medications, and other factors will determine which prophylactic regimen should be used. This decision should be made with a physician's advice.

8. Symptoms that should prompt a suspicion of malaria are fever, with or without associated headache, myalgias, weakness, vomiting or diarrhea, and cough. The symptoms may initially be mild.

9. Anyone staying in a malarious area for longer than 1 month is more likely to catch malaria. It would be a good idea to locate local doctors with experience in prolonged prophylaxis and treatment of malaria.

Dengue and the associated dengue hemorrhagic fever and dengue shock syndrome are mosquito-borne viral illnesses for which there is no effective vaccine. Your only defenses against dengue are avoidance of mosquito bites and prompt, appropriate medical treatment. The mosquito species that carry dengue are much more likely to bite during daylight hours, so travelers to areas where dengue is present should also use mosquito repellents during the daytime. Dengue is characterized by severe, abrupt headache, eye pain, and muscle, bone, and joint pain, and fever. Scleral injection is common. Dengue hemorrhagic fever is more likely to exhibit cough, sore throat, loss of appetite, nausea, vomiting, and abdominal pain rather than bone, joint, or muscle pain. It may progress to spontaneous bleeding and low platelet count, and then to agitation and circulatory failure, followed by profound shock. These latter stages constitute dengue shock syndrome.

Food- and Water-Borne Illnesses

Diarrhea is one of the most common problems to afflict travelers, and is largely preventable. The most important preventive measure is the careful selection and preparation of all food and drink to be consumed. All foods should be cooked thoroughly, and either consumed hot or stored at a temperature below 10°C. Water and other beverages should either be bottled, chemically disinfected and filtered, or boiled. Fruits and vegetables should be considered potentially contaminated unless they can be peeled by you. High-risk foods include raw shellfish, unpasteurized milk, ice cream, and dishes containing raw eggs. Perfectly safe bottled water can be contaminated by using ice made from contaminated water. Some seafood may contain toxins that are not destroyed by cooking; one should consult local authorities before eating unknown species.

Hepatitis A is spread through contaminated food, and persons from developed countries are unlikely to be immune unless they receive proper vaccination or immune globulin pretreatment. Immune globulin offers temporary immunity, the duration of which is dose related. Hepatitis E is also transmitted through contaminated food, but there is no effective vaccine or immune globulin to prevent it. Strict avoidance of potentially contaminated food is the only protection from hepatitis E.

Vaccination against typhoid is recommended for travel anywhere that sanitation may be suspect. An injectable vaccine can be given to those 2 years and older; the newer oral vaccine (if available) is well-tolerated and can be taken by those 6 years and older.

Prophylactic antibiotics are not recommended to *prevent* diarrhea; however, it may be appropriate to take a short course of antibiotic (ciprofloxacin or azithromycin) for severe diarrhea. Protozoal and helminthic infections each require a different medical treatment. Oral rehydration is vitally important in the treatment of diarrheal illnesses, particularly in children; travelers should consider carrying rehydration salts in their medical kit. Oral rehydration therapy is usually available in-country or can be purchased (boxes of 50: $0.55 a piece) from Jianis Brothers (http://rehydrate.org/resources/jianas. htm). Severe cases (such as with cholera) may require intravenous hydration.

Bathing in fresh water (other than chlorinated pools) and walking in bare feet in high-risk areas may expose the traveler to a variety of hazards, and should be avoided.

HIV and Other Sexually Transmitted Infections

The same precautions that apply to sexually transmitted infections (STIs) at home should be used when traveling. Abstinence and sex with one mutually monogamous and non-infected partner are the best ways to prevent STIs. Latex condoms offer some protection against the spread of STIs. Sex with multiple partners or with prostitutes can be extremely hazardous. In many parts of the world, heterosexual intercourse is the most common route of transmission of HIV. Other STIs are also endemic, including hepatitis B, syphilis, gonorrhea, and many others. Many STIs are more resistant to antibiotic therapy overseas.

Human immunodeficiency virus, hepatitis B, and syphilis, among other illnesses, can also be spread by blood products. Transfusions should only be made when absolutely necessary, and then only with blood tested for HIV, hepatitis, and other infectious agents. Poor countries may lack the technology or funds to adequately screen their blood supply. If any injections are required while traveling, one should insist on a brand new, disposable needle, or one that has been thoroughly sterilized. Other medical and dental instruments as well as tattoo needles and equipment for body piercing must also be sterilized to prevent spread of infection. Workers at high risk of exposure (surgeons, operating room nurses, emergency personnel) might consider bringing HIV postexposure medications.

Environmental Hazards

Motion Sickness

Drugs are available to ease the nausea and vomiting associated with the movement of cars, boats, and airplanes. Even over-the-counter medications have associated side effects and should be taken only after reviewing the product instructions and consulting with a physician, if necessary.

Extreme Temperatures

Many travelers will be exposed to extremes of heat or cold during their trip. Typical weather conditions should be inquired about and the proper clothing brought. Extreme heat dramatically increases the body's need for water, and an adequate supply of safe water must be ensured. Protection from sun, particularly in tropical areas where levels of ultraviolet radiation are much higher, can be achieved with long-sleeved, light-colored clothing; hats; and sunscreens. Travelers to hot locations should be familiar with the symptoms and treatment of heat cramps, heat exhaustion, and heat stroke. Similarly, if likely to be exposed to extreme cold, particularly in isolated areas, one should be prepared to prevent, recognize, and treat frostbite and hypothermia.

A small number of travelers will be exposed to high altitudes. The pressurized cabins of commercial airplanes prevent altitude-related problems in flight, but prolonged stays in mountainous areas may expose the traveler to acute mountain sickness, high-altitude pulmonary edema, and high-altitude cerebral edema.

Travelers who will be in remote or wilderness areas should familiarize themselves with potential animal hazards. Sharks, jellyfish, other poisonous marine animals, poisonous snakes, scorpions, spiders, and carnivores are among the many dangerous animals that may be encountered, depending on the location of travel.

Traveler's Medical Kit/Traveling With Chronic Illness

Medical supplies that are inexpensive and readily available at home may be unobtainable while traveling. An adequate supply of such basic items as bandages, disinfectant, nonprescription analgesics and antipyretics, mosquito repellent, and sunscreen should be brought. Depending on the area of travel, appropriate anti-malarial medications, water purification devices, and oral rehydration salts may also be necessities. If prescribed by a physician, antibiotics and anti-diarrheals may be needed.

Persons with chronic health problems or allergies should be sure to bring an adequate supply of their regular medications, and should inquire in advance as to what medical facilities will be available. If injections will be needed (eg, for diabetics), sterile syringes and needles should be brought because they may not otherwise be available. Proper labeling or documentation of a physician's order should accompany needles or controlled substances.

Some serious medical problems should be considered contraindications to travel, particularly by air. Severe anemia, serious infectious diseases, heart failure, recent heart attack or stroke, severe mental illnesses, uncontrolled epilepsy, and other serious medical conditions may make travel too dangerous to attempt.

Health Insurance

Your health insurance may not cover you for illnesses and injuries that occur outside your country of origin. It would be prudent to check with your insurance carrier before traveling, particularly if you have chronic health problems, which are prone to reoccurrence. Even if you are covered, it is unlikely that a foreign provider will bill your insurance carrier. Rather, you are likely to have to pay for care yourself and then submit a claim for reimbursement. Special policies covering medical treatment abroad and/or medical evacuation are commercially available. *Consumer Reports Travel Letter* (October 1999) had an excellent article on health insurance for the traveler. Copies of this issue are available for $5 by calling CRTL at 914/378-2740. Many insurance options are available on the Internet. For example, International SOS provides medical/evacuation insurance (www.internationalsos.com). Also see Medjet Assist (www.medjetassist.com), MEDEX (www.medexassist.com), and CSA Travel Protection (www.csatravelprotection.com).

Chapter 8

Personal Safety Abroad

Introduction

Most health workers are not at serious personal risk while abroad. Studies show that heart attacks and accidents (usually automotive) are by far the most common sources of injury and death to travelers. However, some people choose to work under particularly dangerous conditions—such as war zones or in very high crime areas, where additional precautions are essential. This section provides some practical advice on a variety of security issues and lists references for further study.

General Advice

- Find out about local security conditions including crime, conflict, and attitudes toward foreigners. Ask several different reliable people about local conditions and conservatively follow their advice. US Consular Information Sheets and Travel Warnings are obtainable at US regional passport offices, through airline computer reservation systems, or by sending a self-addressed, stamped envelope to Overseas Citizens Services, Room 4811, Department of State, Washington, DC 20520-4818. In addition, the information is available by phone (202/647-5225) and online (http://travel.state.gov).

- Make a conscious effort to maintain a low profile. Dress conservatively in accordance with local social norms. This does not mean that you must wear local clothing or costumes, but do avoid the appearance of affluence. Don't speak loudly in public or discuss travel plans with strangers.

- Avoid black-market currency exchanges that place you at risk of theft or arrest. If possible, purchase some foreign currency before you leave because exchange opportunities are often not available immediately on arrival.

- Learn how to use local telephones and where they are located before an urgent need arises to do so. This may also include learning how to place collect calls. In many countries, the procedure for telephoning is quite different from what you may be used to, and you may be unable to read any written instructions on the phone.

- Travel "light," and label luggage inside and out. Outside labels should be covered to avoid casual observation by potential thieves and others.

- Carry a separate photocopy of your passport, driver's license (local and international), airline tickets, and other important documents to facilitate replacement. Also carry an extra set of passport photographs.

- Avoid crowds, high-risk areas, and being on the street late at night.

- Learn the layout of your new surroundings using a map. Learn routes to police, hospital, and other sources of assistance both by day and night. Let someone responsible know your daily itinerary and agree beforehand on when and how he or she should act if you are overdue.

- Follow local news events, especially if you are in an unstable region. If there are no local restrictions on radio ownership, consider taking along a shortwave radio to assist in following events.

- Know in advance how to get help. Find out beforehand what your embassy or consulate can do if you need to call on them. Many people do not understand what assistance can and cannot be rendered to them by their nation's representatives. If you are American, be sure to register at the local American embassy or consulate when you arrive. This step will allow officials to give information to your family if needed, to replace lost documents more quickly, and to provide you with up-to-date security advice. If you are not American, follow the advice of your embassy or consular officials.

- If you believe that the local government is likely to be hostile to you, be extra certain that you know in advance how to get help.

- Remember that when you are abroad you are subject to the laws of the country you are visiting, not your own.

- If you are arrested or detained, try to behave in a manner you think best based on your knowledge of local conditions and culture. In some areas a friendly, polite, but confident attitude is best. In other areas "name dropping" can help. Hostile outbursts or refusal to talk are usually not wise. Under international agreement, you have the right to speak to your nation's consul and should do so as soon as possible.

- When taking photographs, be sure to know beforehand what areas are considered sensitive by the local government. Many people inadvertently get into trouble this way. For example, photographing scenes that contain police and military personnel or their vehicles may be prohibited. Failure to obey the rules can mean loss of the film, confiscation of the camera, the imposition of a "fine," or even arrest. Also be sure that local people don't mind being photographed before taking their picture—many do. Some people are so offended that they become hostile or violent; others will demand payment. If you are considering publishing photographs when you return, a simple written release should be obtained or facial features can be masked to avoid identification.

- If you encounter shooting in the street it is usually best to immediately lie down (preferably behind a solid protective object) with your arms over your head. Look up to plan your exit only when things are quiet and seem safe. Then get away fast, staying low. If you are inside of a building when shooting erupts stay low to the ground, away from windows, with lights off. If possible crawl to an interior room or at least behind a protective object. If you should come under shelling, it is usually best to seek interior spaces on lower floors.

- Anticipate and avoid danger—flee if possible; only be brave and tough as a last resort.

Crime

- Don't carry your passport, money, valuables, or camera unless absolutely needed. Leave them in hotel safety boxes when possible.

- Don't wear a watch or jewelry or carry anything that you value or that looks valuable in high crime areas. If you must wear a ring, be certain that you can remove it easily.

- If you must carry money or documents, keep them in a zippered pouch hidden beneath your shirt or in a money belt. Other "body safes" fit onto your thigh like an Ace bandage or hang inside your pants attached to a belt. Access these items only in private.

- Carry a separate wallet or money clip with "mugging money." If you are held up, consider throwing the decoy cash while immediately running in the opposite direction, toward help or at least a lighted, busy area while shouting for assistance.

- You may want to carry a small amount of emergency money and important local addresses and phone numbers hidden in your shoe. If you have been robbed or in an emergency you will still be able to call for help or get a ride even if you don't know the local language.

- Avoid carrying large amounts of cash. Use traveler's checks and credit cards when possible. Traveler's checks have become difficult to cash in some areas, so ask before you leave home. Remember to keep copies of traveler's check numbers both at home and with you, but in a separate location from the checks so that you can report the identification number of stolen or lost checks. Monitor credit card activity online from Internet cafes and destroy copies that contain the full card number.

- ATMs are increasingly available. Check with your bank or credit card company to be certain that you do not need a special PIN. Use caution when leaving the ATM with cash.

- Plan in advance how you will react in given circumstances. Be alert; anticipate problems and avoid them.

Driving

- **Always use seat belts** and head rests. Avoid driving at night or when sick, fatigued, or intoxicated. Drive very defensively; try not to rush or get frustrated with difficult driving conditions.

- Remember to get an international driver's permit for use in the many countries where they are required. They can be obtained through automobile associations such as the American Automobile Association (AAA).

- When renting a car, it is often best to avoid those with conspicuous rental agency markings because these may attract thieves. On the other hand, rental car markings sometimes can be of benefit in areas with frequent checkpoints if local authorities are in the habit of treating tourists well.

- Even if you are a skilled mechanic, choose a reliable, low mileage, commonly available make. Avoid expensive models, which are targets for theft, and lighter models, which fair poorly in collisions. Inspect vehicles (fluids, tool kit, jack, tires, etc) before setting off. Understand clearly how to obtain assistance from the rental agency in case of a breakdown. Know what procedure to follow in case of theft or accident.

- Avoid leaving a vehicle parked with valuables, identification, or bags in plain view.

- Seek off-street, secure parking, especially at night.

- Keep windows closed and doors locked while traveling. Passenger side windows are especially vulnerable to entry by thieves on the curb. Both sides are vulnerable to bicycle- or motorcycle-mounted thieves.

- Be aware that roadside "accidents" may be staged as a ploy to rob you. Some thieves will bump your car or create a "fender bender" accident to get you to stop. Rental companies often have good advice regarding local crime tactics and avoidance.

- When driving, always leave plenty of room in front of you to maneuver, and be ready to take evasive action. When at a stop in traffic, try to leave room in front of you to escape in case of attack.

- Avoid hitchhikers.

- Don't enter a parked vehicle without checking the rear seat area for an intruder.

- Don't exit a vehicle if suspicious individuals are in the vicinity.

- If you are unable to speak the local language, keep 3" x 5" cards with important messages written in the local language in the glove box.

- When in high-threat areas, vary your route and schedule when driving.

Living Quarters

- When sleeping at night, try to secure your room. Sometimes leaving the key partly turned in the lock will prevent insertion of another key from the outside.

- Check to ensure that windows and balcony doors are locked. Close curtains (clothespins come in handy to close any gaps).

- A rubber doorstop, an attachable door lock, an attachable door alarm, or furniture placed in front of a door can lend extra protection to a vulnerable door.

- Don't open doors to unidentified persons.

- Avoid underground parking in multiunit buildings unless security is quite good.

- Plan an escape route in case of fire or hostile assault. Have emergency items for escape in easy reach. Emergency items vary depending on local conditions, but usually include money, phone numbers, important addresses, and a flashlight.

- For theft prevention, rooms above the second floor provide more safety from forced entry. For fire safety, choose a room no higher than local rescue capabilities can handle (usually below the seventh floor).

- Find a neighbor you can trust to turn to for safe haven or at least notification of authorities if needed.

- Apartments are generally easier to make secure than freestanding single homes. Use of intrusion alarms, security lighting, protective metal bars, fencing, and other standard security measures are always desirable.

If your voluntary service will keep you abroad for a considerable time or if your family will be with you, other security concerns should be addressed. Much more detailed advice is available from the US State Department. Additional US government publications regarding travel to specific regions of the world can be obtained from

Superintendent of Documents
US Government Printing Office
Washington DC 20402
Phone: 202/512-1800
Fax: 202/512-2250
Web: http://bookstore.gpo.gov

Resources

Department of State. http://travel.state.gov (Click on International Travel, then safety issues.)

Savage P. *The Safe Travel Book.* Lexington Books; 1999 (ISBN 10-073910053X)

Security Guidelines for American Families Living Abroad. US Dept of State Overseas Security Advisory Council; June 2005. www.osac.gov

Annotated Bibliography for Work in Developing Countries

This bibliography is organized into the following sections:

Administration
Appropriate Technology
Catalogs/Organizations
Dental
Dermatology/Photo Atlases
Drugs/Equipment/Supplies
Lab/Pathology
Nutrition
Obstetrics/Gynecology/Midwives
Ophthalmology
Pediatrics
Relief/Development/Public Health
Refugee/Disaster
Security/Living Abroad/Culture
Surgery/Anesthesia
Training Health Workers
Tropical Medicine
Water/Sanitation/Hygiene
Periodicals

Administration

Goodman H, Waddington C. **Financing Health Care** (Oxford, UK: Oxfam; 1993), index, 80 pages (paperback, ISBN 0-85598-187-3). Intended for managers, health workers, and those involved with nongovernment health programs, this work No. 8 in the *Oxfam Practical Health Guide* series suggests options and poses questions to help readers think through their individual situations. Contains examples from many parts of the world.

Lankester T. **Setting Up Community Health Programmes: A Practical Manual for Use in Developing Countries,** 2nd ed (London: Macmillan; 2000), illustrations, index, 334 pages (paperback, ISBN 0-333-679333-4). Illustrated in a *Where There Is No Doctor* style, this thoroughly revised manual covers many aspects of developing a community health program with cultural sensitivity and plenty of community input. It contains very practical advice on such topics as community survey; diagnosis and plan; managing personnel, supplies, and finance; cooperating with other agencies; and AIDS prevention and control.

Pearson CA. **Medical Administration for Front-Line Doctors,** 2nd ed (Cambridge, UK: FSG Communications Ltd.; 1995), illustrations, index, 290 pages (paperback, ISBN 1-871188-03-20). This practical guide to the management of district-level hospitals in developing countries is packed with extensive technical advice on handling money, personnel, medical records, improving and extending hospital buildings, and outreach programs. The *British Medical Journal* said, "The book's every word speaks of years of on the job experience and of lessons bitterly learned under a blazing sun or in torrential rain."

Witter S, Ensor T, Jowett M, Thompson R. **Health Economics for Developing Countries: A Practical Guide** (London: Macmillan; 2000), index, 296 pages (ISBN 0-333-75205-8). This introduction to health economics and finance for low-income countries presupposes no previous training in economics. Chapter topics (such as Provider Payment Systems) are introduced, then discussed in a humorous fashion by characters in a hypothetical country. Includes an extensive glossary of health economic terms.

Appropriate Technology

Darrow K, Saxenian M. **Appropriate Technology Sourcebook: A Guide to Practical Books for Village and Small Community Technology** (Stanford, CA: Volunteers in Asia; 1993), illustrations, index, 785 pages (paperback, ISBN 0-917704-17-7; hardback, ISBN 0-917704-18-5). More than 50,000 copies of previous editions of this truly remarkable work have been used in more than 130 countries to find a wide range of published technical information that can be used by individuals and small groups. In this revised and expanded version, 1,150 publications from international and US sources are reviewed, covering water supply systems, renewable energy devices, agricultural tools, intensive gardening, and small industries, as well as health care, disaster preparedness, and relief. While many of the publications described are out of print, the Sourcebook serves as the index for the Appropriate Technologies Microfiche library and CD-ROM, which contains the complete text of nearly 1,000 books. Both the Sourcebook and the library are available at very reasonable rates, especially to those working in developing countries. Order from Village Earth—The Consortium for Sustainable Village-based Development, 800/648-8043 or www.villageearth.org (click on Appropriate Technology, then AT Library).

Platt A, Carter N. **Making Health Care Equipment: Ideas for Local Design and Production** (London: Intermediate Technology Publications; 1990), 80 pages (paperback, ISBN 1-85339-067-4), illustrations. This book represents a revision of an earlier text, *How to Make Hospital Equipment,* but is expanded with contributions from many sources. Line drawings and photographs illustrate designs for self-manufactured hospital furniture, wheelchairs, carts, physiotherapy, orthopedic, lab, maternity, and infant care equipment.

Catalogs/Organizations

Global Health Directory
This useful resource is now available only online. More than 500 organizations actively involved in the frontlines of global health are listed. Up-to-date contact information, mission statements, details on service focus, regions/countries

served, and target groups plus expanded indices make the *Global Health Directory* a comprehensive, easy-to-use reference tool. Useful cross-index according to country and 24 activity areas including communicable diseases, disaster relief, medical supplies, and primary health care. Global Health Council, 1701 K St NW, Suite 600, Washington, DC 20006-1503; 202/833-5900 (directory available at www.globalhealth.org/directory).

InterAction Member Profiles
This is a biannual directory of more than 164 private voluntary organizations (PVOs) as well as the unique qualities and distinctions of each individual member organization. Some InterAction PVOs are secular organizations; others represent more than a dozen religious groups. Each member organization profiled features complete contact information, personnel, objectives, program outlines, countries served, financial statements, publications, etc. InterAction, American Council for Voluntary International Action, 1717 Massachusetts Ave NW, 8th Floor, Washington, DC 20036; 202/667-8227 (www.interaction.org).

US PVO Executive Contact List/US Private and Voluntary Organizations Registered With the US Agency for International Development (Annual Report)
Simple directory of about 450 PVO addresses, chief officers, telephone, fax, e-mail, and level of privateness. Largely development oriented. Useful cross-references by state and by such areas of interest as health, nutrition, refugee services, and women in development. Available by calling 202/712-4810 or available online at www.usaid.gov (from drop-down menu under About USAID, link is PVO Registry).

Voluntary Foreign Aid Programs (Report of American Voluntary Agencies Engaged in Overseas Relief and Development Registered With the US Agency for International Development)
This annual online report summarizes PVO activities including their geographic and sectoral focus and their finances. It includes executive contacts, fax numbers, e-mail addresses, and mission statements. US Agency for International Development, 202/712-4810 (www.usaid.gov/our_work/cross-cutting_programs/private_voluntary_cooperation/pub.html). Also available in hard copy.

Dental
Dickinson M. **Where There Is No Dentist** (Palo Alto, CA: Hesperian Foundation; 2006), index, illustrations, 230 pages (paperback, ISBN 0-942364-05-8). This innovative, well-illustrated book provides detailed information on the use of dental equipment, placing fillings, and dental extractions. Dental and nutritional education techniques are also emphasized. Updated 2006 printing features new information on how HIV/AIDS affects the care of teeth and gums. Complete book now available for download from Hesperian (http://hesperian.org/publications_download_dentist.php).

Halestrap DJ. **La santé des dents: notions de soins dentaires élémentaires**
(Zaire: Bureau d'Études et de Recherches our la Pro-motion de la Santé),
illustrations, 59 pages. French translation by P. Duprez of an earlier edition of
Halestrap's work described below with some different illustrations. Useful
teaching tool for French-speaking assistants. Published as *Soins dentaires
elementaires a l'usage des hopitaux ruraux* (London, UK: 1974).

Halestrap DJ. **Simple Dental Care for Rural Hospitals,** 4th ed (London:
Medical Missionary Association; 1981), illustrations, 28 pages (paperback,
ISBN 0-9506100-0; TALC). Written by a British dentist with extensive experience in small African clinics, this very simple booklet is intended for the
medical auxiliary worker whose job it is to treat dental patients. Though written
for those for whom English is not their native language, this work might be
handy for anyone new to dental responsibilities. French edition available from
the Medical Missionary Association, 244 Camden Rd, London, UK NW1 9HE.

Dermatology/Photo Atlases

Ansary MA, et al. **A Colour Atlas of AIDS in the Tropics,** London, UK:
Wolfe Medical Publications; 1989), index, illustrations, 126 pages (ISBN
0-7234-1567-6). Comparatively short on text and long on illustrations, this
visually oriented work helps clinicians recognize HIV-related pathology and
differentiate them from other conditions common in the tropics. This atlas of
diagnostic color photographs also shows the differences in presentation and
disease progression from the Northern hemisphere.

Canizares O. **A Manual of Dermatology for Developing Countries,** 2nd ed
(Oxford, UK: Oxford University Press; 1993), index, illustrations, 370 pages
(ISBN 0-19-262293-5). This practical text is intended for the physician with
little or no access to sophisticated diagnostic procedures and costly therapeutic agents. It strikes a balance between the management of very common infectious diseases and the more rare genetic, degenerative, or malignant processes
that affect the skin. The manual has been updated to cover the dermatologic
consequences of AIDS. Key point summaries and maps in the margin make the
work accessible to students and health workers. Also available in paperback.

Schaller KF, ed. **Colour Atlas of Tropical Dermatology and Venerology**
(Berlin: Springer-Verlag; 1994), index, 601 color photographs, 305 pages (ISBN
0-387-53327-3). This very practical atlas provides succinct descriptions of clinical features, diagnosis and differential diagnosis, and management of skin disorders of the tropics and subtropics. A special feature of this work is the range of
photographs showing the same diseases in patients of different ethnic groups
and skin colors. In addition to the English name of each condition, the Spanish,
German, French, Latin, and local names (as far as they are known) are given.

Drugs/Equipment/Supplies

Dorsch JA, Dorsch SE. **Understanding Anesthesia Equipment,** 4th ed (Baltimore, MD: Williams & Wilkins; 1999), index, illustrations, 1,066 pages (ISBN 0-683-304879). In this comprehensive volume, the authors discuss the equipment about which the least information is readily available as well as the latest innovations. The text is primarily intended for anesthesia residents and certified registered nurse anesthetists, but anyone responsible for maintenance and repair of anesthesia equipment should find it valuable. "While new equipment seems unduly complex, with proper understanding it can be very user-friendly." New topics include automatic noninvasive blood pressure monitoring, design, and equipment selection.

Pinel J, ed, et al. **Essential Drugs: Practical Guidelines** (Paris: Hatier; 2002), index, 338 pages (ISBN 2-906498491). This guide, a translation of one of the Médecins Sans Frontières series, covers the use and management of drugs and medical supplies in dispensaries, health centers, and refugee camps. Part One has chapters on oral drugs, injectable drugs, infusion solutions and electrolytes, vaccines and sera, and drugs for external use and disinfectants; 1 page is devoted to each drug and is written in terms laymen can understand. Part Two covers topics like the organization and management of a pharmacy, prescriptions, costs, and compliance.

Skeet M, Fear D. **Care and Safe Use of Hospital Equipment** (London: VSO Books; 1995), illustrations, 188 pages (ISBN 0-9509050-5-4). Using clear diagrams and charts, Voluntary Service Overseas authors demystify the procedures for maintaining such equipment as autoclaves, incubators, and vacuum extractors. Though the work is written in a British English idiom, its very accessible flow charts, directions, and pictures make it suitable for those who do not have much formal educational background. It contains easy-to-follow checklists, which can be posted near equipment to ensure correct use.

World Health Organization. **Maintenance and Repair of Laboratory, Diagnostic, Imaging, and Hospital Equipment** (Geneva: World Health Organization; 1999), index, illustrations, 158 pages (ISBN 92-4-154463-5). This well-illustrated manual provides practical guidance on the maintenance and repair of a wide range of basic laboratory and diagnostic equipment (from centrifuges to microscopes) as well as anesthetic machines, operating room equipment, and ultrasound and x-ray equipment. It outlines the precautions needed in day-to-day operation and the most common problems likely to be encountered.

Lab/Pathology

Cheesbrough M. **Medical Laboratory Manual for Tropical Countries,** 2nd ed (Doddington: Tropical Health Technology; 1987), index, illustrations. Volume 1,605 pages (ISBN 0750615206). This, the first of a 3-volume series intended to promote the growth of reliable indigenous lab services, covers parasitology, clinical chemistry, anatomy and physiology, and lab equipment. Very comprehensive, yet written in an easy-to-follow style. Volume 2, 479 pages (ISBN 0-9507 434 2 9). This volume focuses on microbiology. In 1990 Cheesbrough published an HIV supplement to this volume. Volume 3 discusses hematology and blood transfusion.

Nutrition

King FS, Burgess A. **Nutrition for Developing Countries,** 2nd ed (Oxford, UK: Oxford University Press; 1993), index, illustrations, 462 pages (ISBN 0-19-262233-1). This work is both an easy-to-access textbook of nutrition with classroom exercises as well as a very practical, detailed guide for nutrition workers. An abundance of black-and-white illustrations makes the volume useful for engaging the interest of those unable to read. Further educational devices include storytelling formats. For example, the chapter "Undernutrition in Women" contrasts the stories of Mari and of Lila and how their differing diets affected their health and the health of their offspring.

McLaren DS, Figg M. **Sight and Life Manual on Vitamin A Deficiency Disorders (VADD)** (Basel, Switzerland: Sight and Life; 2001), index, illustrations, 163 pages (ISBN 3-906412-032). The Swiss Sight and Life Foundation publishes this survey of all the forms and degrees of Vitamin A deficiency, principally xerophthalmia. The control of VADD is discussed under 7 headings: treatment, prophylaxis, prevention and management, fortification, dietary modification, plant breeding, and disaster relief.

World Health Organization. **Management of Severe Malnutrition: A Manual for Physicians and Other Senior Health Workers.** (See entry on page 83.)

Obestetrics/Gynecology/Midwives

Klein S. **A Book for Midwives: A Manual for Traditional Birth Attendants and Community Midwives** (Palo Alto, CA: Hesperian Foundation; 2000), index, hundreds of black-and-white drawings, glossary, 519 pages (ISBN 0-942364-22-8). This extremely down-to-earth paperback was produced by the same people who publish *Where There Is No Doctor.* It is aimed at caregivers like traditional midwives and community health workers, providing them with information and teaching tools to help more women have safer births and healthier babies. It is organized in a "what to do if" format. Apprentice midwives can study this book; practicing midwives can take it along when they work with pregnant women. Illustrations are culturally appropriate. The updated version has been reorganized and extensively revised to better support care during labor and management of obstetric emergencies. Chapters have been expanded and/or updated to cover lifesaving reproductive health information and to recognize the broad role of midwives in providing women's health care. Free download (PDF version) available from Hesperian Foundation (www.hesperian.org/publications_download_midwives.php). Also available in Spanish.

World Health Organization. **Pregnancy, Childbirth, Postpartum and Newborn Care** (Geneva: World Health Organization; 2003), 178 pages (ISBN 13-9789241590846). This is an evidence-based guide for clinical decision-making by skilled attendants working at the primary level of health care. It promotes early detection of complications and initiation of treatment including referral, if necessary.

Ophthalmology

Schwab L. **Eye Care in Developing Nations,** 4th ed (London: Manson Publishing; 2007), index, illustrations, 272 pages (paperback, ISBN 978-1-84076-084-2). Intended as a reference and text for the study of eye care and blindness prevention, this excellent work emphasizes inexpensive methods of diagnosis, treatment, and prevention. It is aimed at general physicians in remote parts of the world who must get along with limited supplies and the simplest equipment (eg, kitchen spoon used as a lid plate). Expanded and updated 4th edition with color photographs and diagrams throughout. Fully revised.

Pediatrics

Barnes PM, Singh H, Stephens AJH. **A Textbook of Paediatrics in the Tropics and Sub-Tropics** (London: Macmillan Education; 1990), illustrations, 282 pages (paperback, ISBN 0-333-51590-0; hardcover, ISBN 0-333-53605-3). A practical text based largely on the authors' experiences in Africa and the Middle East. Written from a British perspective.

Bergström S; Höjer B, Liljestrand J, Tunell R. **Perinatal Health Care with Limited Resources** (London: Macmillan Education; 1994), illustrations, 186 pages (paperback, ISBN 0-333-59594-7). This practical text is written in plain language and illustrated with line drawings. It covers antenatal care, normal delivery care, normal baby care, and breastfeeding, as well as complications.

American Academy of Pediatrics Committee on Infectious Diseases. **Red Book: Report of the Committee on Infectious Diseases,** 27th ed (Elk Grove Village, IL: American Academy of Pediatrics; 2006), index, 992 pages (ISBN 1-58110-039-6). The committee provides "current, relevant, and defensible recommendations for the prevention and management of infectious diseases in children." The book begins with a handy summary of major changes in recommendations. *The Visual Red Book Library* is available online with purchase of *Red Book Online* (available at www.aapredbook.org).

Baker CJ, ed. **Red Book Atlas of Pediatric Infectious Diseases** (Elk Grove Village, IL: American Academy of Pediatrics; 2007), index, color photographs, 450 pages (hardcover, ISBN 158110247X). Based on key content from *Red Book®*, the atlas is a useful quick reference tool for the clinical diagnosis and treatment of more than 75 of the most commonly seen pediatric infectious diseases. It includes more than 500 full-color images adjacent to concise diagnostic and treatment guidelines. Essential information on each condition is presented including clinical manifestations, etiology, epidemiology, incubation period, diagnostic tests, and treatment.

Coovadia HM, ed. **Paediatrics and Child Health: A Handbook for Health Professionals in the Third World,** 3rd ed (Oxford, UK: Oxford University Press; 1992), index, illustrations, 630 pages (paperback, ISBN 0-19-5707311). This straightforward and comprehensive textbook was written by doctors working in southern Africa. This volume would be particularly useful for those working there, but the examples may lack scope for those working in other parts of the world.

Dean P, Ebrahim GJ. **Practical Care of Sick Children: A Manual for Use in Small Tropical Hospitals** (London: Macmillan Education; 1986) illustrations, 348 pages (paperback, ISBN 0-333-42347-X). A British text written by a missionary sister and an academic professor, this manual provides practical advice on a wide range of topics concerning the care of sick children in developing countries.

Ebrahim GJ. **Paediatric Practice in Developing Countries,** 2nd ed (London: Macmillan Education; 1993) illustrations, 345 pages (paperback, ISBN 0-333-57347-1). An excellent practical British text written by an expert in the field. Sections cover relevant social and cultural material, nutrition, and a variety of clinical topics.

Hendrickse RG, Barr DGD, Matthews TS, eds. **Paediatrics in the Tropics** (Oxford, UK: Blackwell Scientific; 1991), index, illustrations, 988 pages (hardcover, ISBN 0-632-02675-8). This sizable hardcover is written from a British perspective (virtually all useful addresses of organizations, for example, are in London). Intended as a principal reference work in the field, it reflects the editors' experience in Africa. The 32 chapters cover a broad range of clinical topics.

King M, King F, Martodipoero S. **Primary Child Care** (Oxford, UK: Oxford University Press; 1978), illustrations, Book One, 315 pages (ISBN 0-19-264229-4); Book Two, 194 pages (ISBN 0-19- 264230-8). Book One is a very practical manual on child health care in the third world, written in as simple English as possible. There is heavy reliance on black-and-white illustrations. Most of Book Two is taken up by multiple-choice tests verifying how much was learned from the study of the first book. Much like *Where There is No Doctor,* the texts seem applicable both for training health assistants and as aids to doctors and nurses working in unfamiliar conditions.

Ressler EM, Boothby N, Steinbock DJ. **Unaccompanied Children: Care and Protection in Wars, Natural Disasters, and Refugee Movements** (Oxford, UK: Oxford University Press; 1988) index, 421 pages (paperback, ISBN 0-19-504937-3). Not a medical text, but a sociological survey, this study summarizes the laws and international agreements that currently bear on displaced children and offers a comprehensive set of recommendations for the international treatment of children in crisis.

Stanfield P, Balldin B, Versluys Z, eds. **Child Health: A Manual for Medical and Health Workers in Health Centers and Rural Hospitals,** 2nd ed (Nairobi: AMREF; 1999), index, illustrations, 538 pages (paperback, ISBN 9966-874-07-0). This revised edition by the African Medical and Research Foundation starts with the most elementary definitions but ends up being quite comprehensive in its scope. Updates in this hefty Africa-specific volume include developments on the progress of the HIV infection, chloroquine-resistant malaria, and some of the newer antituberculous and antihelminthic drugs.

UNICEF. **The State of the World's Children** (Oxford, UK: Oxford University Press; updated annually), illustrations, page count varies. Annual progress report with snapshot articles focusing on different health problems or parts of the world. Invaluable statistical studies on life expectancy, contraception, access to safe water, health services, etc, for every developing nation. Editions can be viewed on UNICEF's Web site (www.unicef.org).

Werner D. **Disabled Village Children: A Guide for Community Health Workers, Rehabilitation Workers and Families** (Berkeley, CA: Hesperian Foundation; 1987, updated 2006), index, black-and-white drawings, photographs, glossary, 672 pages (ISBN 0-942364-06-6). Written with the help of disabled persons and pioneers in rehabilitation in many countries, this book contains a wealth of clear, simple, but detailed suggestions concerning pediatric disabilities, including blindness, deafness, fits, behavior problems, and developmental delay. It gives suggestions for low-cost aids and ways to help disabled children find a role and be accepted in their communities. The illustrations and ideas are especially geared toward rural third-world areas. Available in Spanish.

World Health Organization. **Management of Severe Malnutrition: A Manual for Physicians and Other Senior Health Workers** (Geneva: World Health Organization; 1999) 60 pages (paperback, ISBN 92-4-1545119). Addressed to doctors and auxiliary staff, this extremely practical and compassionate manual gives guidelines for the management of severely malnourished children (though one chapter considers the plight of adolescents and adults). "Successful management requires that both the medical and social problems be recognized and corrected." Appendices cover everything from easy to reproduce sample recording forms to ideas for simple toys.

World Health Organization. **Pocket Book of Hospital Care for Children**
(Geneva: World Health Organization; 2005) 378 pages (paperback, ISBN-
13-9789241546706). Up-to-date evidence-based clinical guidelines for the
management of common illnesses in areas with limited resources. Addressed
to doctors, senior nurses, and senior health care workers at the first referral
level in developing countries. Recommendations are coordinated with
Integrated Management of Childhood Illnesses guidelines.

Relief/Development/Public Health

Desjarlais R, et al. **World Mental Health: Problems and Priorities in Low-
Income Countries** (Oxford, UK: Oxford University Press; 1995), index, charts/
tables, 382 pages (ISBN 0-19-509540-5). This book is the result of several years
of collaboration between experts from more than 19 countries and researchers
in the department of social medicine at Harvard University. The authors examine key findings on mental illness and mental health services; suicide; substance
abuse; the mental health of women, children, and the elderly; violence; disloca-
tion; and health-related behavior in Asia, Latin America, Africa, and the Middle
East. Numerous case studies make the theory more readable.

Green A. **An Introduction to Health Planning in Developing Countries,**
2nd ed (Oxford, UK: Oxford University Press; 1999), index, 318 pages (ISBN
0-19-262161-0). Within the context of a primary health care approach, this
introductory text emphasizes the many factors that impinge on health, the different nongovernmental agencies involved in health activities, and the need for
participation in planning by communities. The need for combining planning
techniques and political analysis is stressed, as is the importance of planning
by a wide variety of health professionals and specialist health planners.

Lankinen KS, Bergström S, Mäkelä PH, Peltomaa M. **Health and Disease in
Developing Countries** (London: Macmillan Education; 1994) illustrated, 586
pages (paperback, ISBN 0-333-58900-9). This excellent text provides both clinical advice and a broad survey of the health problems confronting people in
developing countries and the strategies employed to overcome disease.

Lucas AO, Gilles HM. **Short Textbook of Preventive Medicine for the Tropics,**
4th ed (London: Edward Arnold; 2003), index, illustrations, 318 pages (ISBN
0-340-53591-1). The planning and implementation of health control measures
in the tropics require an understanding of the epidemiology of disease in a tropical environment, the appropriate use of health statistics, and the organization to
target health resources to those most in need. This revised version includes a
large number of illustrations to show geographical distribution and lifecycles
of tropical diseases. It is suitable both as an undergraduate text and as a
quick reference for health professionals practicing in the tropics. This edition
has been thoroughly revised and focuses on recent advances in public health,
retaining the approach from earlier editions in stressing basic principles illus-

trated by selected examples, rather than attempting to provide a detailed comprehensive account. This edition also highlights the global epidemiology of type 2 diabetes and the disease related to cigarette smoking as examples of the growing incidence of chronic diseases in developing countries.

Pratt B, Boyden J. **The Field Directors' Handbook: An Oxfam Manual for Development Workers,** 4th ed (Oxford, UK: Oxford University Press; 1988), illustrations, 512 pages (cased, ISBN 0-19-920-53-6; paperback, 0-85598-073-7). Designed as a set of guidelines for Oxfam's field staff, this book is an excellent relief and development resource. Based on Oxfam's extensive worldwide experience, practical advice is presented in 8 parts: Introduction, Priority Groups, Field Methodologies, Social Development Guidelines, Economic Development Guidelines, Agriculture, Health, and Disaster Guidelines.

Stockman D. **Community Assessment: Guidelines for Developing Countries** (London: Intermediate Technology Publications; 1994) illustrated, 149 pages (paperback, ISBN 1-85339-224-3). A straightforward, introductory text designed to help the reader identify the causes of ill health in the community. Topics include basic demographics, water, food, sanitation, community resources, health, and rapid epidemiologic assessments.

Ulijaszek SJ, ed. **Health Intervention in Less Developed Nations** (Oxford, UK: Oxford University Press; 1995), index, 140 pages (ISBN 0-19-852302-5). This, the seventh volume in Oxford's Biosocial Society series, has 4 main chapters, each with its own extensive bibliography: (1) The Problem of Recurrent Cost in International Aid (2) Nutritional Intervention; (3) International Water Decade; and (4) Development, Modernization and Health Intervention. This text is mostly for those interested in health policy.

Williams CD, Baumslag N, Jelliffe DB. **Mother and Child Health: Delivering the Services,** 3rd ed (Oxford, UK: Oxford University Press; 1994), index, illustrations, 392 pages (ISBN 0-19-508149-8). A wealth of photographs and judicious use of literary references supplement and humanize statistical studies. Many of the studies and examples cited in this book are classic pioneering efforts, which are only now being recognized and replicated in many countries with local adaptation.

Refugee/Disaster

Mears C, Chowdhury S. **Health Care for Refugees and Displaced People** (Oxfam Practical Health Guide No. 9) (Oxford, UK: Oxfam; 1994), index, illustrations, 116 pages (ISBN 0-85598-225-X). Intended as a reference tool for health workers with limited or no experience in emergency situations, this short, practical introduction to health care in relief and refugee programs covers the assessment of health risk factors through a checklist of questions and outline format. Instead of covering immediate medical and surgical care, it focuses instead on sanitation, immunization, etc. Geared primarily toward life in a refugee camp, there are sections on special needs of long-term refugees and on monitoring and evaluation. Detailed information on nutrition, protocols, and other aspects of health care is given in the appendices.

Mandalakas A, Torjesen K, Olness K. **Helping the Children: A Practical Handbook for Complex Humanitarian Emergencies** (Kenyon, MN: Health Frontiers; 1999), 133 pages. This spiral-bound handbook was produced by colleagues at Case Western Reserve with sponsorship from Johnson & Johnson. Chapters can be only a few pages long, but convey information in a warm supportive tone. Available in Spanish as *Como Ayudar a los Niños: Una Guia Practica para las Emergencias Humanitarias Complejas.* To order the book, call the Johnson & Johnson Pediatric Institute at 877/565-5465.

Noji EK, ed. **The Public Health Consequences of Disasters** (Oxford, UK: Oxford University Press; 1997), index, 468 pages (ISBN 0-19-509570-7). Illustrated with examples from recent research, the 20 essays in this work are divided into 4 areas: general issues, geophysical events, weather-related problems, and human-generated disasters. Throughout the book the focus is on the level of epidemiological knowledge about each aspect of disasters. Contributors pay particular attention to prevention and control measures.

The Sphere Program: A set of standards for humanitarian assistance in disaster settings in areas of water supply, nutrition, food, air, shelter, and health services. The very helpful 2004 handbook can be downloaded at www.sphereproject.org.

Security/Living Abroad/Culture

American Society of Tropical Medicine and Hygiene, Wolfe M, ed. **Health Hints for the Tropics** (Northbrook, IL: ASTMH; 1998), 50 pages. A general guide to staying healthy through the knowledge and application of clinical principles, preventive sanitation, and common sense. To order, call 847/480-9592.

Kohls LR. **Survival Kit for Overseas Living,** 3rd ed (Yarmouth, ME: Intercultural Press; 2001) 204 pages (ISBN 1-877864-38-2). This handbook provides straightforward information on the potential perils of going to a new country—culture shock, stereotyping, and misperceptions—and tools for turning things around for a rewarding experience. Excellent both for short-term projects or families moving abroad permanently. To order, go to www.interculturalpress.com.

Piet-Pelon NJ, Hornby B. **Women's Guide to Overseas Living,** 2nd ed (Yarmouth, ME: Intercultural Press; 1992) 210 pages (ISBN 1-877864-05-6). Single women, professional women with families, and homemakers will find plenty of food for thought learning about cultural adjustment, handling stress, loneliness, managing the household, and helping the children cope. This revised edition covers reentry shock and special concerns of minority women. To order, go to www.interculturalpress.com.

Surgery/Anesthesia

Bewes P. **Surgery: A Manual for Rural Health Workers** (Nairobi: AMREF; 1987), index, illustrations, 359 pages (paperback, African Medical and Research Foundation, PO Box 30125, Nairobi, Kenya). This easy-to-read manual is not intended to encourage rural health workers to perform elementary surgery on their own, but might be better suited for those who would assist a surgeon working in a developing nation. It does, however, clearly show "what should and should not be attempted in a health centre."

Cook J, Sankaran B, Wasunna AEO, eds. **General Surgery at the District Hospital** (Geneva: World Health Organization; 1998), index, illustrations, 231 pages (ISBN 92-4-154235-7). One of 3 handbooks published by the World Health Organization for the guidance of doctors providing surgical and anesthetic services in small hospitals subject to constraints on personnel, equipment, drugs, and access to specialized services. The book outlines surgical procedures for the face and neck, chest, abdomen, gastrointestinal tract, and urogenital system. Pediatrics is treated in a special section. Numerous superb illustrations clarify procedures for those who have had little formal surgical training.

Cook J, Sankaran B, Wasunna AEO, eds. **Surgery at the District Hospital: Obstetrics, Gynaecology, Orthopaedics and Traumatology** (Geneva: World Health Organization; 1991), index, illustrations, 207 pages (ISBN 92-4-154413-9). The first section on obstetric/gynecology procedures deals with treatment of the major complications of pregnancy and childbirth. The second section covers both basic orthopedic techniques and management of specific fractures, dislocations, and other injuries including burns. Numerous superb illustrations clarify procedures.

Dobson MB. **Anaesthesia at the District Hospital,** 2nd ed (Geneva: World Health Organization; 2000), index, illustrations, 153 pages (ISBN 92-4-154228 -4). One of 3 handbooks published by the World Health Organization for the guidance of doctors providing surgical and anesthetic services in small hospitals subject to constraints on personnel, equipment, drugs, and access to specialized services. This book covers the immediate and continuing care of critically ill, unconscious, or anesthetized patients and principles of fluid and electrolyte therapy. Special attention is given to pediatric and obstetric anesthesia. The wealth of illustrations is intended to help the medical officer in a small hospital who finds himself or herself responsible for providing anesthesia for both elective and emergency surgery. Thoroughly revised second edition to reflect changes in clinical practice, equipment, and drugs.

King M, ed. **Primary Anesthesia** (Oxford, UK: Oxford University Press; 1986), index, illustrations, 169 pages (paperback, ISBN 0-19-269051-5). This manual of anesthetic methods is intended for nonspecialists working in developing countries or in emergency situations. Many methods of local and regional anesthesia, intubation, and the use of relaxants are discussed. Directions on improvising equipment like vaporizers and "making your own intravenous fluids" included.

King M, Bewes P, Cairns J, Thornton J, eds. **Primary Surgery, Volume One, Non-Trauma** (Oxford, UK: Oxford University Press; 1990; corrected 1993), index, illustrations, 642 pages (paperback, ISBN 0-19-261694-3). Designed for doctors working in developing countries, this impressive volume clearly illustrates methods on procedures from conventional problems like cesarean section and the resection of dead bowel to tackling tropical diseases like leprosy and elephantiasis. It is geared toward the generalist who has never performed any of these procedures before.

King M, Bewes P, eds. **Primary Surgery, Volume Two, Trauma** (Oxford, UK: Oxford University Press; 1987; corrected 1993), index, illustrations, 389 pages (paperback, ISBN 0-19-261598-X). This complete and detailed system of trauma methods is geared toward the nonspecialist physician confronted with having to do an amputation or emergency eye surgery for the very first time. It contains special sections on treating fractures and burns.

Rigal J, ed. **Minor Surgical Procedures in Remote Areas** (Paris: Médecins Sans Frontières; 1989), index, illustrations, 173 pages (ISBN 2-218-021663-3). This outline/cookbook format handbook uses very simple illustrations and text to distill Médecins Sans Frontières' experience in the "most frequent and useful minor surgical procedures practiced by doctors and nurses in remote areas with poor sanitation and no surgical or radiographic equipment." Intended for use in rural hospitals, dispensaries, and refugee camps, this book has appendices that list supplies, equipment, and disinfection and sterilization techniques.

World Health Organization. **Surgical Care at the District Hospital** (Geneva: World Health Organization; 2003) 512 pages (ISBN 9241545755). A compact, comprehensive resource for nonspecialist practitioners focusing on fundamental precepts and practical techniques in surgery, obstetrics/gynecology, orthopedics, trauma, and anesthesia. Illustrations are clear and instructive.

Training Health Workers

Birrell K, Birrell G. **Diagnosis and Treatment: A Training Manual for Primary Health Care Workers** (London: Macmillan; 2000), index, illustrations, 264 pages (ISBN 0-333-722211-6). Based on a training course developed in Tanzania by Voluntary Service Overseas doctors, the lesson plans show health workers how to diagnose common illness and how to prescribe "rationally," enabling practitioners to deliver good patient care with scarce resources. A wide range of experts helped adapt material to make it relevant to conditions throughout the developing world. Medicines recommended are based on World Health Organization guidelines.

Byre M, Beneath FJ. **Community Nursing in Developing Countries: A Manual for the Community Nurse,** 2nd ed (Oxford, UK: Oxford University Press; 1986), index, illustrations, 251 pages (ISBN 0-19-261453). Drawing from their own experience in Uganda, the authors dedicate the first half of the book to community nursing including home management. Chapters then follow on communicable diseases and methods for control as well as health education, community psychiatry, and social welfare. Technical language is avoided as much as possible.

Frankel S, ed. **The Community Health Worker: Effective Programs for Developing Countries** (Oxford, UK: Oxford University Press; 1992), index, 291 pages (paperback, ISBN 0-19-261761-3; hardcover ISBN 0-19-262236-6). This fine text reviews the current state of community health worker programs throughout the world. It provides insight into the reasons for the success and failure of programs. A variety of authors review programs underway in Indonesia, China, Nepal, India, Tanzania, Zimbabwe, Nicaragua, and Honduras. It provides extensive references on the subject of community health workers. With its case studies and analytical overview, this text is recommended for those charged with planning a community health worker program.

Klein S. **A Book for Midwives: A Manual for Traditional Birth Attendants and Community Midwives** (Berkeley, CA: Hesperian Foundation; 2005). See entry on page 80.

Werner D, Bower B. **Helping Health Workers Learn.** (Berkeley, CA: Hesperian Foundation; 1982), index, illustrations, 642 pages (ISBN 0-942364-10-4). Written and illustrated by the author of *Where There Is No Doctor,* this collection of methods, aids and "triggers of the imagination" (including scripts for village theater, instructions for drawing educational cartoons) is geared toward village instructors who themselves may have little formal education. Hundreds of drawings and photographs, based on the author's 16 years of experience with a village-run health program in the mountains of Mexico, make the health education basics very easy to understand and convey.

World Health Organization. **The Community Health Worker** (Geneva: World Health Organization; 1990), illustrations, 486 pages (ISBN 92-4-156097-5). This simply written, but excellent text is divided into 3 parts: (1) a working guide with practical, basic curriculum for the community health worker; (2) guidelines for training community health workers; and (3) advice on adapting this teaching program to local conditions. The book was issued in Arabic, English, French, Spanish, and Russian. It is available locally in many developing countries or from the World Health Organization. The latest revised version features larger print, better layout, and illustrations to aid in the education of community health workers and their community members.

Tropical Medicine

Berkow R, et al, eds. **The Merck Manual of Diagnosis and Therapy,** 18th ed (Rahway, NJ: Merck; 2005). "The most widely used medical text in the world," this work gives a comprehensive overview of medicine, except for details of surgical procedures. The latest revision includes sections on HIV and cross-cultural issues. Its low cost and compact size are major advantages. It is available for free online at www.merck.com/pubs. (Content last updated in May 2007.)

Cook GC, Zumla A. **Manson's Tropical Diseases,** 21st ed (London: WB Saunders; 2002), index, illustrations, 1779 pages (ISBN 0-7020-1764-7). This edition represents an overhaul of former editions stemming from Sir Patrick Manson's classic 1898 text. This "bible of tropical medicine" was written by British doctors with significant input from tropical countries.

Desenclos JC, ed, et al. **Clinical Guidelines: Diagnostic and Treatment Manual** (Paris: Médecins Sans Frontières; 2006), index, illustrations, 320 pages (ISBN 2-218-03480-0). Translated from the French, this clinical manual is part of the highly regarded Médecins Sans Frontières series. It covers the curative and to a lesser extent the preventive aspects of the main conditions encountered in the field. After a brief section on health care organization, the manual covers respiratory diseases, gastrointestinal diseases, skin and eye conditions, parasitic diseases, and bacterial and viral infections. Now available as PDF file from www.refbooks.msf.org.

Eddleston M, Pierini S. **Oxford Handbook of Tropical Medicine,** 2nd ed (Oxford, UK: Oxford University Press; 2004), index, illustrations, 712 pages (ISBN 9-780192-627728). Pocket-sized first edition of a work aimed at "junior doctors working in the developing world." Much of the text is based on World Health Organization–recommended guidelines. Management regimens taken from the World Health Organization's essential Drug Lists. This second edition has major revisions to the cardiology, renal, and endocrine sections. There are new sections on maternal health and ophthalmology and a new color plate section.

Lankinen KS, Bergström S, Mäkelä PH, Peltomaa M. **Health and Disease in Developing Countries** (London: Macmillan Education; 1994), illustrated, 586 pages (paperback, ISBN 0-333-58900-9). This excellent text provides both clinical advice and a broad survey of the health problems confronting people in developing countries and the strategies employed to overcome disease.

Mahmoud AAF. **Tropical and Geographical Medicine Companion Handbook** (New York: McGraw-Hill; 1993), index, 468 pages (ISBN 0-07-039625-6). This pocket-sized handbook provides a quick source of information on the major tropical and geographical diseases, using core information drawn from the parent volume Warren/Mahmoud *Tropical and Geographical Medicine* (1990), supplemented by more recent references. Written by Case Western faculty who did not contribute to the parent text, this portable book emphasizes clinical, diagnostic, and management approaches.

Schull CR. **Common Medical Problems in the Tropics,** 2nd ed (London: Macmillan Education; 1999), illustrated, 522 pages (paperback, ISBN 0-333-41973-1). Based initially on the author's experience in Papua New Guinea, the text has been field tested and expanded to provide practical advice on the care of patients throughout the tropics. The sections on HIV and tuberculosis have been completely rewritten.

Vanderkooi M. **Village Medical Manual: A Layman's Guide to Health Care in Developing Countries** (Pasadena, CA: William Carey Library; 2000), index, illustrations. Volume 1, 249 pages (ISBN 0-87808-251-4, 5th ed). Volume 2, approximately 500 pages (ISBN 0-87808-252-2). This, 2-volume set used for the Missionary Medicine Intensive course is written in an easy-to-follow style, yet it is much more comprehensive than texts such as *Where There is No Doctor* or *Primary Child Care.*

Warren KS, Mahmoud AAF. **Tropical and Geographical Medicine,** 2nd ed (New York: McGraw-Hill; 1990), index, illustrations, 1,159 pages (hardcover, ISBN 0-07-068328-X). This hefty hardcover, authored by 153 contributors from 21 countries, is one of the major reference works on the subject. It is divided into the following sections: Clinical Considerations; Genetics; Parasitism; Protozoan Diseases; Metazoan Diseases; Viral and Chlamydial Diseases; Bacterial, Spirochetal, and Rickettsial Diseases; Fungal Diseases; and Nutritional Diseases. Helpful appendices include Signs and Symptoms, Considerations for Travelers and Immigrants, and a Review of Diseases by Region.

Werner D. **Where There Is No Doctor,** rev. ed (Berkeley, CA: Hesperian Foundation; 2007), index, illustrations, 512 pages (ISBN 0-942364-15-5). This landmark text illustrated by the author and originally written in Spanish was first published in English in 1977. Since then it has been revised and published in more than 50 languages. The book is useful to a broad range of health professionals as well as to village health workers, mothers, midwives, teachers, and village pharmacists. Twenty-three chapters cover many subjects including health education, patient examination, the proper uses of medicines, first aid, nutrition, illness prevention, common illnesses, serious illnesses, skin problems, eyes, teeth, gums and mouth, urogenital problems, family planning, health and sickness in children, health and sickness of older people, and the medicine kit. Excellent appendices cover the usage, dosage, and precautions for medications as well as additional practical information about educating patients. Available online as a PDF file from the Hesperian Foundation (www.hesperian.org/publications_download.php).

World Health Organization. **Management of Severe Malaria,** 2nd ed (Geneva: World Health Organization; 2000), 76 pages (ISBN 9241545232). A pocket-sized guide to the rapid diagnosis and management of severe *Plasmodium falciparum* malaria, offering an at-a-glance reference to the signs, tests, actions, and nursing care required. The book is designed to facilitate rapid decisions and immediate action.

World Health Organization. **TB/HIV: A Clinical Manual,** 2nd ed (Geneva: World Health Organization; 2004) 210 pages (ISBN 9241546344). A pocket-sized guide to the clinical management of tuberculosis, particularly in patients coinfected with HIV. Tables, flow charts, lists of dos and don'ts, Q & A, and numerous practical tips are used to facilitate quick reference and correct decisions. It is primarily addressed to clinicians in sub-Saharan Africa, but is suitable for use in Asia and South America as well.

Water/Sanitation/Hygiene

Delmas G, Courvallet M. **Public Health Engineering in Emergency Situations** (Paris: Médecins Sans Frontières; 1994), illustrations, 178 pages (hardcover). John Adams' translation of the Médecins Sans Frontières French original has minor imperfections and Briticisms, but the spiral-bound book features extremely helpful plans and diagrams that offer concrete technical solutions. After an introduction defining needs in terms of site planning, the book discusses water in camps of displaced people, sanitation in emergency situations, and vector control. There is an English/French/ Spanish glossary defining technical terms that appear in the guide or are used every day in this field.

Davis J, Lambert R. **Engineering in Emergencies: A Practical Guide for Relief Workers,** 2nd ed (London: ITDG Publishing; 2000), index, illustrations, 718 pages (paperback, ISBN 1-85339-222-7). This book aims to give engineers practical information on areas outside their specialty, so that they can provide emergency humanitarian aid, but offers some guidance to non-engineering relief workers. This hefty technical manual is remarkable for its inclusion of advice on personal effectiveness and interpersonal relationships. Water supply, electrical and mechanical plant, refugee camp management, etc, are discussed in great detail. This is a completely revised edition with feedback from users—including experience from cooler climates and European emergencies. The volume has 2 new chapters on personal security and telecommunications, and an improved index for easier use.

Feachem RG, Bradley DJ, Garelick H, Mara DD. **Sanitation and Disease: Health Aspects of Excreta and Wastewater Management** (Chichester: John Wiley & Sons for World Bank; 1983), illustrations, 501 pages (hardcover, ISBN 0-471-90094-X). This, the third volume in a series on appropriate technologies for water supply and sanitation, addresses the public health, microbiological, and parasitological aspects of sanitation. Part One explores Health Hazards of Excreta: Theory and Control. Part Two describes 28 excreted pathogens and the epidemiology and control of the infections these pathogens cause.

Ferron S, Morgan J, O'Reilly M. **Hygiene Promotion: A Practical Manual for Relief and Development** (London: Intermediate Technology/CARE; 2000), index, illustrations, 250 pages (ISBN 1-85339-505-6). Written particularly for fieldworkers trying to reduce incidence of water- and sanitation-related diseases in relief/emergency situations, this lavishly illustrated volume should also prove useful for those working in community development, health, and engineering. The experiences of hygiene promotion by fieldworkers from CARE and other agencies inform the text throughout.

Morgan P. **Rural Water Supplies and Sanitation** (London: Macmillan; 1990), index, illustrations, 358 pages (paperback, ISBN 0-333-48569-6). Part One concerns gaining access to a clean water supply through pumps, wells, and simple water purification systems. Part Two deals with the construction and maintenance of the Blair latrine and its variants. This profusely illustrated work offers a variety of technological options.

Winblad U, Kilama W. **Sanitation Without Water** (London: Macmillan; 1985), index, illustrations, 161 pages (paperback, ISBN 0-333-39140-3). This revised edition contains well-illustrated, practical information on how to design, build, and operate better latrines—simple health measures for those with limited resources. Interesting cultural insights into why different latrine systems are acceptable or not.

World Health Organization. **Surface Water Drainage for Low-income Communities** (England: World Health Organization; 1991), illustrations, 93 pages (paperback, ISBN 92-4-154416-3). This publication describes how low-income communities can take action themselves to construct low-cost drainage systems or rehabilitate one that has fallen into disrepair. Written in nontechnical language and copiously illustrated, it stresses community participation at all stages of the project.

Periodicals

Child Health Dialogue is a quarterly international newsletter on child health and disease prevention focusing on practical information on how to tackle the main causes of child mortality: acute respiratory infections, diarrhea, malaria, malnutrition, and measles. Targeted primarily at health care workers, this accessible publication focuses on diagnosis, management, and procedures in the developing world setting. It provides information on essential drugs and contains tips on training, research updates, a comprehensive review quiz, and letters. This periodical has now ceased publication, but the last 7 issues are available as PDF files and are free downloads (www.healthlink.org.uk).

Community Eye Health, the "International Journal to Promote Eye Health Worldwide" is a 16-page color quarterly free to eye health workers in developing countries. It is available as a PDF download from www.jceh.co.uk/. Chinese, French, Spanish, and Indian editions of the journal are also available.

Footsteps, "a quarterly paper linking health and development workers worldwide," is free of charge to "individuals working to promote health and development." Issues provide practical advice and exchange of news and views.

For example, No. 33 includes step-by step advice on insecticide-treated bed nets, making mosquito nets, and mosquito-proofing homes. To be included on the mailing list, send brief details on your work and preferred language (English, French, Portuguese, Spanish) to Footsteps Mailing List, PO Box 200, Bridgnorth, WV16 4WQ, UK; e-mail: footsteps@tearfund.org. PDF versions of the quarterly paper are available free of charge at http://tilz.tearfund.org. Tearfund International also produces 2 other publication series: (1) **PILLARS** guides are designed for discussion-based learning in small grsoups. They cover issues such as healthy eating, mobilizing the community, and responding more effectively to HIV and AIDS and (2) **ROOTS** books aim to help Christian development organizations in their work. They provide detailed information on relevant topics such as fundraising and project cycle management. They are designed to help staff study and use them together.

Health For the Millions, published bimonthly by the Health for the Millions Trust/Voluntary Health Association of India, an independent Indian commission on health, advocates reform in the public health system of India. Though issues of the periodical may be devoted to topics like diabetes or AIDS, the nontechnical style shows that the publication is aimed at an audience much broader than just the medical community. Each issue contains relevant summaries of Joint United Nations Programme on HIV/AIDS, UNICEF, and World Health Organization reports. Write Health for the Millions Trust c/o VHAI B 40, Qutab Institutional Area south of ITT, New Delhi 110 016. Annual subscription $40, life subscription $360. Phone: 011-26518071-72, e-mail: vhai@del2.vsnl.net.in (www.vhai.org/aboutus1.asp?id=healthforthemillions).

Tropical Doctor, published quarterly by the Royal Society of Medicine, focuses on the prevention, management, and treatment of prevalent diseases in developing countries and endeavors to present a picture of the problems of health and disease in these countries as a step toward lessening the sense of isolation felt by those working far from advanced medical centers. Through its short, practical articles and case studies, the journal functions as a "continuing postgraduate course in the practice of medicine in tropical countries." Contact Tropical Doctor Subscription Department, Royal Society of Medicine, 1 Wimpole St, London, W1M 8AE, UK. Subscription phone: 011 44 (0) 1206 796351; fax: 011 44 (0) 1206 799331. Web: www.rsmpress.co.uk/td.htm. Surface mail North American annual subscription rate: US $180 includes online version; $153 for online version alone.

Update in Anaesthesia, a "journal for anaesthetists in developing countries," is coproduced by World Federation of Societies of Anaesthesiologists and by the International Association for the Study of Pain. Now published only in PDF. For more information, visit their Web site (www.nda.ox.ac.uk/wfsa).

Acronyms in International Health

AAIN
Action Africa in Need (NGO)

AAP
American Academy of Pediatrics (NGO)

ACF
Action Contre la Faim (NGO)

ACET
Advisory Council for the Elimination of Tuberculosis

ACIH
Agency for Co-operation in International Health (Japan)

ACIP
Immunization Practices Advisory Committee (US Public Health Service)

ACMR
Advisory Committee on Medical Research (WHO)

ADB
African Development Bank (IGO)

ADB
Asian Development Bank (IGO)

ADRA
Adventist Development and Relief Agency (NGO)

AED
Academy for Educational Development

AFB
Acid-fast bacilli

AFDB
African Development Bank (IGO)

AFR
Bureau for Africa (USAID)

AFSC
American Friends Service Committee (NGO)

AHRTAG
Appropriate Health Resources and Technologies Action Group
(now Healthlink) (UK)

AI
Amnesty International (NGO)

AICOS
Associazione Interventi di Cooperazione allo Sviluppo (Italy NGO)

AICF
Action Internationale Contre la Faim (NGO)

AID
United States Agency for International Development

AIDS
Acquired immunodeficiency syndrome

AIDSCAP
Acquired Immunodeficiency Syndrome Control and Prevention Program

AIHA
American International Health Alliance (NGO)

AIM
African Inland Mission (NGO)

AIMI
Africa Integrated Malaria Initiative

AJJDC
American Jewish Joint Distribution Committee (NGO)

AJWS
American Jewish World Service (NGO)

AKF
Aga Khan Foundation (NGO)

ALRI
Acute lower respiratory tract infection

AMEL
Lebanese Association for Popular Action (NGO)

AMR
Antimicrobial resistance

AMREF
African Medical and Research Foundation (NGO)

AMSA
American Medical Student Association (NGO)

ANE
Bureau for Asia and the Near East (USAID)

ANM
Auxiliary nurse midwife

APAC
AIDS prevention and control

APHA
American Public Health Association

APLM
Antipersonnel land mine

APO
Aid post orderly

APR
Agency performance report

APUA
Alliance for the Prudent Use of Antibiotics

AR
Attack rate

ARC
American Refugee Committee (NGO)

ARC
American Red Cross, International Service

ARCH
Applied research for child health

ARI
Acute respiratory infections

ASDB
Asian Development Bank

ASEAN
Association of South East Asian Nations

AUI
Action d'Urgence Internationale (International Emergency Action) (NGO)

BASICS
Basic support for institutionalized child support

BBF
Brother's Brother Foundation (NGO)

BCG
Bacille Calmette-Guérin (TB vaccine)

BCI
Behavior change interventions

BHR
Bureau for Humanitarian Response (USAID)

BHS
Basic health services

BMI
Body mass index

BRC
British Refugee Council (NGO)

BRCS
British Red Cross Society

CA
Cooperating agency

C&F
Cost and freight

CARE
Cooperative for Assistance and Relief Everywhere (NGO)

CARICOM
Caribbean community

CBA
Cost-benefit analysis

CBR
Community-based rehabilitation

CBR
Crude birth rate

CCCD
Combating Childhood Communicable Diseases
(USAID program)

CCF
Christian Children's Fund (NGO)

CCH
Community and child health

CDC
Centers for Disease Control and Prevention
(US Department of Health and Human Services)

CDD
Control of diarrheal disease (WHO)

CDR
Center for Documentation of Refugees (IGO)

CEA
Cost-effectiveness analysis

CEDPA
Center for Development and Population Activities (NGO)

CEIS
Centro Italiano di Solidarietá (Italy NGO)

CENTCOM
Central Command (US DOD)

CERF
Central Emergency Revolving Fund (UN)

CFR
Case fatality ratio

CFR
Crude fatality rate

CHE
Complex humanitarian emergency

CHL
Community health leader

CH/N
Child health and nutrition

CHV
Community health volunteer

CHW
Community health worker

CIDA
Canadian International Development Agency

CIF
Cost, insurance, and freight

CIHI
Center for International Health Information

CIMADE
Service Oecuménique d'Entraide (France NGO)

CINC
Commander in chief

CINCPAC
Commander in chief Pacific

CISAS
Centro de Información y Servicios de Asesoria en Salud (Nicaragua NGO)

CL
Cutaneous leishmaniasis

CM
Chief of mission (US)

CMO
Civil military operations (US DOD term)

CMOC
Civil military operations center (US DOD term)

CMOT
Civil military operations team (US DOD term)

CMR
Crude mortality rate

CMS
Center for Migration Studies (NGO)

COMECON
Council for Mutual Economic Assistance

CP
Command post

CPHC
Comprehensive primary health care

CPR
Contraceptive prevalence rate

CRS
Catholic Relief Services (NGO)

CRWRC
Christian Reformed World Relief Committee

CS
Child survival

CSD
Child survival and disease

CSF
Children's Survival Fund (NGO)

CSM
Corn-soya-milk

CSM
Contraceptive social marketing

CSW
Commercial sex worker

CTF
Combined task force (Military)

CTR
Contraceptive technology research

CVI
Children's Vaccine Initiative

CWS
Church World Service

CWS
Community water supply and sanitation unit (WHO)

DAC
Development Assistance Committee (OECD)

DALIS
Disaster assistance logistics information system

DALY
Disability-adjusted life year

DANIDA
Danish International Development Agency

DAP
Drug Action Programme (WHO)

DART
Disaster assistance response team

DC
Developing country

DCM
Deputy chief of mission (US)

DD
Diarrheal disease

DEC
Disasters Emergency Committee (UK NGO consortium)

DEVTA
Deworming and enhanced vitamin A

DFB
Damien Foundation (Belgium NGO)

DFID
Department for International Development (UK)

DHA
Department of Humanitarian Affairs (UN)

DHF
Dengue hemorrhagic fever

DHS
Demographic and health survey

DIRE
Database of items for the relief of emergencies (UN)

DMAT
Disaster medical assistance team

DMF-Index
Decayed-Missed-Filled Index (oral health index)

DMO
District medical officer

DMT
Disaster management team

DOD
Department of Defense (US)

DOS
Department of State (US)

DOTS
Directly observed therapy short-course (TB)

DOW
Doctors of the World (NGO)

DP
Displaced person

DPHO
District public health officer

DPT
Diphtheria, pertussis, tetanus (immunization)

DRD
Disaster Response Division (OFDA)

DRI
Direct Relief International (NGO)

DSM
Dried skimmed milk

DSS
Dengue shock syndrome

EAA
Euro Action-Acord (NGO)

EBV
Epstein-Barr virus

EC
European Community (IGO)

ECHO
Equipment to charity hospitals overseas

ECHO
European Community Humanitarian Office

EDL
Essential drug list

EDRC
Emergency disaster relief coordinator

EEC
European economic community

EH
Environmental health

EHP
Environmental health project

EIS
Epidemic Intelligence Service (CDC)

ENDA CARIBE
Environment and Development in the Third World (Dominican Republic NGO)

ENI
Bureau for Europe and Newly Independent States (USAID)

EPI
Expanded Programme on Immunization (WHO)

ERID
Emerging and reemerging infectious diseases

ERM
Enfants Refugies du Monde (Refugee Children of the World) (NGO)

EU
European Union

EUR
Bureau for Europe and Canadian Affairs (US DOS)

EURCOM
European Command (US DOD)

EXW
Ex-works

FAA
Foreign Assistance Act (US)

FAO
Food and Agriculture Organization (IGO)

FEMA
Federal Emergency Management Agency (US)

FEWS
Famine early warning system

FFH
Food for the Hungry (NGO)

FFP
Office for Food and Peace (BHR)

FFW
Food for work

FGAE
Family Guidance Association of Ethiopia (Ethiopia NGO)

FHI
Food for the Hungry International (NGO)

FHI
Family Health International

FIC
Fully immunized child

FIC
Fogarty International Center (US NIH)

FINNIDA
Finnish International Development Agency

FOB
Free on board

FP
Family planning

FTC
Feed the Children (NGO)
FY
Fiscal year

GAG
Global Advisory Group (EPI)

GAVI
Global Alliance for Vaccines and Immunizations

GDP
Gross domestic product

GNP
Gross national product

GOBI
Growth monitoring, oral rehydration, breastfeeding, immunization

GOBI/FFF
GOBI plus family planning, food production, female education

GPA
Global Programme on AIDS (WHO)

GSK
Gonoshasthaya Kendra (Bangladesh NGO)

GTZ
German Technical Assistance Agency

HA
Health Aide

HAST
Humanitarian Assistance Survey Team (DOD)

HAV
Hepatitis A virus

HBV
Hepatitis B virus

HDR
Humanitarian daily ration

HEED
Health, Education, Economic Development Bangladesh (Bangladesh NGO)

HFA
Health for All (WHO)

HFA2000
Health for All by the Year 2000 (WHO)

HIS
Health information system

HIV
Human immunodeficiency virus

HKI
Hellen Keller International (US NGO)

HMD
Health Manpower Development (WHO)

HMIS
Health management information system

HMMWV
Highly mobile multipurpose wheeled vehicle ("hum vee") (DOD)

HQ
Headquarters

HRA
Humanitarian and Refugee Affairs Office (US DOD)

IAA
Inter-agency agreement

IAM
International Assistance Mission (Afghanistan NGO)

IAPSO
Inter-Agency Procurement Services Office

IARA
Islamic African Relief Agency

IARC
International Agency for Research on Cancer (WHO)

IAS
International Aid Sweden (NGO)

IATA
International Air Transport Association

IBRD
International Bank for Reconstruction and Development (World Bank)

ICCE
Intracapsular cataract extraction

ICDDR,B
International Centre for Diarrhoeal Disease Research, Bangladesh

ICHF
International Child Health Foundation (NGO)

ICM
Intergovernmental Committee on Migration

ICMC
International Catholic Medical Commission (NGO)

ICMR
Indian Council of Medical Research

ICRC
International Committee of the Red Cross (NGO)

ICS
Immunochromatographic strip (TB test)

ICVA
International Council of Voluntary Agencies (NGO)

ID
Infectious disease

IDA
International Dispensary Association

IDA
International Development Association (UN)

IDB
Inter-American Development Bank

IDD
Iodine deficiency disorder

IDP
Internally displaced person

IEF
International Eye Foundation (NGO)

IFAD
International Fund for Agricultural Development

IFPMA
International Federation of Pharmaceutical Manufacturers Associations

IFRCS
International Federation of Red Cross and Red Crescent Societies

IGO
Intergovernmental organization

IHE
International Health Exchange (UK NGO)

ILO
International Labour Organisation

IMA
Interchurch Medical Assistance (NGO)

IMC
International Medical Corps (NGO)

IMCI
Integrated Management of Childhood Illness (WHO initiative)

IMF
International Monetary Fund

IMPACT
An International Initiative Against Avoidable Disability (Switzerland NGO)

IMR
Infant mortality rate

IMVA
International Medical Volunteers Association (NGO)

INCAP
Institute of Nutrition of Central America and Panama

INCLEN
International Clinical Epidemiology Network

IND
Investigational new drug

INN
International nonproprietary name (of medications)

INRUD
International Network for the Rational Use of Drugs

INSTRAW
International Research and Training Institute for the Advancement of Women

IO
International organization

IOM
International Organization for Migration

IPA
International Pediatric Association

IPM
Integrated pest management

IPPF
International Planned Parenthood Federation (UK NGO)

IPV
Inactivated polio vaccine (Salk)

IPVO
Indigenous private voluntary organization

IRB
Institutional review board (for studies on human subjects)

IRC
International Rescue Committee (NGO)

IRH/FP
Integrated rural health and family planning

ISRA
Islamic Relief Agency (NGO)

ISTI
International Sciences and Technology Institute

ITBN
Insecticide treated bed nets

ITN
Insecticide treated nets

IUAT
International Union Against Tuberculosis

IUD
Intrauterine device

IUGR
Intrauterine growth retardation

IWHC
International Women's Health Coalition (US NGO)

JAIDO
Japan International Development Organization

JICA
Japan International Cooperation Agency

JRS
Jesuit Refugee Service (NGO)

JSI
John Snow Incorporated

KAP
Knowledge, attitude, and practices

KPV
Killed polio virus (IPV)

LAC
Latin America and the Caribbean

LBRF
Louse-borne relapsing fever

LBW
Low birth weight

LDC
Less or least developed country

LEB
Life expectancy at birth

LICROSS
League of Red Cross/Crescent Societies (NGO)

LLDC
Least developed country

LPO
Local purchase order

LWF
Lutheran World Federation

LWR
Lutheran World Relief (NGO)

MA
Medical assistant

MAC
Mid-arm circumference

MAF
Mission Aviation Fellowship

MAL
Malaria unit (WHO)

MAP
Medical Assistance Program (NGO)

MAP
Malaria Action Programme (WHO)

MCC
Mennonite Central Committee (NGO)

MCD
Medical Care Development (NGO)

MCH
Maternal and child health

MCH
Maternal and Child Health Programme (WHO)

MCI
Mercy Corps International (NGO)

MCL
Mucocutaneous leprosy

MDB
Multilateral Development Bank

MDM
Médecins du Monde (NGO, Doctors of the World)

MDRO
Mission disaster relief officer

MDT
Multiple drug therapy

MHW
Multipurpose health worker

MMB
Medicus Mundi Belgium (Belgium NGO)

MMR
Mumps, measles, rubella (vaccine)

MMR
Maternal mortality rate

MNH
Maternal and neonatal health

MOH
Medical officer of health

MOH
Ministry of Health

MOPH
Ministry of Public Health

MRE
Meal-ready-to-eat (DOD)

MSF
Médecins Sans Frontières (NGO, Doctors Without Borders)

MSF-H
Médecins Sans Frontières Holland (NGO, Doctors Without Borders)

MSH
Management sciences for health

MT
Metric ton

MUAC
Mid-upper arm circumference

MVDP
Malaria Vaccine Development Program

MVI
Malaria Vaccine Initiative

NACP
National AIDS Control Program

NATO
North Atlantic Treaty Organization

NCIH
National Council for International Health (US)

NGO
Nongovernmental organization

NHA
National health accounts

NHS
National Health Service (UK)

NID
National immunization days

NIH
National Institutes of Health (US)

NIS
Newly Independent States (former Soviet states)

NN
Neonatal

NNMR
Neonatal mortality rate

NNT
Neonatal tetanus

NOAA
National Oceanographic and Atmospheric Administration (US)

NORAD
Norwegian Agency for Development Co-operation

NPA
Norwegian People's Aid

NRC
Norwegian Refugee Council (NGO)

NUT
Nutrition Programme (WHO)

OAS
Organization of American States (IGO)

OAU
Organization of African Unity (IGO)

OC
Oral contraceptive

OCP
Oral contraceptive pill

OCP
Onchocerciasis Control Program

ODA
Overseas Development Administration

ODA
Official development assistance

ODM
Overseas Development Ministry (UK)

ODP
Orderly Departure Programme

OECD
Organization for Economic Cooperation and Development (IGO)

OED
Austrian Service for Development Cooperation (Austria NGO)

OFDA
Office of Foreign Disaster Assistance (USAID)

OHI
Operation Handicap Internationale (NGO)

OHS
Occupational Health Services

OIH
Office of International Health (US Public Health Service)

OLS
Operation Lifeline Sudan (UN)

ONG
French and Spanish acronym for NGO

OPV
Oral polio vaccine (Sabin)

OR
Odds ratio

ORA
Oromo Relief Association (Ethiopia NGO)

ORC
Open Relief Centre

ORH
Oral Health Programme (WHO)

ORS
Oral rehydration salts

ORS
Oral rehydration solution

ORT
Oral rehydration therapy

OS
Operations support

OSOCC
On-site operations coordination center

OTI
Office for Transition Initiatives (USAID/BHR)

Oxfam
Oxford Committee for Famine Relief

PA
Physician assistant

PADF
Pan American Development Foundation

PAHO
Pan American Health Organization (IGO)

PASB
Pan American Sanitary Bureau

PATH
Program for Appropriate Technology in Health

PCI
Project Concern International (US NGO)

PDA
Population and Community Development Association (Thailand NGO)

PDP
Parasitic Diseases Programme (WHO)

PEI
Polio Eradication Initiative

PEM
Protein-energy malnutrition

PHC
Primary health care

PHN
Public health nurse

PHN
Population, Health and Nutrition Department (World Bank)

PHR
Partnership for Health Reform

PK/HA
Peace keeping/humanitarian assistance

PMPP
Prevention, Mitigation, Preparedness and Planning Division (OFDA)

PNN
Postneonatal

PNNMR
Postneonatal mortality rate

PPD
Purified protein derivative

PRICOR
Primary Health Care Operations Research

PRITECH
Technologies for primary health care

PRM
Bureau for Population, Refugees and Migration (US DOS)

PROWID
Promoting Women in Development

PSC
Personal services contractor

PTB
Pulmonary tuberculosis

PTSD
Post-traumatic stress disorder

PVD
Programme for Vaccine Development (WHO)

PVO
Private voluntary organization (US term for NGO)

PYLL
Potential years of life lost

QALY
Quality adjusted life years

QIP
Quick impact project

QPS
Quaker Peace and Service (UK NGO)

QUIP
Quick impact project

RBM
Roll Back Malaria

RCO
Rural community organizer

RDF
Revolving Drug Fund

REA
Rapid epidemiological assessment

RECPHEC
Resource Center for Primary Health Care (Nepal NGO)

RedR
Registered Engineers for Disaster Relief

RH
Reproductive health

RHC
Rural health center

RI
Relief International (NGO)

RPC
Refugee processing center

RPM
Rational pharmaceutical management

RR
Relative risk

RSV
Respiratory syncytial virus

RTI
Reproductive tract infection

RTI
Respiratory tract infection

SADC
Southern Africa Development Community

SAT
Satellite

SAT
Southern Air Transport

SAWSO
Salvation Army World Service Office (NGO)

SCF
Save the Children Federation (NGO)

SFC
Supplementary feeding center

SFP
Supplementary feeding program

SHS
Division of Strengthening Health Services (WHO)

SIDA
Swedish International Development Authority

SOICH
Section on International Child Health (AAP)

SM
Safe motherhood

SNID
Subnational immunization days

SOM
Sovereign Order of Malta

SOUTHCOM
Southern Command (DOD)

SPHC
Selective primary health care

STI
Sexually transmitted infections

TA
Travel authorization

TA
Technical assistance

TALC
Teaching Aids at Low Cost (UK NGO)

TAPS
Associação Brasileira de Tecnologia Alternativa na Promoção da Saude
(Brazil NGO)

TB
Tuberculosis

TBA
Traditional birth attendant

TBM
Tuberculous meningitis

TBRF
Tick-borne relapsing fever

TCDC
Technical cooperation among developing countries

TDR
Special Programme for Research and Training in Tropical Diseases (UN)

TDY
Temporary duty

TFC
Therapeutic feeding center

TFP
Therapeutic feeding program

TFR
Total fertility rate

TM
Traditional midwife

TU
Tropical ulcer

TU
Tuberculin unit

U5MR
Under 5 mortality rate

UCI
Universal childhood immunization

UMCOR
United Methodist Committee on Relief (NGO)

UNAIDS
Joint United Nations Programme on HIV/AIDS

UN
United Nations (IGO)

UN-DMT
United Nations Disaster Management Team

UNCSH
United Nations Centre for Human Settlements (IGO)

UNDHA
United Nations Department of Humanitarian Affairs (IGO)

UNDOS
United Nations Development Office for Somalia (IGO)

UNDP
United Nations Development Programme (IGO)

UNDRO
United Nations Disaster Relief Office—now UNDHA (IGO)

UNEP
United Nations Environment Program (IGO)

UNESCO
United Nations Educational, Scientific and Cultural Organization (IGO)

UNFPA
United Nations Fund for Population Activities (IGO)

UNHCR
United Nations High Commissioner for Refugees (IGO)

UNICEF
United Nations Children's Fund (IGO)

UNIFEM
United Nations Development Fund for Women (IGO)

UNIPAC
United Nations Packing & Assembly Center (Denmark) (IGO)

UNIPAC
United Nations Procurement & Assembly Center (Denmark) (IGO)

UNITAR
United Nations Institute for Training and Research (IGO)

UNRISD
United Nations Research Institute for Social Development (IGO)

UNTAG
United Nations Transition Assistance Group (IGO)

UNU
United Nations University (IGO)

UNV
United Nations Volunteers (IGO)

USACE
United States Army Corps of Engineers (DOD)

USAF
United States Air Force (DOD)

USAID
United States Agency for International Development

USG
United States Government

USGS
United States Geological Survey (US Department of the Interior)

USPHS
US Public Health Service

UXO
Unexploded ordinance

VAD
Vitamin A deficiency

VADD
Vitamin A deficiency disease

VB
Vector borne

VCW
Village community worker

VHAI
Voluntary Health Association of India (India NGO)

VHF
Viral hemorrhagic fever

VHP
Village health post

VHW
Village health worker

VITA
Volunteers in technical assistance

VOLAG
Voluntary agency (PVO or NGO)

WASH
Water and Sanitation for Health Project (US NGO)

WCC
World Council of Churches (NGO)

WCDO
World Concern Development Organization (NGO)

WDR
World Development Report (World Bank)

WFC
World Food Council (UN)

WFP
World Food Programme (UN)

WHA
World Health Assembly (WHO)

WHC
Ward Health Committee

WHO
World Health Organization (IGO)

WMO
World Meteorological Organization (IGO)

WRC
World Relief Corporation

WSB
Wheat-soya blend

WVRD
World Vision Relief and Development (NGO)

YARH
Young adult reproductive health

YLL
Years of life lost

YMCA
Young Men's Christian Association (NGO)

YPLL
Years of productive life lost

Appendix C

Child Survival Indicators

Adequate nutritional status: An individual child of a certain age is said to be adequately nourished if his or her weight is greater than the weight corresponding to 2 Z-scores (2 SDs) below the median weight achieved by children of that age. The median weight and the distribution of weights around that median in a healthy population are taken from a standard established by the National Center for Health Statistics, or other reference populations endorsed by the World Health Organization. The indicator for the population as a whole is the proportion of children 12 through 23 months of age who are adequately nourished.

Continued breastfeeding: An estimate of the proportion of children breastfed for at least 1 year.

Contraceptive prevalence rate (CPR): An estimate of the proportion of women, aged 15 through 44 (or, in some countries, 15 through 49) in union or married, currently using a method of contraception. Where sources fail to distinguish modern and traditional methods, the combined rate is often shown.

Complementary feeding: An estimate of the proportion of infants 6 to 9 months of age (181 days–299 days) still breastfeeding, but also receiving complementary weaning foods.

DTP drop-out rate: An estimate of the proportion of living children between the ages of 12 and 23 months who received at least one DTP (diphtheria, tetanus, pertussis) vaccination but who did not receive the entire series of 3 vaccinations before their first birthdays.

Exclusive breastfeeding: An estimate of the proportion of infants younger than 4 months (120 days) who receive no foods or liquids other than breast milk.

Oral rehydration salts (ORS) access rate: An estimate of the proportion of the population younger than 5 years with reasonable access to a trained provider of oral rehydration salts that receives adequate supplies. This is a particularly difficult indicator to measure and, therefore, it may fluctuate dramatically from year to year as improved methods of estimation are devised.

Oral rehydration therapy (ORT) use rate: An estimate of the proportion of all cases of diarrhea in children younger than 5 years treated with ORS and/or a recommended home fluid. ORT use may be determined using administrative means or surveys. In general, administrative estimates are based on estimates of the number of episodes of diarrhea in the target population for a given year and the quantity of ORS available. Thus changes in the estimates of the frequency of diarrhea episodes can alter the ORT use rate as well as real changes in the pattern of use. Surveys are more precise in that they focus on the actual behavior of mothers in treating diarrhea in the 2-week period prior to the survey.

Vaccination coverage rate in children: An estimate of the proportion of living children between the ages of 12 and 23 months who have been vaccinated before their first birthday—3 times in the cases of polio and DTP and once for both measles and bacille Calmette-Guérin. Vaccination coverage rates are calculated in 2 ways. Administrative estimates are based on reports of the number of inoculations of an antigen given during a year to children who have not yet reached their first birthday divided by an estimate of the pool of children younger than 1 year eligible for vaccination. Survey estimates are based on samples of children between the ages of 12 and 23 months.

Vaccination coverage rate in mothers, tetanus toxoid 2+ (TT2+): An estimate of the proportion of women in a given period who have received 2 doses of tetanus toxoid during their pregnancies. This indicator is being changed in many countries to account for the cumulative effect of tetanus toxoid boosters. A woman and her baby are protected against tetanus when a mother has had only one or perhaps no boosters during a given pregnancy so long as the woman had received the appropriate number of boosters in the years preceding the pregnancy in question. (The appropriate number of boosters required during any given pregnancy varies with number received previously and the time elapsed.) The revised indicator is referred to as TT2+. Rates are computed using administrative methods or surveys.

Demographic Indicators

Annual infant deaths: An estimate of the number of deaths occurring among children younger than 1 year in a given year.

Average annual rate of growth: An estimate of the rate at which a population is increasing (or decreasing) in a given year.

Crude birth rate: An estimate of the number of live births per 1,000 population in a given year.

Crude death rate: An estimate of the number of deaths per 1,000 population in a given year.

Infant mortality rate: The estimated number of deaths in infants (children <1 year) in a given year per 1,000 live births in that same year. This rate may be calculated by direct methods (counting births and deaths) or by indirect methods (applying well-established demographic models).

Life expectancy at birth: An estimate of the average number of years a newborn can expect to live. Life expectancy is computed from age-specific death rates for a given year. It should be noted that low life expectancies in developing countries are, in large part, due to high infant mortality.

Maternal mortality rate: The estimated number of maternal deaths per 100,000 live births where a maternal death is one that occurs when a woman is pregnant or within 42 days of termination of pregnancy from any cause related to or aggravated by the pregnancy or its management. Although commonly referred to as a rate, this measure is actually a ratio because the unit of measurement of the numerator (women) is different than that of the denominator (births). Extremely difficult to measure, maternal mortality can be derived from vital registration systems (usually underestimated), community studies and surveys (requires very large sample sizes), or hospital registration (usually overestimated).

Number of births: An estimate of the number of births occurring in a given year.

Total fertility rate: An estimate of the average number of children a woman would bear during her lifetime given current age-specific fertility rates.

Total population: The mid-year estimate of the total number of individuals in a country.

Under 5 mortality rate: The estimated number of children born in a given year who will die before reaching 5 years of age per 1,000 live births in that same year. This rate may also be calculated by direct or indirect methods.

Disaster and Refugee Terminology

Absorptive capacity: The ability of a recipient country to effectively manage outside assistance.

Affected population: People requiring immediate emergency assistance from outside sources as a result of a disaster situation or event.

Anticipatory refugees: Individuals who flee their country based on the anticipation of persecutory events.

Assisting country: A country providing aid to an affected country. Assisting countries may or may not be a donor country (eg, assisting country provides shipping of food given by donor nation).

Asylum: Protection extended to persons fleeing political persecution.

Creeping disaster: Slow-onset disaster (eg, drought).

Cyclone: A violent rotating wind storm.

Damage assessment: An evaluation of the damages and losses caused by a disaster.

Displaced persons: Persons made homeless by disaster or upheaval, but still remaining within their own country.

Donor country: A nation giving money, materials, or supplies.

Famine: An acute and widespread lack of food causing hunger and starvation.

Famine early warning systems: Programs used to monitor and warn of possible impending famine.

Host country: Country hosting a development or disaster assistance program.

Hurricane: Severe tropical storm in the eastern Pacific and western Atlantic.

Mitigation: The reduction of the harmful effects of a disaster (eg, improving building standards in earthquake zones).

Needs assessment: Evaluation of the needs of the affected population.

Prevention: Activities undertaken to prevent a natural phenomenon or potential hazard from producing harmful effects (eg, construction of dams or dikes to eliminate flooding, or the safe disposal of hazardous materials).

Refugee: Generally refers to a person outside of his or her own country because of disaster or upheaval.

Situation assessment: Evaluation of the situation caused by a disaster, such as the number killed, injured, and affected.

Sitrep: A situation report on the current disaster situation.

Slow-onset disaster: Disaster that develops over time (eg, famine, civil strife, and insect infestations).

Sudden-onset disaster: Fast-onset disaster (eg, cyclone, earthquake, or volcanic eruption).

Typhoon: Severe tropical storm in the western Pacific, China Seas, or India.

Unaccompanied minors: Generally refers to refugee children without parents or guardians.

Vulnerable groups: Groups of people, often in a refugee or disaster context, who are particularly at risk of disease, starvation, or exploitation (eg, unaccompanied children, disabled, elderly, pregnant women).

Nutrition Terms and Acronyms

Basic food ration: A ration of cereal grain (eg, wheat or sorghum).

Body mass index (BMI): Weight in kilograms per height in meters squared.

Complementary ration: Foods that improve the taste or nutritional quality of the basic ration.

Corn-soya-blend (CSB): A fortified cereal blend used for general food distribution.

Corn-soya-milk (CSM): A protein-fortified blended dry food used for supplementary feeding.

Low birth weight: Below 2,500 g.

Maize: Corn.

Mid-upper arm circumference (MUAC): A rapid nutritional assessment screening tool used to identify malnourished children.

Nutrition survey: An assessment of the nutritional situation. It usually employs anthropometric (body) surveys of children to determine the prevalence of malnutrition in a population. Commonly used nutrition indices are weight for height, weight for length, or mid-upper arm circumference.

Protein-energy malnutrition (PEM): Major cause of death among infants and young children, usually caused by low food intake and infection. There are 3 types of PEM: nutritional marasmus, kwashiorkor, and marasmic kwashiorkor.

Pulse: The edible seeds of leguminous plants such as peas, beans, or lentils. Used in reference to feeding supplements.

Selective feeding: A collective term used for all feeding/food distribution programs in which food is provided to specifically selected beneficiaries. It typically includes both supplementary and therapeutic feeding.

Stunting: Low height for age.

Supplementary feeding program (SFP): Feeding program offering extra calories for vulnerable populations of displaced persons.

Therapeutic feeding program (TFP): Intensive feeding program offering total calories for severely malnourished infants and small children in a health care setting (sometimes referred to as *nutritional rehabilitation).*

Underweight: *Moderate* underweight is between -2 and -3 SDs from the median of weight for age of the reference population. *Severe* underweight is below -3 SDs from the median of weight for age of the reference population.

Wasting: Low weight for height.

Z-scores (SD scores): Express a child's weight as a multiple of the SD of the reference population. They are statistically more accurate than percentage of weight for height, but harder to calculate and understand. They are usually calculated by computer because reference population data are more manageable electronically. For example, a weight for height Z-score may be calculated as follows:

$$Z\ Score = \frac{(Weight\ of\ individual)\ minus\ (Average\ weight\ of\ children\ of\ same\ height\ from\ reference\ population)}{SD\ of\ children\ of\ same\ height\ of\ reference\ population}$$

Other Health Indicators and Terminology

Access to health services: Percentage of the population that can reach appropriate local health services by means of local transportation within 1 hour.

Access to potable water, urban: An estimate of the proportion of all persons living in urban areas (defined roughly as population centers of ≥2,000 persons) who live within 200 m of a standpipe or fountain source of water.

Access to potable water, rural: An estimate of the proportion of all persons not living in urban areas with a source of water close enough to home that family members do not spend a disproportionate amount of time fetching water.

Access to sanitation, urban: An estimate of the proportion of all persons living in urban areas with sanitation service provided through sewer systems or individual in-house or in-compound excreta disposal facilities (latrines).

Access to sanitation, rural: An estimate of the proportion of all persons not living in urban areas with sanitation coverage provided through individual in-house or in-compound excreta disposal facilities (latrines).

Adult literacy rate: The percentage of persons aged 15 years or older who can read and write.

Case fatality rate: The proportion of cases of a specified condition that are fatal within a specific time.

Census: An enumeration or survey of the entire population.

Cold chain: The refrigerated transportation system for vaccines from the manufacturer to the patient.

Coverage: The extent to which health services cover the need in the community.

Deliveries by trained attendants: An estimate of the proportion of deliveries attended by at least one physician, nurse, midwife, or trained traditional birth attendant.

Ex-pat (expatriate): Person residing in country other than his or her own.

HIV-1 seroprevalence, urban: An estimate of the proportion of all persons living in urban areas infected with HIV-1, the most virulent and globally prevalent strain of the human immunodeficiency virus. Where data are disaggregated by risk group, data for low-risk population are typically drawn from test results among pregnant women, the general population, or blood donors. High-risk population includes persons with known risk factors; these estimates are typically drawn from test results among commercial sex workers, their clients, or patients at sexually transmitted infection clinics.

HIV-1 seroprevalence, rural: An estimate of the proportion of all persons living in rural areas infected with HIV-1.

Index case: The first case in a group to come to the attention of the investigator.

Oral rehydration salts (ORS): Electrolyte-replenishing salts that may come in premixed packages or are made on demand from basic ingredients. Used in ORT.

Oral rehydration therapy (ORT): Treatment used for dehydrated patients, usually children, to prevent death from dehydration, which is often the result of diarrheal diseases.

Seeds and tools: A relief intervention (distribution of seeds and tools) designed to give an affected population the opportunity to gain self-sufficiency in food production.

Surveillance: The regular collection of information about a given health problem.

Target population: The group of individuals for whom an intervention is planned.

Urban percent: Percentage of population living in urban areas as defined according to the national definition used in the most recent population census.

Vector: A living organism (often an insect) that transports an infectious agent from an infected organism or its waste to a susceptible individual, its food, or immediate surroundings.

Appendix D

Resources

Internet Resources

Travel

www.embassy.org
The Electronic Embassy site provides information about foreign embassies in Washington, DC.

www.lonelyplanet.com
Lonely Planet travel books site offers lively news from many cities and countries.

www.tripprep.com
Travel Health OnLine has a lot of useful travel information including country information, travel clinic locations, and travel health concerns.

www.worldtravelguide.net
World Travel Guide Online has country profiles that include details on electricity and available communication services (mobile phones, fax, etc).

www.xe.com/ucc
The universal currency converter.

www.intellicast.org
This site provides weather information.

Governmental and Intergovernmental

www.cdc.gov
The Centers for Disease Control and Prevention site has superb travel health information, including geographic health recommendations, publications, disease information, and general information on staying healthy abroad.

www.rmis.com
The Center for International Health Information site has country health profiles and information about US Agency for International Development programs.

www.paho.org
The Web site of the Pan American Health Organization. It contains several useful features including publications and country health profiles.

www.cia.gov
This site provides country information by accessing the CIA World Factbook.

http://travel.state.gov/travel
The US State Department Web site has passport, visa, and travel warning information. It also lists hospitals and doctors in various nations.

www.reliefweb.int
ReliefWeb provides information on complex humanitarian emergencies, natural disasters, country backgrounds, and more.

www.unicef.org
UNICEF's Web site has extensive information on child health including the annual State of the World's Children and Progress of Nations reports.

www.unhcr.org
The United Nations High Commissioner for Refugees Web site specializes in refugee information.

www.unv.org
The United Nations Volunteers Web site.

www.usaid.gov
The US Agency for International Development (USAID) Web site.

www.usaid.gov/our_work/humanitarian_assistance/disaster_assistance
Office for Foreign Disaster Assistance information, including their Field Operations Manual.

www.worldbank.org/html/extpb/publications.htm
The World Bank Publications site.

www.who.org
The World Health Organization site has a wide range of health information and reports.

Nongovernmental Organizations and Other Sites

www.aap.org/sections/ich
The American Academy of Pediatrics Section on International Child Health Web site contains a searchable list of organizations needing medical volunteers, including pediatricians (www.aap.org/cgi-bin/overseas/aapartcl.cfm). The Directory of Overseas Opportunities is reproduced in the back of this book.

www.ichn.org
The International Child Health Network brings together workers in child health from all over the world to share advice and cooperate on projects.

www.hvousa.org
The Health Volunteers Overseas Web site.

www.cfhi.org
The Child Family Health International Web site.

www.dwb.org
The Doctors Without Borders (Médecins Sans Frontières) Web site.

www.medweb.emory.edu/MedWeb
MEDWEB has extensive health resources.

www.imva.org
The International Medical Volunteers Association Web site has a lot of volunteer-related material.

www.healthtraining.org
Medicus Mundi provides a comprehensive searchable listing of international health courses/programs.

www.pedschat.org
The international pediatrics chat site links pediatricians from more than 100 different countries and hosts weekly, live interactive medical presentations.

www.healthlink.org.uk
Web site of Healthlink Worldwide (low-cost international health publications including *Child Health Dialogue).*

www.globalhealth-ec.org
The Global Health Medical Education Consortium Web site.

www.ipa-world.org
The Web site of International Pediatrics Association, now headquartered in Paris.

Additional Resources

Healthlink Worldwide (formerly AHRTAG) publishes a variety of practical journals and newsletters. Makes available lists of community health resources, publications, and equipment worldwide. Provides an information consultancy and issues an annual directory of training courses in community health.

> 56 Leonard St, London EC2A 4LT, UK
> Phone: 01144 20 7549 0240, fax: 011 44 171 7549 0241
> E-mail: publications@healthlink.org.uk
> Web: www.healthlink.org.uk

IDA Foundation is an independent not-for-profit organization established by a group of Amsterdam pharmacists with the objective of providing high-quality, essential drugs and medical supplies at the lowest possible price to the not-for-profit health care sector in developing countries.

> PO Box 37098, 1030 AB Amsterdam, the Netherlands
> Phone: +31 020 4033051, fax: +31 020 403184
> E-mail: service@idafoundation.org
> Web: www.idafoundation.org

CHILD2015 (www.dgroups.org/groups/CHILD2015) is a free e-mail discussion group with the goal that "by 2015, every child will have access to an informed health care provider." As of spring 2008, there are more than 800 members in 90 countries and from all professions exploring the information and learning needs of health members in developing countries. It is organized in collaboration with the Royal College of Paediatrics and Child Health. One can join by sending an e-mail to child2015-admin@dgroups.org.

Global Health Council (formerly NCIH) is a Washington-based nongovernmental organization created in 1973 to identify priority health problems and to report on them to the US public, Congress, international and domestic government agencies, academic institutions, and the global health community. Their network includes hundreds of private and public organizations as well as several thousand professionals based inside and outside of the United States. Their Web site lists job opportunities both domestic and abroad.

> 1701 K St NW, Suite 600, Washington, DC 20006-1503
> Phone: 202/833-5900
> Web: www.globalhealth.org

Interaction is a well-established Washington-based coalition of more than 160 not-for-profit organizations working worldwide in the fields of relief, development, and refugee assistance. It is one of the leading US advocates for humanitarian assistance to the world's poor. Their **InterAction Member Profiles** provides details on member organizations including program activities and contacts.

> 1400 16th St NW, Suite 210, Washington DC 20036
> Phone: 202/667-8227
> Web: www.interaction.org

Lehman's Non-Electric "Good Neighbor" Heritage Catalog is a folksy catalog that visually resembles quaint old Sears and Roebuck with Amish flavor. "Everything old is new again," but also includes portable water filters, household and agricultural tools, solar-powered items, non-electric refrigerators, lanterns, etc.

> One Lehman Circle, PO Box 41, Kidron, OH 44636
> Phone: 888/438-5346, fax: 330/857-5785
> E-mail: GetLehmans@aol.com
> Web: www.lehmans.com

Magellan's Catalog of travel supplies lists hundreds of personal travel-related items.

> 110 W Sola St, Santa Barbara, CA 93101-3007
> Phone: 800/962-4943
> Web: www.magellans.com

Pan American Health Organization has many publications focused on the Americas, including Country Health Profiles, available free online.

> 525 23rd St, NW, Washington DC, 20037
> Phone: 202/974-3000
> Web: www.paho.org

Schumacher Center for Technology and Development publishes works on solid waste management, health care infrastructure support, water supply and sanitation, construction, energy, etc.

> Bourton on Dunsmore, RUGBY, CV23 9QZ, UK
> Phone: 011 44 (0) 1926 634400, fax: 011 44 (0) 1926 634401
> E-mail: practicalaction@practicalaction.org.uk
> Web: www.practicalaction.org

TALC (Teaching-aids At Low Cost) offers a wealth of materials: books, videos, slide sets, charts, and even low-priced complete libraries for community hospitals. Topics include tropical medicine, child health, child-to-child, and health care services management.

> PO Box 49, St Albans, Herts AL1 5TX, UK
> Phone: 011 44 172 785 3869, fax: 011 44 172 784 6852
> E-mail: talcuk@btinternet.com
> Web: www.talcuk.org

World Health Organization is the definitive United Nations agency that advises governments worldwide on all aspects of health care. The WHO publishes a huge number of books, journals, reports, and other publications, and has specialists available to advise on almost any health-related subject.

> Distribution and Sales, 1211 Geneva 27, Switzerland
> Web: www.who.org

The World Bank prints the *Index of Publications & Guide to Information Products and Services*. Though there are few specific works on health, there is much relevant material on nutrition, housing, nongovernmental organizations, water supply and sanitation, etc.

> Book Orders, PO Box 960, Herndon, VA 20172-0960
> Phone: 800/645-7247 or 703/661-1580, fax: 703/661-1501
> E-mail: books@worldbank.org
> Web: www.worldbank.org

Important Programs for Improving Child Health in Underserved Countries

Integrated Management of Childhood Illness (IMCI): A broad strategy to promote well-child interventions, especially nutrition and vaccine needs, at child health visits in hospital and clinic settings (www.who.int/child-adolescent-health/integr.htm).

Global Immunization Vision and Strategy 2006–2015 (GIVS): The latest strategic initiative to improve immunization delivery. Previous efforts include the elimination of smallpox (1967–1977), Global Polio Eradication Initiative (1988–present), and Expanded Immunization Program (EIP), which has recently added hepatitis B and *Haemophilus influenzae* vaccines to the standard DTP, polio, measles, and tuberculosis (www.who.int/immunization/givs).

The Sphere Program: A set of standards for humanitarian assistance in disaster settings in areas of water supply, nutrition, food, air, shelter, and health services. The very helpful 2004 handbook can be downloaded at www.sphereproject.org.

United Nations Convention of the Rights of the Child: A 1989 UN document outlining civil, political, economic, social, and cultural rights for all children (www.unicef.org/crc).

UN Millennium Development Goals Related to Children (MDGs): A 2002 action plan to eradicate poverty; achieve universal primary education; promote gender equality; reduce child mortality; improve maternal health; combat HIV/AIDS, malaria, and other diseases; ensure environmental sustainability; and develop a global partnership for development.

Periodical Subscriptions

Acta Tropica
Elsevier Science
PO Box 945
New York, NY 10159-0945
Phone: 888/4ES-INFO
E-mail: usinfo@scidirect.com
Web: www.elsevier.com

The American Journal of Tropical Medicine and Hygiene
The American Society of Tropical Medicine and Hygiene
60 Revere Dr, Suite 500
Northbrook, IL 60062
Phone: 847/480-9592
Web: www.ajtmh.org

Annals of Tropical Pediatrics
Vanessa Coulter
Editorial Assistant
Liverpool School of Tropical Medicine
Pembroke Place, Liverpool, L3 5QA, UK
Web: www.ingentaconnect.com

The Journal of Tropical Pediatrics
Journals Marketing
Oxford University Press
2001 Evans Rd
Cary, NC 27513
Phone: 800/852-7323
Web: http://tropej.oxfordjournals.org

Tropical Medicine and Hygiene News
The American Society of Tropical Medicine and Hygiene
60 Revere Dr, Suite 500
Northbrook, IL 60062
Phone: 847/480-9592
E-mail: astmh@aol.com
Web: www.astmh.org

Tropical Medicine & International Health
Note: In 1996 this journal combined *Annales de le Societe Belge de Medecine Tropicale; the Journal of Tropical Medicine and Hygiene, Tropical and Geographical Medicine;* and *Tropical Medicine and Parisitology.*
Blackwell Publishing, Ltd.
Journals Subscriptions
PO Box 1354
Oxford OX4 2XG, UK
Phone: +44 1865 778315
E-mail: orders@ames.blackwellpublishing.com

World Health
The magazine of the World Health Organization is published 6 times per year in English, French, and Spanish and 4 times per year in Arabic and Farsi.

World Health Organization
CH-1211 Geneva 27 Switzerland
Web: www.who.org

Selected International Health/Tropical Medicine Training Centers

Selected International Health/Tropical Medicine Training Centers

Asterisk (*) denotes schools with American Society of Tropical Medicine and Hygiene (ASTMH)–approved diploma course in clinical tropical medicine.

Europe

Christian Medical Fellowship, International Health Exchange
1st Floor 134 Lower Marsh
London SE 17 AE, UK
Phone: 011 44 171 620 3333
Fax: 011 44 171 620 2277
E-mail: info@ihe.org.uk
Web: www.ihe.org.uk

International Health Exchange
157 Waterloo Rd
London SE1 8XN, UK
Phone: +44 (0) 207 928 4694
Fax: +44 (0) 207 620 2453
E-mail: mailto:info@ihe.org
Web: www.ihe.org.uk/

Institut de Médecine Tropicale
155 Nationale Strasse
200 Antwerp
Belgium
Phone: +32-3-247.66.6
Fax: +32-3-216.14.31
E-mail: info@itg.be
Web: www.itg.be/

Liverpool School of Tropical Medicine*
Pembroke Place
Liverpool L3 5QA, UK
Phone: +44 (0) 151 705 3100
Fax: +44 (0) 151 705 3370
Web: www.liv.ac.uk/lstm

London School of Hygiene and Tropical Medicine*
Registry
Keppel St
London WC1E 7HT, UK
Phone: +44 (0) 20 7636 8636
Fax: +44 (0) 20 7436 5389
E-mail: registry@lshtm.ac.uk
Web: www.lshtm.ac.uk

RedR
1 Gt. George St
London SW1P 3AA, UK
Phone: +44 (0) 20 7233 3116
Fax: +44 (0) 20 7233 3590
Web: www.redr.org.uk

Swiss Tropical Institute
Course Secretariat
PO Box
CH 4002 Basel Switzerland
Phone: +41 61 284 82 80
Fax: +41 61 284 81 06
E-mail: courses-sti@unibas.ch
Web: www.sti.unibas.ch

USA

Boston University School of Public Health
Dept of International Health
715 Albany St, Talbot Bldg
Boston, MA 02218
Phone: 617/638-4640
Fax: 617/638-5299
E-mail: ih@bu.edu
Web: http://sph.bu.edu

Case Western Reserve University*
Center for International Health
2103 Cornell Rd
Cleveland, OH 44106-4978
Phone: 216/368-6321
Fax: 216/368-4825
E-mail: asr7@case.edu
Web: www.case.edu

Gorgas Memorial Institute*
University of Alabama at Birmingham
1530 Third Ave South, BBRB 203
Birmingham, AL 35294-2170
Phone: 800/822-6478
E-mail: info@gorgas.org
Web: http://gorgas.dom.uab.edu

Harvard University
School of Public Health
677 Huntington Ave
Boston, MA 02115
Phone: 617/432-4515
Web: www.hsph.harvard.edu

Johns Hopkins University*
Bloomberg School of Public Health
615 North Wolfe St
Baltimore, MD 21205
Phone: 410/955-6878
Fax: 410/955-4749
E-mail: mphprog@jhsph.edu
Web: www.jhsph.edu

Tulane University*
School of Public Health & Tropical Medicine
1501 Canal St
New Orleans, LA 70112
Phone: 800/676-5389
Web: www.sph.tulane.edu

Uniformed Services University of Health Sciences*
Division of Tropical & Public Health
4301 Jones Bridge Rd
Bethesda, MD 20814-4799
Phone: 800/772-1743
Web: www.usuhs.mil/medschool/fehsom.html

University of Arizona College of Medicine
Dept of Family & Community Medicine
PO Box 245052
Tucson, AZ 85724-5025
Phone: 520/626-7864
Fax: 520/626-2030
Web: www.globalhealth.arizona.edu

University of Virginia*
Dept of Infectious Diseases
PO Box 800738
Charlottesville, VA 22908
Phone: 434/924-2181
Web: www.healthsystem.virginia.edu/internet/inf-diseases

West Virginia University*
International Health Program
Byrd Health Sciences Center
PO Box 9100
Morgantown, WV 26506-9100
Phone: 304/293-5916
Fax: 304/293-2209
E-mail: nsanders@hsc.wvu.edu
Web: www.hsc.wvu.edu/som/tropmed

Directory of Overseas Opportunities

Aloha Medical Mission*

Jorge Camara, MD
810 N Vineyard Blvd
Honolulu, HI 96817
Phone: 808/847-3400
E-mail: jkia@alohamedicalmission.org
Web: www.alohamedicalmission.org

Minimum time: 10 days
Usual time: 2 weeks
Maximum time: 2 weeks
Who pays transportation: Volunteer
Who pays housing: Volunteer
Who pays food: Volunteer
Language requirements: No
Religious requirements: No
Countries: Marshall Islands, Micronesia, Myanmar, Papua New Guinea, Philippines, Vietnam
Regions: Asia/Pacific
Comments: A secular organization that provides health care to underserved patients in Hawaii and 11 Asian Pacific countries. The group organizes 3 to 5 international missions a year and works with local facilities and nongovernmental organizations.
Paid or volunteer: Volunteer
Residents or medical students accepted: Residents
Last update: January 2008

Amazon Promise

Jacqueline Carroll, Volunteer Coordinator
PO Box 1304
Newburyport, MA 01950
Phone: 800/775-4704
E-mail: expeditions@amazonpromise.org
Web: www.amazonpromise.org

Minimum time: 1 week
Usual time: 4 weeks
Maximum time: NA
Who pays transportation: Volunteer
Who pays housing: $1,100 for 1 week/$1,995 for 2 weeks/$2,750 for 4 weeks
(covers all expenses and travel insurance)
Who pays food: See Housing.
Language requirements: Spanish. Translators are available on most expeditions.
Religious requirements: No
Countries: Peru
Regions: Latin America
Comments: Volunteers work as part of health care teams in impoverished
villages along the Amazon River and in the city of Belen, Peru. There are
two 4-week medical student trips each summer and 5 other trips during
the year.
Paid or volunteer: Volunteer
Residents or medical students accepted: Residents
Last update: January 2008

American Baptist Board of International Ministries

Jonathan Hilsher, Coordinator of Volunteers
588 N Gulph Rd
King of Prussia, PA 19406
Phone: 800/ABC-3USA, ext 2367, or 610/768-2000
E-mail: jhilsher@abc-usa.org
Web: www.internationalministries.org

Minimum time: 2 weeks
Usual time: 3 months
Maximum time: Missionaries: indefinite amount of time
Who pays transportation: Varies
Who pays housing: Varies
Who pays food: Varies
Language requirements: Sometimes
Religious requirements: Baptist

Countries: Democratic Republic of the Congo, Dominican Republic, Haiti, India, Nepal, Nicaragua, Philippines, Thailand

Regions: Africa, Asia/Pacific, Caribbean, Latin America

Comments: Work with partners and nongovernmental organizations worldwide. Some placements are in hospitals.

Paid or volunteer: Paid and volunteer

Residents or medical students accepted: Residents and medical students

Last update: January 2008

American Jewish World Service (AJWS)

Andrea Richardson
45 W 36th St, 11th Floor
New York, NY 10018-7904
Phone: 212/792-2900 or 800/889-7146
E-mail: volunteer@ajws.org
Web: www.ajws.org

Minimum time: 2 months

Usual time: 4 months

Maximum time: 1 year

Who pays transportation: Organization

Who pays housing: Volunteer

Who pays food: Volunteer

Language requirements: Spanish or French in some countries

Religious requirements: Jewish

Countries: Cambodia, El Salvador, Ghana, Guatemala, Honduras, India, Mexico, Nicaragua, Senegal, South Africa, Thailand, Uganda

Regions: Africa, Asia/Pacific, Latin America

Comments: AJWS places professional Jewish men and women, including retirees, with local nongovernmental organizations (NGOs) in developing countries. Medical volunteers train NGO staff and local health providers in best medical practices and public health. Volunteers do not provide direct medical services to community members. Goal is sustainable development of community-based NGOs.

Paid or volunteer: Volunteer

Residents or medical students accepted: Residents

Last update: January 2008

American Refugee Committee (ARC)

Anthony Indelicato
430 Oak Grove St, Suite 204
Minneapolis, MN 55403
Phone: 612/872-7060 or 800/875-7060
E-mail: archq@archq.org
Web: www.arcrelief.org

Minimum time: 3 months
Usual time: 1 year
Maximum time: Years
Who pays transportation: Organization
Who pays housing: Organization
Who pays food: Volunteer
Language requirements: Varies
Religious requirements: No
Countries: Guinea, Liberia, Pakistan, Sierra Leone, Sudan, Sri Lanka, Thailand,
   Uganda
Regions: Africa, Asia/Pacific
Comments: ARC provides primary health care and training to refugees and
   internally displaced persons. ARC provides a monthly stipend, round-trip
   transportation, medical insurance, and group housing. Internships are
   rarely available.
Paid or volunteer: Paid
Residents or medical students accepted: No
Last update: January 2008

Angkor Hospital for Children (see Friends Without a Border)

Asociacion Ak'tenamit/Pueblo Nuevo

Maria Fernandez Trueba
Apartado Postal 2675, Zona 1
Ciudad de Guatemala, Guatemala
Phone: 502/5908-4358
E-mail: info@aktenamit.org
Web: www.aktenamit.org

Minimum time: 2 months
Usual time: 3 months
Maximum time: 1 year
Who pays transportation: Volunteer
Who pays housing: Organization

Who pays food: Organization
Language requirements: Spanish (must be fluent)
Religious requirements: No
Countries: Guatemala
Regions: Latin America
Comments: Medical doctor or final year medical student will help local health care workers in rural clinics and attend remote village outreach clinics.
Paid or volunteer: Volunteer
Residents or medical students accepted: Residents and 4th-year medical students
Last update: January 2008

Baptist General Conference

Curt Hansen
2002 S Arlington Heights Rd
Arlington Heights, IL 60005
Phone: 800/323-4215 or 847/228-0200
E-mail: chansen@baptistgeneral.org
Web: www.bgcworld.org

Minimum time: 6 months Africa; 1 month Haiti
Usual time: 1 to 2 years
Maximum time: Career
Who pays transportation: Short term, volunteer; long term, organization
Who pays housing: Volunteer
Who pays food: Volunteer
Language requirements: Local language encouraged for long-term volunteers.
Religious requirements: Baptist; short term: must be recommended by an evangelical church
Countries: Brazil, Cameroon, Cote d'Ivoire, Ethiopia, Haiti
Regions: Africa, Caribbean, Latin America
Comments: Need strong recommendation from volunteer's home church. Career positions are available and they are supported by the organization.
Paid or volunteer: Paid and volunteer
Residents or medical students accepted: Residents and medical students sometimes
Last update: January 2008

Baylor International Pediatric Aids Initiative

Texas Children's Hospital Clinical Care Center
6621 Fannon 001210
Houston, TX 77030
Phone: 832/822-1038
E-mail: mkline@bcm.edu
Web: www.bayloraids.org

Minimum time: 1 year
Usual time: 2 years
Maximum time: 2 years
Who pays transportation: Organization
Who pays housing: Organization
Who pays food: Organization
Language requirements: English/French
Religious requirements: No
Countries: Botswana, Burkina Faso (French preferred), China, Kenya, Lesotho, Malawi, Romania, Swaziland, Tanzania, Uganda
Regions: Africa, Asia, Eastern Europe
Comments: Pediatric AIDS Corps doctors work at one of Baylor's Clinical Centers of Excellence, where more than 20,000 HIV-infected children and family receive care. There is a 4-week preservice training in Houston in July and August.
Paid or volunteer: Paid: $40,000 plus benefits; student loan debt relief
Residents or medical students accepted: 1-month rotations for medical students and residents
Last update: January 2008

Board of World Mission of the Moravian Church

Lisa Mixon
PO Box 1245
Bethlehem, PA 18016-1245
Phone: 610/868-1732
E-mail: lisa@mcnp.org or dr_sam_marx@juno.com
Web: www.moravianmission.org

Minimum time: 2 weeks
Usual time: 1 to 2 months
Maximum time: 6 months
Who pays transportation: Volunteer
Who pays housing: Varies
Who pays food: Volunteer
Language requirements: Spanish for Honduras, Nicaragua
Religious requirements: Yes

Countries: Caribbean, Honduras, Nicaragua, Tanzania
Regions: Africa, Caribbean, Latin America
Comments: Christian faith commitment required.
Paid or volunteer: Volunteer
Residents or medical students accepted: Residents and medical students
Last update: January 2008

Brethren in Christ World Missions

Mike Holland
431 Grantham Rd, PO Box 390
Grantham, PA 17027-0390
Phone: 717/697-2634, ext 5411
E-mail: mholland@messiah.edu
Web: www.bic-church.org

Minimum time: 1 month
Usual time: 3 years for career missionaries
Maximum time: Career
Who pays transportation: Volunteer
Who pays housing: Volunteer
Who pays food: Volunteer
Language requirements: No
Religious requirements: No for short term
Countries: Zambia, Zimbabwe
Regions: Africa
Comments: Evangelical Christian organization that helps staff hospitals, operates a malaria research institute, and has a nurses' training school. John Spurrier in Zambia (hospital director) e-mail: spurrier@mmh.macha.org.zm.
Paid or volunteer: Volunteer
Residents or medical students accepted: Residents and 4th-year medical students
Last update: January 2008

Bridges to Community

Executive Director
95 Croton Ave
Ossining, NY 10562
Phone: 914/923-2200
E-mail: info@bridgestocommunity.org
Web: www.bridgestocommunity.org

Minimum time: 1 week
Usual time: 10 days
Maximum time: 3 weeks
Who pays transportation: Volunteer
Who pays housing: Volunteer
Who pays food: Volunteer
Language requirements: No
Religious requirements: No
Countries: Kenya, Nicaragua
Regions: Africa, Latin America
Comments: Organizes service trips primarily to Nicaragua. Professionals of all levels (including medical students) and families are welcome.
Paid or volunteer: Volunteer
Residents or medical students accepted: Residents and medical students
Last update: January 2008

Cameroon Baptist Convention Health Board (CBC)

George Ngwang
PO Box 1, Bamenda
NW Province
Cameroon, Africa
Phone: 237 77 13 32 82
E-mail: cbcvisitors@gmail.com
Web: www.mtctplus.org

Minimum time: 1 month
Usual time: 1 to 2 months
Maximum time: None
Who pays transportation: Volunteer
Who pays housing: Organization
Who pays food: Volunteer
Language requirements: No
Religious requirements: Christian
Countries: Cameroon
Regions: Africa

Comments: CBC runs 5 hospitals and 66 health centers. Sometimes much-needed volunteers receive a stipend.
Paid or volunteer: Paid and volunteer
Residents or medical students accepted: Residents and 4th-year medical students pay fee of $800 to $1,100 to cover housing, food, and supervision.
Last update: April 2008

Cape Cares

Martha Baxley, Administrator
PO Box 310
West Barnstable, MA 02668
Phone: 508/982-1207
E-mail: mebbax@hotmail.com
Web: www.capecares.com

Minimum time: 1 week
Usual time: 1 week
Maximum time: 1 week
Who pays transportation: Volunteer
Who pays housing: Volunteer
Who pays food: Volunteer
Language requirements: No
Religious requirements: No
Countries: Honduras
Regions: Latin America
Comments: This is a smaller-scale service organization based on Cape Cod, MA. Cape Cares has adopted several communities in Honduras and sends teams of health care workers and support personnel to these communities 9 or so times a year.
Paid or volunteer: Volunteer
Residents or medical students accepted: Sometimes
Last update: January 2008

Caring Partners International

Rhonda Reed, Vice President
PO Box 44707
Middletown, OH 45044-0707
Phone: 513/727-1400
E-mail: r.reed@caringpartners.org
Web: www.caringpartners.org

Minimum time: 1 week
Usual time: 10 days
Maximum time: 2 weeks
Who pays transportation: Varies
Who pays housing: Varies
Who pays food: Varies
Language requirements: No. Interpreters provided.
Religious requirements: Christian Evangelical; statement of faith required
Countries: Cuba, Ecuador, Guatemala, Nicaragua, Ukraine
Regions: Caribbean, Eastern Europe, Latin America
Comments: Hands-on clinic and conferences.
Paid or volunteer: Volunteer
Residents or medical students accepted: Residents and medical students
Last update: January 2008

Carolina Honduras Health Foundation

Chris Zawacki
Box 528
Barnwell, SC 29812
Phone: 803/259-3513
E-mail: Czawacki@aol.com

Minimum time: 1 week
Usual time: 1 week
Maximum time:
Who pays transportation: Volunteer
Who pays housing: Organization
Who pays food: Volunteer
Language requirements: No
Religious requirements: No
Countries: Honduras
Regions: Latin America
Comments: Established by a South Carolina–based family physician in 1995, the foundation's seaside clinic in Limon, Honduras, treats an impoverished, underserved population. Physicians in all specialties are needed to join US medical teams that travel to Honduras.

Paid or volunteer: Volunteer
Residents or medical students accepted: Residents and medical students
Last update: January 2008

Casa Clinica de la Mujer

Angelica del Valle
Domicilio Conocido
Chacala, Nayarit, Mexico 63715
Phone: 800/257-0532, direct line in Mexico: +52(327)219-4000
E-mail: info@mardejade.com
Web: www.mardejade.com

Minimum time: 2 weeks
Usual time: 2 weeks
Maximum time:
Who pays transportation: Volunteer
Who pays housing: Host facility (rates on Web site)
Who pays food: Host facility
Language requirements: Spanish grammar and medical Spanish are taught as part of the program.
Religious requirements: No
Countries: Mexico
Regions: Latin America
Comments: The clinic volunteer program is directed by the founder and medical director of the clinic, Laura del Valle, MD, MPH, who is an assistant professor of family and community medicine at University of California San Francisco. Good place to improve Spanish language interviewing skills and volunteer in a rural primary health clinic.
Paid or volunteer: Volunteer
Residents or medical students accepted: Residents and medical students
Last update: January 2008

Catholic Medical Mission Board

Rosemary DeConstanzo
10 W 17th St
New York, NY 10011-5765
Phone: 212/242-7757 or 800/678-5659
E-mail: info@cmmb.org
Web: www.cmmb.org

Minimum time: 1 month
Usual time: 1 year
Maximum time: Career
Who pays transportation: Long term, organization; short term, volunteer
Who pays housing: Host facility
Who pays food: Host facility
Language requirements: Sometimes
Religious requirements: No
Countries: Latin America: Belize, Bolivia, Brazil, Dominican Republic,
    Ecuador, El Salvador, Guatemala, Guyana, Haiti, Honduras, Jamaica,
    Mexico, Nicaragua, Peru. Africa: Cameroon, Ghana, Kenya, Malawi,
    Nigeria, South Africa, Swaziland, Tanzania, Uganda, Zambia, Zimbabwe.
    Asia: Cambodia, China, India, Papua New Guinea, South Korea, Thailand
Regions: Africa, Asia/Pacific, Caribbean, Latin America
Comments: Volunteers need not be Catholics but must abide by moral and
    ethical teachings of Catholic Church. All volunteers receive insurance:
    Medivac, liability, accidental life, and malpractice (where applicable).
    Volunteers of 1 year or more receive a stipend and hospitalization.
Paid or volunteer: Volunteer
Residents or medical students accepted: No
Last update: January 2008

Catholic Network of Volunteer Service (CVNS)

Jim Lindsay, Executive Director
6930 Carroll Ave, Suite 820
Takoma Park, MD 20912-4423
Phone: 800/543-5046 or 301/270-0900
E-mail: cnvsinfo@cnvs.org
Web: www.cnvs.org

Minimum time: 1 month
Usual time: 1 year
Maximum time: Varies (average few years)
Who pays transportation: Varies
Who pays housing: Varies
Who pays food: Varies

Language requirements: Sometimes
Religious requirements: Sometimes
Countries: Worldwide
Regions: Africa, Asia/Pacific, Caribbean, Eastern Europe, Latin America, Middle East
Comments: CVNS is a membership network of more than 200 programs with volunteers serving in all 50 states and more than 100 countries worldwide.
Paid or volunteer: Paid and volunteer
Residents or medical students accepted: Some programs may accept
Last update: January 2008

Center for Personal Restoration

David Krier, MD
18891 River Rd, NE
St Paul, OR 97137
Phone: 503/703-4745
E-mail: dbkmd@earthlink.net
Web: www.cprestoration.org

Minimum time: 1 week
Usual time: 2 weeks
Maximum time: Varies (longer stays can be arranged individually)
Who pays transportation: Volunteer
Who pays housing: Volunteer
Who pays food: Volunteer
Language requirements: English. Spanish is helpful, but interpreters used.
Religious requirements: No
Countries: Honduras, Peru, others in planning phases
Regions: Latin America
Comments: The center's mission statement is, "To provide personal renewal for health care professionals through volunteer service." This is done by organizing campaigns (group experiences) to underserved areas so health care can be provided to those who have rare or no access.
Paid or volunteer: Volunteer
Residents or medical students accepted: Residents and medical students
Last update: January 2008

Child Family Health International (CFHI)

David Tozer
995 Market St, Suite 1104
San Francisco, CA 94103
Phone: 415/957-9000, ext 301, or 866/345-4674
E-mail: students@cfhi.org
Web: www.cfhi.org

Minimum time: 1 month
Usual time: 1 to 2 months
Maximum time:
Who pays transportation: Volunteer
Who pays housing: Homestay
Who pays food: At homestay
Language requirements: Spanish
Religious requirements: No
Countries: Bolivia, Ecuador, India, Mexico, Nicaragua, South Africa
Regions: Africa, Asia/Pacific, Latin America
Comments: Since 1993 CFHI has run global health, service-learning electives for premedical, medical, and other students of the health professions. Students are immersed in new cultural contexts and learn how health care is practiced and experienced worldwide.
Paid or volunteer: Volunteer
Residents or medical students accepted: ONLY residents and medical students
Last update: January 2008

Children of Peace International

PO Box 2911
Loveland, CO 80539-2911
Phone: 970/667-3716
E-mail: childrenofpeace@hotmail.com
Web: www.childrenofpeace.org

Minimum time: 2 weeks
Usual time: 4 weeks
Maximum time: Varies
Who pays transportation: Volunteer
Who pays housing: Volunteer
Who pays food: Volunteer
Language requirements: No
Religious requirements: No
Countries: Vietnam
Regions: Asia/Pacific

Comments: Humanitarian organization that sponsors medical teams to deliver dental and medical care to orphans and poor people of neighboring communities. They also built the first pediatric HIV treatment center in Ho Chi Minh City.
Paid or volunteer: Volunteer
Residents or medical students accepted: Residents
Last update: January 2008

Children's Cross Connection

Pamela Rundle
220 Avon Dr
Fayetteville, GA 30215
Phone: 770/716-1926
E-mail: info@ChildrensCross.org
Web: www.cccinternational.org

Minimum time: 1 week
Usual time: 2 weeks
Maximum time: 2 weeks
Who pays transportation: Volunteer
Who pays housing: Varies
Who pays food: Varies
Language requirements: No
Religious requirements: Jewish or Christian
Countries: El Salvador, Ethiopia, Nicaragua
Regions: Africa, Latin America
Comments: Our organization provides primary medical and dental care to rural areas of Ethiopia and Nicaragua through mobile medical dental teams as well as surgical support for long-term teaching projects within El Salvador.
Paid or volunteer: Volunteer
Residents or medical students accepted: No
Last update: January 2008

Christian and Missionary Alliance/CAMA Services

Phil Skellie
PO Box 35000
Colorado Springs, CO 80935-3500
Phone: 719/265-2093
E-mail: CAMA@CAMAservices.org
Web: www.CAMAservices.org

Minimum time: 2 weeks
Usual time: 2 years
Maximum time: Career
Who pays transportation: Varies
Who pays housing: Varies
Who pays food: Varies
Language requirements: Local language for long term
Religious requirements: Protestant for long term
Countries: Burkina Faso, Cambodia, Guinea, Mali
Regions: Africa, Asia/Pacific
Comments: Some short-term medical-surgical teams, hospital work in Mali, Cambodia clinic.
Paid or volunteer: Paid and volunteer
Residents or medical students accepted: Resident electives
Last update: January 2008

Christian Emergency Relief Teams International (CERT)

George Willis, Recruiter
PO Box 1129
Crossville, TN 38557
Phone: 888/299-8502 or 931/707-9328
E-mail: george@certinternational.org
Web: www.certinternational.org

Minimum time: 1 week
Usual time: 2 weeks
Maximum time: Varies
Who pays transportation: Volunteer
Who pays housing: Volunteer (program fee $1,300)
Who pays food: Volunteer
Language requirements: No
Religious requirements: No
Countries: Mexico, Peru, Romania
Regions: Eastern Europe, Latin America
Comments: Nondenominational Christian organization that provides free medical and dental services to people in need.

Paid or volunteer: Volunteer
Residents or medical students accepted: Residents and medical students
Last update: January 2008

Christian Medical & Dental Society (CMDA)

Susan Carter (long term), Alicia Trivett (short term)
PO Box 7500
Bristol, TN 37621
Phone: 888/230-2637 or 423/844-1000
E-mail: main@cmda.org
Web: www.cmda.org

Minimum time: 1 week
Usual time: 2 weeks
Maximum time: 2 weeks (varies for long term)
Who pays transportation: Volunteer
Who pays housing: Volunteer
Who pays food: Volunteer
Language requirements: Sometimes
Religious requirements: Christian
Countries: Afghanistan, Bangladesh, Belize, Cambodia, Chad, China, El
   Salvador, Ecuador, Egypt, Ethiopia, Ghana, Guatemala, Guyana, Haiti,
   Honduras, Iraq, Kenya, Malawi, Nepal, Nicaragua, Nigeria, South Sudan,
   Vietnam, Yemen, Zambia
Regions: Africa, Asia/Pacific, Caribbean, Latin America, Middle East
Comments: In addition to its short-term medical missions, CMDA provides
   resources, networking opportunities, and education for Christian health
   care professionals and students.
Paid or volunteer: Volunteer
Residents or medical students accepted: Residents and medical students
Last update: January 2008

Commonwealth Health Center

Chief of Staff
PO Box 500-409
Saipan MP 96950-0409
Phone: 670/234-8950
E-mail: rsalas@cnmidph.net
Web: www.dphsaipan.com

Minimum time: Varies
Usual time: 2 years
Maximum time: Career
Who pays transportation: Organization
Who pays housing: Organization
Who pays food: Volunteer
Language requirements: No
Religious requirements: No
Countries: Saipan
Regions: Asia/Pacific
Comments: US-accredited hospital with level 3 neonatal intensive care unit and coronary unit, dialysis. Serves 60,000 residents. Only US or Canadian citizens with US or Canadian training/certificates are eligible.
Paid or volunteer: Paid and volunteer
Residents or medical students accepted: No
Last update: January 2008

Complete Basic Health 2000

Manny Tuffuor, MD
1831 Foresthills Blvd, Suite 102
Cleveland, OH 44112
Phone: 216/541-3600
E-mail: etuffuor@aol.com
Web: www.ghanacare.org

Minimum time: 1 month
Usual time: 6 months
Maximum time: 1 year or longer
Who pays transportation: Varies
Who pays housing: Organization
Who pays food: Varies
Language requirements: No
Religious requirements: No
Countries: Ghana
Regions: Africa
Comments: Travel costs paid if working for longer than 1 year.

Paid or volunteer: Volunteer
Residents or medical students accepted: Residents
Last update: January 2008

Concern America

Recruitment Coordinator
2015 N Broadway, PO Box 1790
Santa Ana, CA 92702
Phone: 714/953-8576 or 800/CONCERN
E-mail: concamerinc@earthlink.net
Web: www.concernamerica.org

Minimum time: 2 years
Usual time: 2 years or 1 month (immersion program)
Maximum time: 3 years or longer
Who pays transportation: Organization
Who pays housing: Organization
Who pays food: Organization
Language requirements: Spanish (except Mozambique)
Religious requirements: No
Countries: Bolivia, Colombia, El Salvador, Guatemala, Honduras, Mexico,
   Mozambique
Regions: Africa, Latin America
Comments: Small monthly stipend and a repatriation allowance of $50 per
   month the first year, $100 per month the second year, and $150 per month
   the third year. Volunteer professionals share skills and knowledge in health
   promotion. A 3-week immersion program is available twice yearly in Bolivia
   and Guatemala for health professionals, including residents and medical
   students (cost: $1,600).
Paid or volunteer: Volunteer
Residents or medical students accepted: Residents and medical students
   (see comments)
Last update: January 2008

Cross Cultural Solutions

Dava Antoniotti
2 Clinton Place
New Rochelle, NY 10801
Phone: 800/380-4777 or 914/632-0022
E-mail: info@crossculturalsolutions.org
Web: www.crossculturalsolutions.com

Minimum time: 2 weeks
Usual time: 2 weeks to 3 months
Maximum time: 3 months
Who pays transportation: Volunteer
Who pays housing: Volunteer
Who pays food: Volunteer
Language requirements: No
Religious requirements: No
Countries: Brazil, China, Costa Rica, Ghana, Guatemala, India, Morocco, Peru, Russia, South Africa, Tanzania, Thailand
Regions: Africa, Asia/Pacific, Latin America, Middle East
Comments: Partner with sustainable community initiatives to operate volunteer programs in health and social services. International not-for-profit organization with no political or religious affiliations.
Paid or volunteer: Volunteer
Residents or medical students accepted: Residents and medical students
Last update: January 2008

Cross World

Karen Holmes
PO Box 306, 306 Bala Ave
Bala-Cynwyd, PA 19004
Phone: 610/667-7660
E-mail: info@crossworld.org
Web: www.crossworld.org

Minimum time: 6 months
Usual time: 2 years
Maximum time: Career
Who pays transportation: Volunteer
Who pays housing: Volunteer
Who pays food: Volunteer
Language requirements: Varies
Religious requirements: Christian, Evangelical
Countries: Democratic Republic of Congo, Haiti, Papua/Indonesia, Senegal
Regions: Africa, Asia/Pacific, Caribbean

Comments: Christian organization that promotes faith through medical work, teaching, and building infrastructure.
Paid or volunteer: Paid and volunteer
Residents or medical students accepted: Residents and medical students
Last update: January 2008

Curamericas

Jeanne Lawson
2245 North Hills Dr, Suite E
Raleigh, NC 27612
Phone: 919/510-8787 or 877/510-4787
E-mail: jlawson@curamericas.org
Web: www.curamericas.org

Minimum time: 1 week
Usual time: 2 weeks
Maximum time: 3 months (special circumstances)
Who pays transportation: Volunteer
Who pays housing: Volunteer (arranged by Curamericas)
Who pays food: Volunteer (arranged by Curamericas)
Language requirements: No
Religious requirements: No
Countries: Bolivia, Guatemala
Regions: Latin America
Comments: Expeditions have 6 to 15 participants and last 10 to 14 days. Fee of $750 to $900 covers in-country travel and expenses.
Paid or volunteer: Volunteer
Residents or medical students accepted: Residents and medical students
Last update: January 2008

Doctors for Global Health (DGH)

PO Box 1761
Decatur, GA 30031
Phone: 404/377-3566
E-mail: volunteer@dghonline.org
Web: www.dghonline.org

Minimum time: 1 to 4 months
Usual time: Varies
Maximum time: 1 year or longer
Who pays transportation: Volunteer
Who pays housing: Varies
Who pays food: Varies
Language requirements: Spanish for Latin countries
Religious requirements: No
Countries: Argentina, El Salvador, Guatemala, Mexico, Nicaragua, Peru, Uganda
Regions: Africa, Latin America
Comments: DGH is a private nonprofit organization that promotes health, human rights, and social justice throughout the world. They work with local organizations in hospitals and rural clinics.
Paid or volunteer: Volunteer
Residents or medical students accepted: Residents and medical students
Last update: January 2008

Doctors of the World (DOW)

Jackie MacLeod
80 Maiden Lane
New York, NY 10038
Phone: 212/226-9890
E-mail: humanresources@dowusa.org
Web: www.doctorsoftheworld.org

Minimum time: 1 month
Usual time: 1 to 3 months
Maximum time: 6 months to 1 year
Who pays transportation: Organization
Who pays housing: Organization
Who pays food: Volunteer
Language requirements: Sometimes
Religious requirements: No
Countries: Bulgaria, India, Kenya, Kosovo, Mexico, Nepal, Romania, Russia, Sri Lanka, Ukraine
Regions: Africa, Asia, Eastern Europe

Comments: DOW brings American health professionals to provide essential care while training community residents. DOW is affiliated with Medecins du Monde.
Paid or volunteer: Volunteer
Residents or medical students accepted: No
Last update: January 2008

Doctors on Call for Service, Inc. (DOCS)

Caroline Howser
Box 24597
St Simons Island, GA 31522
Phone: 912/634-0065
E-mail: docs@docs.org
Web: www.docs.org

Minimum time: 2 weeks
Usual time: 2 to 4 weeks
Maximum time: Several months
Who pays transportation: Volunteer
Who pays housing: Volunteer
Who pays food: Volunteer
Language requirements: No
Religious requirements: Christian
Countries: Democratic Republic of the Congo, Rwanda, Zimbabwe
Regions: Africa
Comments: DOCS, a Christian nonprofit organization, is improving public health care in Africa by providing medical educational opportunities and postgraduate medical training for physicians in regions where these opportunities are not readily available.
Paid or volunteer: Volunteer
Residents or medical students accepted: No
Last update: January 2008

Doctors Without Borders (Médecins Sans Frontières) (DWB)

Human Resources
333 7th Ave, 2nd Floor
New York, NY 10001-5004
Phone: 212/679-6800
E-mail: doctors@newyork.msf.org
Web: www.doctorswithoutborders.org

Minimum time: 6 months (surgeons and anesthesiologists accepted for shorter missions)
Usual time: 6 to 12 months
Maximum time: Career
Who pays transportation: Organization
Who pays housing: Organization
Who pays food: Organization
Language requirements: French, Spanish, Portuguese, or Arabic is helpful.
Religious requirements: No
Countries: Worldwide
Regions: Africa, Asia/Pacific, Caribbean, Eastern Europe, Latin America, Middle East
Comments: DWB is the world's largest independent international voluntary emergency relief service. About 2,000 doctors volunteer a year through this program. DWB is usually one of the first relief organizations on the scene of conflicts and famines.
Paid or volunteer: Volunteer
Residents or medical students accepted: No
Last update: January 2008

El Buen Pastor International Medical

Manuel A. Galquers, MD
International Corporate Park
10125 NW 19th St
Doral, FL 33172
Phone: 305/513-3940
E-mail: medical@mebpi.net
Web: www.mebpi.net/medical

Minimum time: 2 days
Usual time: 2 to 5 days
Maximum time: 5 days
Who pays transportation: Volunteer
Who pays housing: Volunteer
Who pays food: Volunteer

Language requirements: Spanish
Religious requirements: No
Countries: Argentina, Dominican Republic, Honduras, Mexico, Nicaragua
Regions: Latin America
Comments: Christian nongovernmental organization sponsors medical trips to support ongoing basic care in Latin America.
Paid or volunteer: Volunteer
Residents or medical students accepted: Sometimes
Last update: January 2008

Emergency International

Rohith Malya, External Relations, or Sandro Greblo, Human Resources Department
Via Meravigli 14
Milan, Italy 20123
Phone: 39-2881881 or 39-02-863161
E-mail: rohith@emergency.it or sandro@emergency.it
Web: www.emergency.it or www.emergencyusa.org

Minimum time: 3 months
Usual time: 6 months
Maximum time: Career
Who pays transportation: Organization
Who pays housing: Organization
Who pays food: Organization
Language requirements: English. Knowledge of regional languages is helpful.
Religious requirements: No
Countries: Afghanistan, Iraq, Sierra Leone, Sudan. 2008 pediatrics positions at new hospital in Khartoum, Sudan, and Afghanistan (Anabah hospital, Panshir Valley).
Regions: Africa, Asia/Pacific
Comments: Interview required at headquarters in Milan, Italy, before placement. Full international living stipend provided for selected candidates. Emergency International is an independent, neutral, and nonpolitical organization founded to provide free, high-quality medical and surgical treatment to the civilian victims of war, land mines, and poverty. Mission: to promote a culture of peace and solidarity.
Paid or volunteer: Paid
Residents or medical students accepted: Residents (Harvard Humanitarian Initiative: e-mail hcranmer@partners.org)
Last update: January 2008

Emergency USA

10592 Perry Highway #112
Wexford, PA 10509
Phone: 724/766-4518
E-mail: info@emergencyusa.org
Web: www.emergencyusa.org

Minimum time: 3 months
Usual time: 6 months
Maximum time: Career
Who pays transportation: Organization
Who pays housing: Organization
Who pays food: Organization
Language requirements: Local language helpful.
Religious requirements: No
Countries: Afghanistan, Sierra Leone, Sudan. 2008 vacancies Afghanistan (Anabah hospital, Panshir Valley), Sudan (Mayo clinic inside internally displaced persons camp). New neonatal hospital in Nicaragua is planned soon.
Regions: Africa, Asia
Comments: Emergency USA is a branch of Emergency International and is an independent, neutral, and nonpolitical organization founded to provide medical care to victims of war and poverty and to train and supervise local staff.
Paid or volunteer: Paid
Residents or medical students accepted: Residents (see Emergency International listing)
Last update: January 2008

Evangelical Lutheran Church in America (ELCA)/Global Mission Volunteers

Y. Franklin Ishida
8765 W Higgins Rd
Chicago, IL 60631-4192
Phone: 800/638-3522, ext 2639 or +1 773-380-2639 (outside US)
E-mail: franklin.ishida@elca.org
Web: www.elca.org/globalmission (downloadable application form) or www.elca.org/globalserve

Minimum time: 2 months
Usual time: 2 to 3 months
Maximum time: 2 years
Who pays transportation: Varies
Who pays housing: Organization
Who pays food: Varies

Language requirements: French, Spanish, Portuguese, or Arabic is helpful depending on country.
Religious requirements: Christian, compatible with ELCA mission theology
Countries: Bangladesh, Cameroon, Liberia, Madagascar,Tanzania
Regions: Africa, Asia/Pacific, Caribbean, Eastern Europe, Latin America, Middle East
Comments: See Web site for current personnel needs. Contact directly for resident or student placement.
Paid or volunteer: Volunteer, occasional stipend
Residents or medical students accepted: Residents and medical students in Tanzania only
Last update: January 2008

Fellowship of Associates of Medical Evangelism (FAME)

Lonnie Burley
PO Box 33548, 4545 Southeastern Ave
Indianapolis, IN 46203
Phone: 317/358-2480
E-mail: trips@fameworld.org
Web: www.fameworld.org

Minimum time: None
Usual time: Varies
Maximum time: 3 weeks
Who pays transportation: Volunteer
Who pays housing: Volunteer
Who pays food: Volunteer
Language requirements: No
Religious requirements: Christian
Countries: Albania, Brazil, Dominican Republic, Ghana, Haiti, Honduras, India, Nigeria, Panama, Ukraine, Zimbabwe
Regions: Africa, Asia/Pacific, Eastern Europe, Latin America
Comments: FAME works to provide medical facilities, medicines, and equipment, as well as mobilizing medical personnel and evangelistic teams to the poorest of the poor around the world. See Web site for current needs.
Paid or volunteer: Volunteer
Residents or medical students accepted: Residents and medical students
Last update: January 2008

Feed the Children

Larry Bieler, MD
333 North Meridian
Oklahoma City, OK 73107-6568
Phone: 888/210-7734 or 405/721-3728
E-mail: ftc@feedthechildren.org
Web: www.feedthechildren.org

Minimum time: 2 weeks
Usual time: 2 weeks
Maximum time: 2 weeks
Who pays transportation: Volunteer
Who pays housing: Volunteer
Who pays food: Volunteer
Language requirements: No
Religious requirements: Christian
Countries: Four countries a year: In 2008 Bolivia, Ecuador, Malawi, Nicaragua.
  See Web site.
Regions: Africa, Latin America
Comments: Evangelical nonprofit relief organization that offers four 2-week
  trips a year. Physicians, dentists, pharmacists, and ophthalmologists travel
  to new villages daily to dispense care and faith.
Paid or volunteer: Volunteer
Residents or medical students accepted: Residents and medical students
Last update: January 2008

Fight for the Children

Kathryn Morgan
18725 136th Pl SE
Renton, WA 98058
Phone: 425/306-2572
E-mail: kathryn@fightforthechildren.org
Web: www.fightforthechildren.org

Minimum time: 2 weeks
Usual time: 1 month
Maximum time: Career
Who pays transportation: Volunteer
Who pays housing: Volunteer
Who pays food: Volunteer
Language requirements: English; Swahili helpful
Religious requirements: No
Countries: Kenya, Rwanda, Tanzania, Uganda

Regions: Africa
Comments: We establish children's clinics in the developing world and currently are operating in East Africa. We need volunteers of all skill levels in 2008 to help establish new clinics in Rwanda and Tanzania.
Paid or volunteer: Volunteer
Residents or medical students accepted: Residents and medical students
Last update: January 2008

Florida Association of Voluntary Agencies for Caribbean Action (FAVACA)

International Programs Coordinator
NW 36th St, Suite 535
Miami, FL 3166
Phone: 350/470-5070
E-mail: favaca@favaca.org
Web: www.favaca.org

Minimum time: 3 days
Usual time: 1 week
Maximum time: 3 weeks
Who pays transportation: Organization
Who pays housing: Organization
Who pays food: Organization
Language requirements: No (Spanish, French, or Kreyol helpful)
Religious requirements: No
Countries: Antigua and Barbuda, Bahamas, Barbados, Belize, Colombia, Costa Rica, Dominica, Dominican Republic, El Salvador, Grenada, Guatemala, Guyana, Haiti, Honduras, Jamaica, Montserrat, Nicaragua, Panama, St Kitts and Nevis, St Lucia, St Vincent and the Grenadines, Trinidad and Tobago
Regions: Caribbean, Latin America
Comments: FAVACA is a nonprofit organization that arranges short-term technical assistance and training in health, agriculture, social services, education, and more by Florida professionals as requested by partners in the Caribbean and Central America.
Paid or volunteer: Volunteer
Residents or medical students accepted: Residents
Last update: January 2008

Forward Edge International (FEI)

Kay Moore
15121-A NE 72nd Ave
Vancouver, WA 98686
Phone: 360/574-3343
E-mail: fei@forwardedge.org
Web: www.forwardedge.org

Minimum time: 1 week
Usual time: 2 weeks
Maximum time:
Who pays transportation: Volunteer
Who pays housing: Volunteer
Who pays food: Volunteer
Language requirements: No
Religious requirements: No
Countries: Nicaragua
Regions: Latin America
Comments: FEI is a Christian relief organization that supports short-term medical and surgical trips to remote villages in Nicaragua.
Paid or volunteer: Volunteer
Residents or medical students accepted: Residents and medical students if mentored
Last update: January 2008

The Flying Doctors

Al Longoria
PO Box 24007
San Jose, CA 95154
Phone: 408/279-8445
E-mail: fernal95@aol.com

Minimum time: 1 week
Usual time: 2 weeks
Maximum time: None
Who pays transportation: Volunteer
Who pays housing: Volunteer (some homestays)
Who pays food: Volunteer
Language requirements: Spanish
Religious requirements: No
Countries: Mexico
Regions: Latin America
Comments: Volunteers work in Tonala, Chiapas. Volunteers can stay in Pacific beach hotel and drive 10 miles inland to work, or stay with a family.

Paid or volunteer: Volunteer
Residents or medical students accepted: Residents
Last update: January 2008

Flying Samaritans International

13595 San Antonio Rd
Atascadero, CA 93422-5317
Phone: 888/FLY-SAMS
Web: www.flyingsamaritans.org

Minimum time: 1 weekend
Usual time: 2 to 3 clinics per year
Maximum time: 12 weekends
Who pays transportation: Volunteer
Who pays housing: Volunteer
Who pays food: Volunteer
Language requirements: Spanish is helpful.
Religious requirements: No
Countries: Baja, Mexico
Regions: Latin America
Comments: The Flying Samaritans is an all-volunteer organization that operates free 1-day medical clinics in Baja California, Mexico. Doctors, dentists, nurses, translators, pilots, and support personnel fly to clinics in private aircraft.
Paid or volunteer: Volunteer
Residents or medical students accepted: Sometimes
Last update: January 2008

Foundation for Sustainable Development (FSD)

517 Potrero Ave, Suite B
San Francisco, CA 94110
Phone: 415/283-4873
E-mail: info@fsdinternational.org
Web: www.fsdinternational.org

Minimum time: 1week
Usual time: 2 months
Maximum time: 1 year
Who pays transportation: Volunteer
Who pays housing: Volunteer (program fee)
Who pays food: Volunteer
Language requirements: Sometimes
Religious requirements: No
Countries: Argentina, Bolivia, Ecuador, India, Kenya, Nicaragua, Peru, Uganda
Regions: Africa, Asia, Latin America
Comments: FSD offers internships, short-term volunteer opportunities, and longer project development programs that include training in needs assessment, cross-cultural differences, project design, and grant writing.
Paid or volunteer: Volunteer
Residents or medical students accepted: Residents and medical students
Last update: January 2008

Foundation Human Nature

Erin Lunde
1823 Westridge Rd
Los Angeles, CA 90049
E-mail: volunteers.medical.ec@f-h-n.org
Web: www.f-h-n.org

Minimum time: 6 months
Usual time: 6 months
Maximum time: None
Who pays transportation: Volunteer
Who pays housing: Organization
Who pays food: Volunteer
Language requirements: Spanish for Ecuador
Religious requirements: No
Countries: Ghana, Ecuador
Regions: Africa, Latin America
Comments: This nongovernmental organization supports sustainable health development at 2 project sites in Ecuador and Ghana. Volunteer physicians work with local staff to provide primary, emergency, and obstetric care to the remote communities they serve.

Paid or volunteer: Volunteer
Residents or medical students accepted: No
Last update: January 2008

Friends Without a Border

Akiko Arai (NY) or Varun Kumar (Cambodia)
1123 Broadway Suite 1210
New York, NY 10010
Phone: 212/691-0909
E-mail: varun@angkorhospital.org or leakhena@angkorhospital.org
Web: www.fwab.org or www.angkorhospital.org

Minimum time: Varies
Usual time: 2 to 4 weeks
Maximum time: Varies
Who pays transportation: Volunteer
Who pays housing: Volunteer
Who pays food: Volunteer
Language requirements: English
Religious requirements: No
Countries: Cambodia
Regions: Asia/Pacific
Comments: Pediatric hospital near the Angkor Wat monuments. Doctors and nurses are needed to teach. Volunteers have 2 days a week free. This site is available through Health Volunteers Overseas.
Paid or volunteer: Volunteer
Residents or medical students accepted: Residents and medical students
Last update: January 2008

General Baptist International

Jack Eberhardt
100 Stinson Dr
Popular Bluff, MO 63901
Phone: 573/785-7746
E-mail: jack.eberhardt@generalbaptist.com
Web: www.generalbaptist.com

Minimum time: 7 to 10 days
Usual time: 2 weeks
Maximum time: Varies
Who pays transportation: Volunteer
Who pays housing: Varies
Who pays food: Varies
Language requirements: No (short term)
Religious requirements: Baptist
Countries: Honduras, Jamaica, Mexico, Philippines, Saipan
Regions: Asia, Caribbean, Latin America
Comments: Mobile health teams visit rural villages and set up clinics.
Paid or volunteer: Volunteer
Residents or medical students accepted: Residents and medical students
Last update: January 2008

General Board Global Ministries, UMMC *(see Evangelical Lutheran Church in America/Global Mission Volunteers)*

Global Healing: Roatan Volunteer Pediatric Clinic (RVPC)

Arup Roy-Burman MD
PO Box 2166
Orinda, CA 94563
Phone: 925/327-7889
E-mail: arup@roatanclinic.org
Web: www.globalhealing.org

Minimum time: 3 weeks
Usual time: 4 weeks
Maximum time: 1 year
Who pays transportation: Organization
Who pays housing: Organization
Who pays food: Organization or volunteer
Language requirements: Spanish is helpful.
Religious requirements: No

Countries: Honduras
Regions: Latin America
Comments: The RVPC is a pediatric outpatient clinic within the Roatan public hospital, staffed year-round by volunteer pediatricians, 3rd-year residents, and medical students.
Paid or volunteer: Volunteer
Residents or medical students accepted: Residents and medical students
Last update: January 2008

Global Health Ministries

3805 West Chester Pike, Suite 100
Newtown Square, PA 19073
Phone: 610/335-2003
E-mail: mmcginley@che.org
Web: www.globalhealthministry.org

Minimum time: 1 week
Usual time: 2 weeks
Maximum time: Varies
Who pays transportation: Volunteer
Who pays housing: Volunteer
Who pays food: Volunteer
Language requirements: No
Religious requirements: No
Countries: Guatemala, Haiti, Jamaica, Peru
Regions: Caribbean, Latin America
Comments: Medical and surgical teams provide care and education in partnership with local health care providers. Application, interview, and orientation weekend required.
Paid or volunteer: Volunteer
Residents or medical students accepted: Residents and medical students accepted
Last update: January 2008

Global Mission Volunteers

Sonya Lindquist
8765 W Higgins Rd
Chicago, IL 60631
Phone: 773/380-2765
E-mail: globalserve@elca.org
Web: www.elca.org/globalserve

Minimum time: 2 months
Usual time: 3 months
Maximum time: 2 years
Who pays transportation: Volunteer
Who pays housing: Varies
Who pays food: Volunteer
Language requirements: Sometimes
Religious requirements: Sometimes
Countries: Africa, Asia, Latin America, Pacific
Regions: Africa, Asia/Pacific, Caribbean, Latin America, Middle East
Comments: Evangelical Lutheran Church makes matches for Christian doctors and other medical personnel as requested by their overseas partners.
Paid or volunteer: Volunteer
Residents or medical students accepted: Varies with site needs.
Last update: January 2008

Global Outreach

Brian Tyndall
PO Box 1
Tupelo, MS 38802
Phone: 662/842-4615
E-mail: go@globaloutreach.org
Web: www.globaloutreach.org

Minimum time: 1 week
Usual time: 1 week to 2 months
Maximum time: Career
Who pays transportation: Volunteer
Who pays housing: Volunteer
Who pays food: Volunteer
Language requirements: No
Religious requirements: Christian, Evangelical
Countries: Africa, Asia, Central America, Europe, South America
Regions: Africa, Asia, Eastern Europe, Latin America

Comments: Short-term projects originate in a local church and are generally traveling clinics to rural areas. Longer trips may be arranged through the central office.
Paid or volunteer: Volunteer
Residents or medical students accepted: Residents and medical students
Last update: January 2008

Global Partners

John Steppe
PO Box 50434
Indianapolis, IN 46250-0434
Phone: 800/707-7715 or 317/774-7950
E-mail: globalpartners@wesleyan.org
Web: www.praygivego.com

Minimum time: 2 weeks
Usual time: 1 year
Maximum time: Career
Who pays transportation: Volunteer
Who pays housing: Volunteer
Who pays food: Volunteer
Language requirements: No
Religious requirements: Christian
Countries: Haiti, Sierra Leone, Zambia
Regions: Africa, Caribbean
Comments: Mission trips are organized to local hospitals.
Paid or volunteer: Volunteer
Residents or medical students accepted: Residents
Last update: January 2008

Global Volunteers

Volunteer Coordinators
375 East Little Canada Rd
St Paul, MN 55117-1627
Phone: 800/487-1074 (toll free) or 651/407-6100 (local)
E-mail: email@globalvolunteers.org
Web: www.globalvolunteers.org

Minimum time: 1 week
Usual time: 2 weeks
Maximum time: 3 weeks
Who pays transportation: Volunteer
Who pays housing: Volunteer (service program fees $1,500–$2,500)
Who pays food: Volunteer (see Housing)
Language requirements: No
Religious requirements: No
Countries: Cook Islands, Ghana, Jamaica, Peru (plus other countries where nonmedical personnel can serve)
Regions: Africa, Asia/Pacific, Latin America
Comments: Health care volunteers are needed to provide basic services in developing countries where medical treatment is often inaccessible and inadequate.
Paid or volunteer: Volunteer
Residents or medical students accepted: Residents and medical students
Last update: January 2008

Haiti Medical Mission of Wisconsin

Joan Fordham
125 15th Ave
Baraboo, WI 53913
Phone: 608/356-8927
E-mail: dfordham@chorus.net
Web: www.haitimedicalmission.com

Minimum time: 1 week
Usual time: 1 week
Maximum time:
Who pays transportation: Volunteer
Who pays housing: Volunteer (fee covers housing and food)
Who pays food: Volunteer (see Housing)
Language requirements: No
Religious requirements: No
Countries: Haiti
Regions: Caribbean

Comments: Volunteers provide health care in Southern Haiti, Village of Thiotte. Pediatricians needed for the clinic, which is staffed by Haitian nurses. Usually do 6 trips per year.

Paid or volunteer: Volunteer

Residents or medical students accepted: Residents and medical students

Last update: January 2008

Hands Together

Douglas Campbell
PO Box 80985
Springfield, MA 01138
Phone: 413/731-7716
E-mail: info@handstogether.org
Web: www.handstogether.org

Minimum time: 1 week

Usual time: 2 to 3 weeks

Maximum time: 1 year

Who pays transportation: Volunteer

Who pays housing: Organization

Who pays food: Organization

Language requirements: French helpful, Haitian Kreyol ideal

Religious requirements: Catholic preferred

Countries: Haiti

Regions: Caribbean

Comments: Experienced medical personnel are needed for treatment and training of Haitian staff.

Paid or volunteer: Volunteer

Residents or medical students accepted: No

Last update: January 2008

HBS Foundation, Inc./Hopital Bon Samaritain

Paul Hodges
PO Box 1290
Lake Worth, FL 33460
Phone: 561/533-0883
E-mail: info@hbslimbe.org
Web: www.hbslimbe.org

Minimum time: 2 weeks
Usual time: 3 to 6 months
Maximum time: Career
Who pays transportation: Volunteer
Who pays housing: Organization
Who pays food: Organization
Language requirements: French/Kreyol preferred
Religious requirements: No
Countries: Haiti
Regions: Caribbean
Comments: Hopital Bon Samaritain (HBS), a nonprofit primary health care center, is situated in the river valley of Limbe, Haiti. There is a 130-bed hospital and outpatient clinics.
Paid or volunteer: Paid and volunteer
Residents or medical students accepted: Residents and medical students
Last update: January 2008

Heal A Child

Lauren Faig
1900 Byrd Ave, Suite 204
Richmond, VA 23230
Phone: 888/300-6917
E-mail: l.faig@healachild.org
Web: www.healachild.org

Minimum time: 1 week
Usual time: 2 weeks
Maximum time: Varies
Who pays transportation: Volunteer
Who pays housing: Volunteer
Who pays food: Volunteer
Language requirements: No
Religious requirements: No
Countries: Belize, Dominican Republic, East Caribbean, Guyana, Honduras
Regions: Caribbean, Latin America

Comments: Nonprofit humanitarian organization sends surgical and diagnostic teams to poor areas. Teams also teach and mentor local providers.
Paid or volunteer: Volunteer
Residents or medical students accepted: Residents
Last update: January 2008

Healing the Children National Headquarters

Carol Borneman or Dr Donald VanNimwegen, Medical Director
PO Box 9065
Spokane, WA 99209
Phone: 800/992-0324
E-mail: MedVolunteers@healingthechildren.org
Web: www.healingthechildren.org

Minimum time: 1 week
Usual time: 10 days
Maximum time: 10 days
Who pays transportation: Volunteer
Who pays housing: Organization
Who pays food: Organization
Language requirements: No
Religious requirements: No
Countries: Cambodia, Guatemala, Nicaragua, Vietnam
Regions: Asia, Latin America
Comments: Pediatricians assist surgical teams, primarily plastic; dental; ear, nose, throat; eye; neurosurgery; urologic; and orthopedic.
Paid or volunteer: Volunteer
Residents or medical students accepted: Residents and medical students
Last update: January 2008

HealthCare Nepal

Jack Starmer
PO Box 4455 George School
Newtown, PA 18940
Phone: 215/579-8765
E-mail: js@healthcarenepal.org
Web: www.healthcarenepal.org

Minimum time: 2 weeks
Usual time: 3 weeks
Maximum time: 1 month
Who pays transportation: Volunteer
Who pays housing: Volunteer
Who pays food: Volunteer
Language requirements: No
Religious requirements: No
Countries: Nepal
Regions: Asia/Pacific
Comments: Involves short-term medical/surgical "camps" in remote villages.
    Two per year are planned, in the fall and spring.
Paid or volunteer: Volunteer
Residents or medical students accepted: Residents and 4th-year medical
    students
Last update: January 2008

Health Extension and Learning (University of Florida)

PO Box 100014
Gainsville, FL 32610-0243
Phone: 352/392-2761
E-mail: webmaster@dean.med.ufl.edu
Web: www.med.ufl.edu/international

Minimum time: 2 weeks
Usual time: 1 month
Maximum time: Varies
Who pays transportation: Volunteer
Who pays housing: Volunteer
Who pays food: Volunteer
Language requirements: No. Spanish is helpful.
Religious requirements: No
Countries: Dominican Republic, Ecuador, Haiti
Regions: Caribbean, Latin America

Comments: Programs sponsored by University of Florida health services establish outreach and training programs. Traveling clinics in Haiti treat and educate on nutrition and HIV/AIDS prevention. Formal arrangement with University of San Francisco in Quito for ongoing training programs.
Paid or volunteer: Volunteer
Residents or medical students accepted: Residents and medical students
Last update: January 2008

Health Talents International

Julie Wheetley
PO Box 59871
Birmingham, AL 35259
Phone: 615/397-5447
E-mail: juliewheetley@healthtalents.org
Web: www.healthtalents.org

Minimum time: 2 weeks
Usual time: 2 weeks
Maximum time: Varies
Who pays transportation: Volunteer
Who pays housing: Volunteer
Who pays food: Varies
Language requirements: Spanish helpful
Religious requirements: No
Countries: Guatemala, Nicaragua
Regions: Latin America
Comments: Christian organization that supports health care and education. Three medical-dental teams and 9 surgical teams per year. Volunteer health education program trains health promoters.
Paid or volunteer: Volunteer
Residents or medical students accepted: Residents
Last update: January 2008

Health Teams International

Richard Charlick, DDS
10056 Applegate Lane
Brighton, MI 48114
Phone: 810/229-9247
Web: www.healthteamsintl.org

Minimum time: 1 week
Usual time: 2 weeks
Maximum time: 1 month
Who pays transportation: Volunteer
Who pays housing: Volunteer
Who pays food: Varies
Language requirements: No
Religious requirements: Christian
Countries: Benin, Cameroon, China, Colombia, Dominican Republic,
     Myanmar, Mongolia, Sudan
Regions: Africa, Asia, Latin America
Comments: Evangelical and Ecumenical. We strive to provide health care to
     those who have never heard of Christ. Medical and dental trips to evangelize
     remote areas.
Paid or volunteer: Volunteer
Residents or medical students accepted: Sometimes
Last update: January 2008

Health Volunteers Overseas (HVO)

Jenny Kelley
1900 L Street, NW Suite 310
Washington, DC 20036
Phone: 202/296-0928
E-mail: j.kelley@hvousa.org
Web: www.hvousa.org

Minimum time: 2 weeks
Usual time: 1 month
Maximum time: 3 months or more
Who pays transportation: Volunteer
Who pays housing: Varies
Who pays food: Varies
Language requirements: No
Religious requirements: No
Countries: Cambodia, Malawi, St Lucia, Uganda
Regions: Africa, Asia/Pacific, Caribbean

Comments: By emphasizing teaching rather than service, HVO aims to train local health providers who can teach others. This builds an ongoing capacity that will benefit the population long after the volunteer and HVO have departed.

Paid or volunteer: Volunteer

Residents or medical students accepted: Residents accepted at some sites with mentor

Last update: January 2008

Heart to Heart International

Steve Hower
5915 NW 23rd St, Suite 205
Oklahoma City, OK 73127
Phone: 405/787-5200, ext 100
E-mail: amanda.keeter@hearttoheart.org
Web: www.hearttoheart.org

Minimum time: 10 days

Usual time: 10 days

Maximum time: 10 days

Who pays transportation: Volunteer

Who pays housing: Volunteer

Who pays food: Volunteer

Language requirements: No

Religious requirements: No

Countries: China, Tajikistan, Zambia

Regions: Africa, Asia/Pacific

Comments: Heart to Heart International is a humanitarian relief organization that mobilizes volunteers to serve the poor around the world. On international projects, which last about 10 days, volunteers deliver medicines and medical supplies, conduct medical symposia.

Paid or volunteer: Volunteer

Residents or medical students accepted: No

Last update: January 2008

Helping Hands Health Education

Narayan Shrestha
948 Pearl St
Boulder, CO 80302
Phone: 303/448-1811
E-mail: helpinghands@sannr.com
Web: www.helpinghandsusa.org

Minimum time: 2 weeks
Usual time: 1 month
Maximum time: 2 years or more with adjusted fee
Who pays transportation: Volunteer (a fee covers all expenses)
Who pays housing: Volunteer (included in fee)
Who pays food: Volunteer (included in fee)
Language requirements: No
Religious requirements: No
Countries: Nepal, Nicaragua, Vietnam
Regions: Asia/Pacific, Latin America
Comments: Helping Hands seeks physicians and medical students in all specialties. A typical program in Nepal is 2 weeks of volunteer work in a permanent clinic and 2 weeks of trekking in the mountains. Established clinics in Vietnam and Nicaragua have basic services.
Paid or volunteer: Volunteer
Residents or medical students accepted: Residents and medical students
Last update: January 2008

Helps International

Rita Martin
15301 Dallas Pkwy, Suite 200
Addison, TX 75001
Phone: 800/414-3577 or 972/386-2901
E-mail: rmartin@helpsintl.org or info@helpsintl.org
Web: www.helpsintl.org

Minimum time: 7 days
Usual time: 2 weeks
Maximum time:
Who pays transportation: Volunteer
Who pays housing: Volunteer
Who pays food: Volunteer
Language requirements: No
Religious requirements: No
Countries: Guatemala

Regions: Latin America
Comments: Helps International, founded in 1983, assists indigenous peoples in the Guatemalan highlands. During 12-day medical missions undertaken January through May, and July and Oct, its teams treat as many as 10,000 patients in local and US government-built hospitals.
Paid or volunteer: Volunteer
Residents or medical students accepted: Residents and medical students
Last update: January 2008

Hillside Healthcare Center

Joyce Lopez
Box 27
Punta Gorda, Toledo District, Belize
Phone: 011-501-722-2312
E-mail: info@hillsidebelize.net
Web: www.hillsidebelize.com

Minimum time: 2 weeks
Usual time: Varies
Maximum time: 1 year or longer
Who pays transportation: Volunteer
Who pays housing: Volunteer (organization for long-term volunteers)
Who pays food: Volunteer
Language requirements: English
Religious requirements: No
Countries: Belize
Regions: Latin America
Comments: Hillside Healthcare Center provides a free on-site health care clinic for the people of the Toledo District in southern Belize. Mobile clinics serve remote rain forest villages.
Paid or volunteer: Paid (some long term) and volunteer
Residents or medical students accepted: Residents and medical students— 4-week elective precepted by medical director (contact jahartman@wisc.edu)
Last update: January 2008

Himalayan Healthcare

David Johnson
PO Box 737
Planetarium Station
New York, NY 10024
E-mail: info@himalayan-healthcare.org or dnjsailor@hotmail.com
Web: www.himalayan-healthcare.org

Minimum time: 3 weeks
Usual time: 3 weeks
Maximum time: 3 weeks
Who pays transportation: Volunteer
Who pays housing: Volunteer
Who pays food: Volunteer
Language requirements: No
Religious requirements: No
Countries: Nepal
Regions: Asia/Pacific
Comments: Physicians may volunteer at a clinic in Ilam in eastern Nepal that
    was opened in 2004. Medical treks to remote areas resumed in 2007.
Paid or volunteer: Volunteer
Residents or medical students accepted: Sometimes
Last update: January 2008

Himalayan Health Exchange (HHE)

Ravi Singh
PO Box 610
Decatur, GA 30031-0610
Phone: 404/929-9399
E-mail: info@himalayanhealth.com
Web: www.himalayanhealth.com

Minimum time: 2 weeks
Usual time: 3 weeks
Maximum time: 1 month
Who pays transportation: Volunteer
Who pays housing: Volunteer
Who pays food: Volunteer
Language requirements: No
Religious requirements: No
Countries: India, Nepal
Regions: Asia/Pacific

Comments: HHE organizes expeditions to provide medical and dental care to remote regions of the Indian and Nepal Himalayan and to uplift 2 orphanages in Himachal Pradash.
Paid or volunteer: Volunteer
Residents or medical students accepted: Residents and medical students
Last update: January 2008

Honduras Outreach, Inc

Beth Barnwell
4105 Briarcliff Rd NE
Atlanta, GA 30345
Phone: 404/327-5768
E-mail: bbarnwell@hoi.org
Web: www.hoi.org

Minimum time: 1 week
Usual time: 1 week
Maximum time: 2 weeks
Who pays transportation: Volunteer
Who pays housing: Volunteer ($600 fee covers food and housing)
Who pays food: Volunteer
Language requirements: Spanish is helpful.
Religious requirements: No
Countries: Honduras
Regions: Latin America
Comments: Christian organization supports medical care for 38 Honduran villages in 5 medical clinics. Volunteers treat patients and train Honduran medical staff. Specialized medical teams are planned for 2008.
Paid or volunteer: Volunteer
Residents or medical students accepted: Residents and medical students sometimes through Emory University program.
Last update: January 2008

Hope Worldwide

Mandy Jordan
353 West Lancaster Ave, Suite 200
Wayne, PA 19087
Phone: 610/254-8800
E-mail: hope_worldwide@HOPEww.org
Web: www.HOPEww.org

Minimum time: 1 week
Usual time: Varies
Maximum time: Career
Who pays transportation: Volunteer
Who pays housing: Volunteer
Who pays food: Volunteer
Language requirements: No
Religious requirements: No
Countries: Worldwide. 2007 sites for pediatrician: Afghanistan, Brazil,
    Cambodia, China, India, Indonesia, Ivory Coast, Jamaica, Kenya, Malaysia,
    Philippines, PNG, Russia, Singapore, South Africa
Regions: Africa, Asia/Pacific, Caribbean, Eastern Europe, Latin America
Comments: HOPE worldwide Healthcorps offers an annual continuing medical
    education course combined with service opportunities.
Paid or volunteer: Paid and volunteer
Residents or medical students accepted: No
Last update: January 2008

Hopital Albert Schweitzer

Rona Watts
PO Box 81046
Pittsburgh, PA 15217
Phone: 412/361-5200
E-mail: info@hashaiti.org
Web: www.hashaiti.org

Minimum time: 1 month
Usual time: Varies
Maximum time: Varies
Who pays transportation: Volunteer
Who pays housing: Volunteer
Who pays food: Volunteer
Language requirements: No. French or Haitian Kreyol is helpful.
Religious requirements: No
Countries: Haiti

Regions: Caribbean
Comments:
Paid or volunteer: Paid and volunteer
Residents or medical students accepted: Residents may apply.
Last update: January 2008

Intercristo

19303 Fremont Avenue N MS# 20
Seattle, WA 98133
Phone: 206/546-7330
E-mail: jobhunter@intercristo.com
Web: www.intercristo.com

Minimum time: 2 weeks
Usual time: Varies
Maximum time: Career
Who pays transportation: Varies
Who pays housing: Varies
Who pays food: Varies
Language requirements: Sometimes
Religious requirements: Christian
Countries: Worldwide
Regions: Africa, Asia/Pacific, Caribbean, Eastern Europe, Latin America, Middle East
Comments: Intercristo is a placement service that provides a connection between Christian job hunters and Christian employers.
Paid or volunteer: Paid and volunteer
Residents or medical students accepted: No
Last update: January 2008

International Center for Equal Healthcare Access (ICEHA)

Katrina Glaser
101 West 23rd St, Suite 179
New York, NY 10040
Phone: 212/243-7234
E-mail: volunteer@iceha.org
Web: www.iceha.org

Minimum time: 6 weeks
Usual time: 1 to 3 months
Maximum time: 12 months
Who pays transportation: Organization
Who pays housing: Organization
Who pays food: Organization
Language requirements: No
Religious requirements: No
Countries: Burundi, Congo, Nepal, South Africa, Vietnam, Zambia
Regions: Africa, Asia/Pacific
Comments: The ICEHA is an international not-for-profit organization that engages health care professionals to rapidly transfer their expertise on HIV care and infectious diseases to colleagues in developing countries, using an innovative method of clinical training.
Paid or volunteer: Volunteer (all overseas expenses are covered by ICEHA)
Residents or medical students accepted: No
Last update: January 2008

International Health Service (IHS)

Cheryl Schraeder or Gary Ernst
PO Box 44339
Eden Prairie, MN 55344
Phone: 952/996-0977 (Cheryl), 952/239-4361 (Gary)
E-mail: cschraeder@earthlink.net
Web: www.ihsofmn.org

Minimum time: 2 weeks
Usual time: 2 weeks
Maximum time: None
Who pays transportation: Volunteer
Who pays housing: Volunteers can stay with host families or at a hotel at their own expense.
Who pays food: 2 designated restaurants and IHS pick up the tab.
Language requirements: Spanish is helpful.
Religious requirements: No
Countries: Honduras

Regions: Latin America
Comments: IHS does a 2-week medical mission in Honduras each February. We take approximately 100 people to make up 6 medical/dental teams, surgery teams, eyeglass teams, and a general work team that does work in a children's home.
Paid or volunteer: Volunteer
Residents or medical students accepted: Residents and medical students
Last update: January 2008

International Medical Corps (IMC)

Maryn Perryman
1919 Santa Monica Blvd, Suite 300
Santa Monica, CA 90404
Phone: 310/826-7800
E-mail: imc@imcworldwide.org
Web: www.imcworldwide.org

Minimum time: 2 to 4 weeks
Usual time: 3 months
Maximum time: 6 months to 1 year (staff positions)
Who pays transportation: Varies
Who pays housing: Varies
Who pays food: Varies
Language requirements: Sometimes (French, Spanish, Portuguese at some assignments)
Religious requirements: No
Countries: Afghanistan, Angola, Bosnia/Croatia, Burundi, Rwanda, Somalia, Sudan
Regions: Africa, Asia/Pacific, Eastern Europe
Comments: IMC dispenses medical teams and support staff to help rebuild health care systems and restore self-sufficiency and independence to regions where few relief organizations serve. View openings at www.cytiva.com/cejobs/cojobsIMC.asp.
Paid or volunteer: Paid and volunteer
Residents or medical students accepted: No
Last update: January 2008

International Relief Teams

Rose Uranga
4560 Alvarado Canyon Rd, Suite 2G
San Diego, CA 92120
Phone: 619/284-7979
E-mail: info@irteams.org
Web: www.irteams.org

Minimum time: 1 week
Usual time: 10 days
Maximum time: 3 weeks
Who pays transportation: Organization (participation fee of $100–$500)
Who pays housing: Varies
Who pays food: Varies
Language requirements: No
Religious requirements: No
Countries: Armenia, Ecuador, Guatemala, Honduras, Latvia, Lithuania, Mexico, Pakistan, South Africa, Romania, Uganda
Regions: Africa, Asia/Pacific, Eastern Europe, Latin America
Comments: Mobilizes medical and nonmedical volunteers to aid victims of disaster, poverty, and neglect worldwide. Provides medical training and education (including Neonatal Resuscitation Program), surgical outreach, health promotion, disease prevention, and disaster relief.
Paid or volunteer: Volunteer
Residents or medical students accepted: No
Last update: January 2008

International Rescue Committee (IRC)

Christian Bowman
122 East 42nd St
New York, NY 10168-1289
Phone: 212/551-3000
E-mail: Christian.Bowman@theirc.org
Web: www.theirc.org

Minimum time: 2 months
Usual time: 3 months to 1 year
Maximum time:
Who pays transportation: Organization
Who pays housing: Organization
Who pays food: Volunteer
Language requirements: English and/or French
Religious requirements: No

Countries: Afghanistan, Azerbaijan, Burundi, Central African Republic, Chad, Colombia, Democratic Republic of Congo, Ethiopia, Guinea, Indonesia, Ivory Coast, Jordan, Kenya, Liberia, Nepal, Northern Caucasus, Pakistan, Rwanda, Sierra Leone, Somalia, Sudan, Tanzania, Thailand, Uganda
Regions: Africa, Asia/Pacific, Latin America, Middle East
Comments: Founded in 1933, IRC is a global leader in emergency relief, protection of human rights, post-conflict development, resettlement services, and advocacy for those uprooted or affected by violent conflict and oppression. Learn more about what we do at www.theirc.org.
Paid or volunteer: Paid and volunteer
Residents or medical students accepted: Residents and medical students
Last update: January 2008

Interplast, Inc.

Beverly Kent
857 Maude Ave
Mountain View, CA 94043
Phone: 888/467-5278 or 650/962-0123
E-mail: info@interplast.org
Web: www.interplast.org

Minimum time: 2 weeks
Usual time:
Maximum time:
Who pays transportation: Volunteer pays $325 toward transportation and housing, organization pays remainder
Who pays housing: See Transportation
Who pays food: Volunteer
Language requirements: Varies
Religious requirements: No
Countries: Bangladesh, Ecuador, Ghana, India, Nepal, Nicaragua, Peru, Sri Lanka, Zambia
Regions: Africa, Asia/Pacific, Latin America
Comments: Interplast brings surgical teams to disadvantaged countries to provide free repair of clefts, disabling burns, and hand injuries.
Paid or volunteer: Volunteer
Residents or medical students accepted: No
Last update: January 2008

Jewish Renaissance Foundation (JRF)/Operation Lifeline International

Alan Goldsmith, PhD
149 Kearny Ave
Perth Amboy, NJ 08861
Phone: 732/324-2114
E-mail: jrfmed@aol.com
Web: www.jrfmed.org

Minimum time: 1 week
Usual time: 1 to 2 weeks
Maximum time: None
Who pays transportation: Volunteer
Who pays housing: Volunteer
Who pays food: Volunteer
Language requirements: No
Religious requirements: Jewish
Countries: Africa, Caribbean, Eastern Europe, India, former Soviet Union
Regions: Africa, Asia/Pacific, Caribbean, Eastern Europe
Comments: JRF seeks volunteer physicians in all specialties for its medical missions to crisis-ridden areas and to underserved areas overseas.
Paid or volunteer: Volunteer
Residents or medical students accepted: Residents and medical students
Last update: January 2008

Lalmba Association

Marc Seidman
7685 Quartz St
Arvada, CO 80007
Phone: 303/420-1810
E-mail: lalmba@lalmba.org or marcseidman@yahoo.com
Web: www.lalmba.org

Minimum time: 6 months
Usual time: 1 to 2 years
Maximum time: 3 years
Who pays transportation: Organization
Who pays housing: Organization
Who pays food: Organization
Language requirements: No
Religious requirements: No
Countries: Eritrea, Ethiopia, Kenya
Regions: Africa

Comments: In existence for more than 43 years, Lalmba (La-lum-ba) is one of the world's smallest international development agencies. Its focus is primary care health projects in Africa, but other projects include children's homes, schools, orphanages, and education.
Paid or volunteer: Volunteer
Residents or medical students accepted: No
Last update: January 2008

LIGA International

Jim Ott
1464 N Fitzgerald Hanger # 2
Rialto, CA 92376
Phone: 909/875-6300
E-mail: j.OTT@Ligainternational.org
Web: www.ligainternational.org

Minimum time: 3 days
Usual time: 3 days
Maximum time: 4 days
Who pays transportation: Volunteer
Who pays housing: Volunteer
Who pays food: Volunteer
Language requirements: No. Spanish is helpful.
Religious requirements: No
Countries: Mexico
Regions: Latin America
Comments: Volunteers are flown in small privately owned aircraft from California to treat the rural poor of Northern Mexico. Trips leave the first Friday of each month, October through June, and return on Sunday.
Paid or volunteer: Volunteer
Residents or medical students accepted: Residents and medical students
Last update: January 2008

Maluti Adventist Hospital

Wilber Hurlow, MD
Private Bag X019
Ficksburg, OFS 9730
Rep S Africa
Phone: 266/2254-0203
E-mail: info@malutiadventisthospital.org
Web: www.malutiadventisthospital.org

Minimum time: 1 month
Usual time: Varies
Maximum time: None
Who pays transportation: Volunteer
Who pays housing: Volunteer
Who pays food: Volunteer
Language requirements: No
Religious requirements: No
Countries: Lesotho
Regions: Africa
Comments: Volunteers work full time in hospital and outpatient department, sharing call. Hospital has operating room, x-ray, lab, and an associated center for HIV/AIDS.
Paid or volunteer: Volunteer
Residents or medical students accepted: Residents
Last update: January 2008

Maryknoll Lay Missioners

Kathy Wright
PO Box 307
Maryknoll, NY 10545-0307
Phone: 914/762-6364 or 800/818-5276, ext 114
E-mail: kwright@mklm.org
Web: www.mklm.org

Minimum time: 3 years
Usual time: 3 years
Maximum time: Career
Who pays transportation: Organization
Who pays housing: Organization
Who pays food: Organization
Language requirements: No
Religious requirements: Catholics interested in being missionaries
Countries: Bolivia, Brazil, Cambodia, Chile, East Timor, El Salvador, Kenya, Mexico, Peru, Tanzania, Thailand, Vietnam, Zimbabwe

Regions: Africa, Asia/Pacific, Latin America
Comments: For those with a family, a maximum of 2 children, 8 years or younger. In the past organization paid for everything. Now volunteers are expected to do some fundraising. Volunteers receive a stipend while working overseas. Generally volunteers are aged 23 to 60. Volunteers are expected to learn local language. Organization provides an orientation prior to going overseas.
Paid or volunteer: Volunteer
Residents or medical students accepted: No
Last update: January 2008

Med Commission

Tom and Nancy Loveless
3771 Spring Park Rd
Jacksonville, FL 32207
Phone: 904/398-6559, ext 1117
Web: www.gotonations.com

Minimum time: 1 week
Usual time: 1 to 2 weeks
Maximum time: Lifetime
Who pays transportation: Volunteer
Who pays housing: Volunteer
Who pays food: Volunteer
Language requirements: No
Religious requirements: Christian
Countries: Worldwide
Regions: Africa, Asia, Eastern Europe, Latin America, Middle East
Comments: A ministry of Calvary International, Med Commission mobilizes volunteer health care professionals to staff primary care facilities, provide health education, and perform surgery in underdeveloped communities around the world.
Paid or volunteer: Volunteer
Residents or medical students accepted: No
Last update: January 2008

Medical Benevolence Foundation (MBF)

Chip Lambert, MD, Church Outreach Coordinator
3100 S Gessner #210
Houston, TX 77063-3743
Phone: 866/866-0430
E-mail: clambert@mbfoundation.org
Web: www.mbfoundation.org

Minimum time: 2 to 3 weeks
Usual time: 3 to 4 weeks
Maximum time: 11 months
Who pays transportation: Volunteer
Who pays housing: Volunteer
Who pays food: Volunteer
Language requirements: Sometimes
Religious requirements: Christian
Countries: Cameroon, Democratic Republic of Congo, Egypt (in development), Kenya, Malawi
Regions: Africa, Middle East
Comments: The MBF/Presbyterian Church (PC) (USA) International Short Term Volunteer program is currently in development and operating on an interim basis. It links with PC (USA), requiring application through MBF and the PC (USA) One Door (http://onedoor.pcusa.org). Primary care, teaching, and community health issues are the main activities of volunteer pediatricians.
Paid or volunteer: Volunteer
Residents or medical students accepted: Residents and medical students
Last update: January 2008

Medical Expeditions International (MEI)

Rachel Friday
1235 N Decatur Rd
Atlanta, GA 30306
Phone: 404/815-7044
E-mail: info@medexinternational.org
Web: www.medexinternational.org

Minimum time: 1 week
Usual time: 1 to 2 weeks
Maximum time: 2 weeks
Who pays transportation: Volunteer
Who pays housing: Volunteer
Who pays food: Volunteer
Language requirements: No (interpreters)

Religious requirements: No
Countries: Ecuador, India
Regions: Asia, Latin America
Comments: A private, nonprofit nonsectarian medical aid organization, MEI is dedicated to providing health care to some of the most remote regions of the world. Currently missions are planned to India, Ecuador, and Mexico.
Paid or volunteer: Volunteer
Residents or medical students accepted: Sometimes
Last update: January 2008

Medical Ministry International (MMI)

Brian Piecuch
400 N Allen Dr, Suite 204
Allen, TX 75013
Phone: 972/727-5864
E-mail: mmitx@mmint.org
Web: www.mmint.org

Minimum time: 1 week
Usual time: 2 weeks
Maximum time: 2 weeks
Who pays transportation: Volunteer
Who pays housing: Organization
Who pays food: Organization
Language requirements: No. Basic knowledge of the language of the country is helpful.
Religious requirements: No; Christian organization
Countries: Armenia, Azerbaijan, Bolivia, Cambodia, Colombia, Costa Rica, Dominican Republic, Ecuador, Ethiopia, Fiji, Ghana, Guatemala, Haiti, India, Indonesia, Jamaica, Jordan, Lebanon, Madagascar, Mexico, Mozambique, Myanmar, Nepal, Nicaragua, Peru, Philippines, Rwanda, Sudan, Tanzania, Thailand, Vietnam
Regions: Africa, Asia/Pacific, Caribbean, Latin America, Middle East
Comments: MMI volunteers work alongside national doctors and helpers from the countries we go to, joining the efforts of the local church where possible.
Paid or volunteer: Volunteer
Residents or medical students accepted: Residents and medical students
Last update: January 2008

Medical Teams International (formerly Northwest Medical Teams)

Eve Ford, International Volunteer Recruiter
PO Box 10
Portland, OR 97207-0010
Phone: 800/959 HEAL, ext 1201 or 503/624-1201
E-mail: eford@medicalteams.org
Web: www.medicalteams.org

Minimum time: 1 to 4 weeks
Usual time: 2 to 4 weeks
Maximum time: Varies
Who pays transportation: Varies
Who pays housing: Varies
Who pays food: Varies
Language requirements: No
Religious requirements: No; must support organization's mission statement
Countries: Worldwide
Regions:
Comments: The mission statement of Medical Teams International is to demonstrate the love of Christ to people affected by disaster, conflict, and poverty. We send medical and dental professionals and various lay worker teams to poverty and crisis areas all over the world. We have a strong emphasis on training and equipping the local in-country health care system and also send disaster teams around the world.
Paid or volunteer: Volunteer
Residents or medical students accepted: No
Last update: January 2008

MEDICO (Medical, Eye & Dental International Care Organization)

Lynda Peters, Director
2955 Dawn D, Suite D
Georgetown, TX 78628
Phone: 512/930-1893
E-mail: director@medico.org
Web: www.medico.org

Minimum time: 1 week
Usual time: 1 week
Maximum time: 1 week
Who pays transportation: Volunteer
Who pays housing: Volunteer
Who pays food: Volunteer

Language requirements: Spanish is helpful, not required.
Religious requirements: No
Countries: Honduras, Nicaragua
Regions: Latin America
Comments: Any specialty is welcome. This is a popular program. Trips are booked well in advance. This is a particularly good trip for students. Teams often take several students along to assist the doctors, dentists, and nurses. MEDICO serves the rural populations where there is little or no access to medical care.
Paid or volunteer: Volunteer
Residents or medical students accepted: Residents and medical students
Last update: January 2008

Mennonite Mission Network

Diana Cook
1611 W Beardsley, PO Box 370
Elkart, IN 46515-0370
Phone: 316/283-5100 or 866/866-2872
E-mail: mmninternationalministries@mennonites.org
Web: www.mennonitemission.net

Minimum time: 2 weeks
Usual time: 3 months
Maximum time: 2 to 3 years
Who pays transportation: Varies
Who pays housing: Varies
Who pays food: Varies
Language requirements: Training given
Religious requirements: Christian; Mennonite for long term
Countries: Worldwide, Brazil, China, Congo, Japan, Nepal, Senegal. Medical needs vary.
Regions: Africa, Asia/Pacific, Latin America
Comments: Short-term volunteers are expected to pay their own expenses. Long-term volunteers (>2 years) receive a stipend.
Paid or volunteer: Paid (stipend for long-term volunteers)
Residents or medical students accepted: Residents and medical students possible at times
Last update: January 2008

Mercy Airlift

Mr Pike, Medical Team Coordinator/Recruiter
PO Box 90452
Los Angeles, CA 90009
Phone: 800/637-2945
E-mail: info@mercyairlift.org
Web: www.flyinghospital.org

Minimum time: 1 week
Usual time: 2 weeks
Maximum time: 4 weeks
Who pays transportation: Varies
Who pays housing: Varies
Who pays food: Varies
Language requirements: Sometimes
Religious requirements: Varies
Countries: Worldwide
Regions: Africa, Asia/Pacific, Caribbean, Eastern Europe, Latin America, Middle East
Comments: Humanitarian organization provides complete logistical services and air transportation to other humanitarian organizations worldwide. Medical response teams provide free medical and surgical care in developing countries.
Paid or volunteer: Volunteer
Residents or medical students accepted: Residents and medical students
Last update: January 2008

Mercy Ships

Angie Fadely
PO Box 2020
Garden Valley, TX 75771-2020
Phone: 800/MERCYSHIPS (info) or 903/939-7000
E-mail: jobs@mercyships.org
Web: www.mercyships.org

Minimum time: 2 weeks
Usual time: 2 weeks to 3 months
Maximum time: 9 months without entry training
Who pays transportation: Volunteer
Who pays housing: Volunteer
Who pays food: Volunteer
Language requirements: No
Religious requirements: Christian
Countries: Benin, Ghana, Liberia, Sierra Leone

Regions: West Africa

Comments: Mercy Ships, a global charity, has operated hospital ships in developing nations since 1978 to bring hope and healing to the poor worldwide.

Paid or volunteer: Volunteer

Residents or medical students accepted: No

Last update: January 2008

Mexican Medical Ministries

Kristi Libby
7850 Lester Ave
Lemon Grove, CA, 91945
Phone: 619/463-4777
E-mail: information@mexicanmedical.com
Web: www.mexicanmedical.com

Minimum time: 1 day to weekender teams

Usual time: 1- to 4-week surgical teams

Maximum time: Varies

Who pays transportation: Volunteer

Who pays housing: Volunteer

Who pays food: Volunteer

Language requirements: Sometimes, Spanish

Religious requirements: Christian for long term

Countries: Mexico (Baja and Palenque)

Regions: Latin America

Comments: This organization drives volunteer doctors to Tijuana for "weekenders" and may treat hundreds of medical, dental, and eye patients in a day at the health fair. They also have a small hospital and operating room in Palenque, where surgical teams with medical and pediatric support do 1-week trips.

Paid or volunteer: Volunteer

Residents or medical students accepted: Residents

Last update: April 2008

MIMA Foundation

Mary Kay Thomas
Box 7133
Jupiter, FL 33468
Phone: 561/747-3343
E-mail: mimafoundation@hotmail.com
Web: www.mimafoundation.com

Minimum time: 1 week
Usual time: 2 weeks
Maximum time: 4 weeks
Who pays transportation: Volunteer
Who pays housing: Volunteer
Who pays food: Volunteer
Language requirements: No
Religious requirements: No
Countries: Bolivia, Guatemala
Regions: Latin America
Comments: MIMA runs medical outreach and surgical projects twice a year and involves local health care providers to ensure continuity of care.
Paid or volunteer: Volunteer
Residents or medical students accepted: Residents
Last update: January 2008

Minnesota International Health Volunteers (MIHV)

Executive Director
122 W Franklin Ave, Suite 510
Minneapolis, MN 55404-2480
Phone: 612/871-3759
E-mail: info@mihv.org
Web: www.mihv.org

Minimum time: 3 to 4 months
Usual time: 1 year
Maximum time: Varies
Who pays transportation: Varies
Who pays housing: Varies
Who pays food: Varies
Language requirements: Sometimes
Religious requirements: No
Countries: Tanzania, Uganda—limited positions available
Regions: Africa

Comments: Shorter-term service available for those able to pay own way. MIHV aims at development rather than dependence so volunteers are typically involved in education and organization as much as direct health care service, especially in the areas of maternal and child health, malaria, and HIV/AIDS.

Paid or volunteer: Paid and volunteer

Residents or medical students accepted: Residents

Last update: January 2008

Mission Doctors Association (MDA)

Elise Frederick, Program Coordinator
3435 Wilshire Blvd, Suite 1035
Los Angeles, CA 90010
Phone: 213/368-1875
E-mail: missiondrs@earthlink.net
Web: www.MissionDoctors.org

Minimum time: 1 month

Usual time: 1 to 3 months

Maximum time: 2 years

Who pays transportation: Varies

Who pays housing: Organization

Who pays food: Organization

Language requirements: Training available for long-term assignment; Spanish for short-term Latin American assignments

Religious requirements: Catholic

Countries: Cameroon, Ecuador, Ghana, Guatamala, Uganda, Zimbabwe

Regions: Africa, Latin America

Comments: MDA was founded in 1959 to assist Catholic physicians and their families in their desire to serve in mission hospitals and clinics. All physicians are invited to apply. Some specialties may only be appropriate for short-term assignment.

Paid or volunteer: Volunteer

Residents or medical students accepted: Residents (4th year)

Last update: January 2008

Nazarene Health Care Fellowship

Erika Rios
6401 The Paseo
Kansas City, MO 64131
Phone: 816/333-7000, ext 2509
E-mail: nmo@nazarene.org
Web: www.nazareneworldmission.org

Minimum time: 1 week
Usual time: 2 weeks
Maximum time: 1 year
Who pays transportation: Volunteer
Who pays housing: Volunteer
Who pays food: Volunteer
Language requirements: No
Religious requirements: Christian members of the Church of the Nazarene
Countries: Caribbean, Central America, India, Kenya, South Africa
Regions: Africa, Asia, Caribbean, Latin America
Comments: Some short-term medical mission trips and other placements at established facilities.
Paid or volunteer: Volunteer
Residents or medical students accepted: Residents and medical students
Last update: January 2008

North American Baptist Conference

Eric Larsen
1 S 210 Summit Ave
Oakbrook Terrace, IL 60181
Phone: 630/495-2000, ext 208
E-mail: serve@nabconf.org
Web: www.NABConference.org

Minimum time: 2 weeks
Usual time: 2 months
Maximum time: 2 years
Who pays transportation: Volunteer
Who pays housing: Volunteer
Who pays food: Volunteer
Language requirements: Local language for long term
Religious requirements: Christian preferred
Countries: Cameroon, Nigeria
Regions: Africa
Comments: Hospitals and clinics need pediatricians.
Paid or volunteer: Volunteer

Residents or medical students accepted: Residents and medical students
in Cameroon
Last update: January 2008

Northwest Medical Teams International
(see Medical Teams International)

Omni Med

Edward O'Neil, MD
81 Wyman St
Waban, MA 02468
Phone: 617/332-9614
E-mail: ejoneil@comcast.net or ejoneil@omnimed.org
Web: www.omnimed.org

Minimum time: 1 week
Usual time: 2 weeks
Maximum time: Varies
Who pays transportation: Volunteer
Who pays housing: Varies
Who pays food: Varies
Language requirements: No
Religious requirements: No
Countries: Belize, Guyana, Kenya, Thailand
Regions: Africa, Asia/Pacific, Latin America
Comments: Except Thailand, which is an eye surgery program, these are
teaching trips to hospitals in Guyana and Kenya and at 7 sites around Belize.
Paid or volunteer: Volunteer
Residents or medical students accepted: No
Last update: January 2008

Operation Rainbow

Laura Escobosa
4200 Park Blvd PmB157
Oakland, CA 94602
Phone: 510/273-2485
E-mail: info@operationrainbow.org
Web: www.operationrainbow.org

Minimum time: 10 days
Usual time: 10 days
Maximum time: 10 days
Who pays transportation: Volunteer
Who pays housing: Volunteer
Who pays food: Volunteer
Language requirements: No. Spanish is helpful, not required.
Religious requirements: No
Countries: China, Ecuador, El Salvador, Guatemala, Honduras, Mexico, Nicaragua, Peru, Philippines
Regions: Asia/Pacific, Latin America
Comments: Operation Rainbow organizes surgical missions to provide orthopedic surgery to poor children. In addition to providing free surgery, the medical teams pass on skills to local health care workers. A pediatrician is needed on every trip.
Paid or volunteer: Volunteer
Residents or medical students accepted: Residents
Last update: January 2008

Operation Smile

Ronda Shelby, Medical Credentialing
6435 Tidewater Dr
Norfolk, VA 23509
Phone: 757/321-7617
E-mail: rshelby@operationsmile.org
Web: www.operationsmile.org

Minimum time: 2 weeks
Usual time: 2 weeks
Maximum time: 3 weeks
Who pays transportation: Volunteer
Who pays housing: Organization ($500 team fee)
Who pays food: Volunteer
Language requirements: No
Religious requirements: No

Countries: Bolivia, Brazil, Cambodia, China, Honduras, India, Kenya, Laos, Myanmar, Nicaragua, Philippines (2008 schedule)
Regions: Africa, Asia/Pacific, Latin America
Comments: This private not-for-profit medical service organization provides reconstructive surgery and related health care to indigent children and young adults in developing countries and the United States. Operation Smile provides education and training to promote long-term self-sufficiency. Pediatricians and pediatric intensivists are needed.
Paid or volunteer: Volunteer
Residents or medical students accepted: Residents and 4th-year medical students
Last update: January 2008

Our Little Brothers and Sisters

Frank J. Krafft, President
PO Box 3134
Alexandria, VA 22302
Phone: 703/580-8850
E-mail: fkrafft@olbsus.org
Web: www.nph.org

Minimum time: 1 year
Usual time: 1 year
Maximum time: 10 years
Who pays transportation: Volunteer
Who pays housing: Organization
Who pays food: Organization
Language requirements: French for Haiti, Spanish for other countries
Religious requirements: Christian
Countries: Dominican Republic, El Salvador, Guatemala, Haiti, Honduras, Mexico, Nicaragua
Regions: Caribbean, Latin America
Comments: We have a children's hospital in Haiti and clinics at all of our other orphanages. Description of programs and application forms are available on request.
Paid or volunteer: Volunteer
Residents or medical students accepted: Medical students and residents (1 year of service required)
Last update: January 2008

Palestine Children's Relief Fund (PCRF)

Stephen Sosebee
PO Box 1926
Kent, OH 44240
Phone: 330/678-2645
E-mail: pcrf1@pcrf.net
Web: www.pcrf.net

Minimum time: Varies
Usual time: Varies
Maximum time: Varies
Who pays transportation: Organization
Who pays housing: Organization
Who pays food: Organization
Language requirements: No
Religious requirements: No
Countries: Lebanon
Regions: Middle East
Comments: While the PCRF brings children injured in war or crippled by
  birth defects for treatment in US hospitals, it also sends teams of doctors,
  particularly surgeons, to train local physicians from the West Bank and the
  Gaza Strip. PCRF also sends medical supplies.
Paid or volunteer: Volunteer
Residents or medical students accepted: Residents and medical students
Last update: January 2008

Partners of the Americas (National Office)

1424 K St NW, Suite 700
Washington, DC 20005
Phone: 202/628-3300
E-mail: info@partners.net
Web: www.partners.net

Minimum time: Varies
Usual time: Varies
Maximum time: Varies
Who pays transportation: Volunteer
Who pays housing: Volunteer
Who pays food: Volunteer
Language requirements: Varies
Religious requirements: None
Countries: Argentina, Barbados, Belize, Bolivia, Brazil, Chile, Columbia,
  Costa Rica, Dominican Republic, Ecuador, El Salvador, Guatemala, Guyana,
  Haiti, Honduras, Jamaica, Mexico, Nicaragua, Panama, Paraguay, Peru,
  Uruguay, Venezuela

Regions: Caribbean, Latin America
Comments: Partners of the Americas links US states with countries in the western hemisphere to promote understanding and development. Each state sponsors specific programs with their partner country, many of which are health care related.
Paid or volunteer: Volunteer
Residents or medical students accepted: Varies
Last update: January 2008

Peacework (Placement Service)

209 Otey St
Blacksburg, VA 02406-7426
Phone: 800/272-5519
E-mail: mail@peacework.org
Web: www.peacework.org

Minimum time: Any
Usual time: 1 to 2 weeks
Maximum time: None
Who pays transportation: Volunteer (in program budget)
Who pays housing: Volunteer (in program budget)
Who pays food: Volunteer
Language requirements: Sometimes
Religious requirements: No
Countries: Belize, Cameroon, Dominican Republic, Ghana, Guatemala, Honduras, India, Kenya, Nepal, Russia, Vietnam, and others.
Regions: Africa, Asia/Pacific, Latin America
Comments: Peacework arranges and manages international volunteer projects for medical groups. Occasionally, individual professionals may join one of these groups. Many sites are suitable for medical students and faculty. Peacework makes all arrangements and provides logistical support.
Paid or volunteer: Paid and volunteer
Residents or medical students accepted: Residents and medical students
Last update: January 2008

Peruvian American Medical Society (PAMS)

6488 Tamerlane Dr
West Bloomfield, MI 48322-2379
Phone: 248/851-2709
E-mail: PAMS1AMS@comcast.net or miguelpro@aol.com
Web: www.pamsnational.org

Minimum time: 1 week
Usual time: 1 to 2 weeks
Maximum time: None
Who pays transportation: Volunteer
Who pays housing: Volunteer
Who pays food: Volunteer
Language requirements: Spanish is helpful.
Religious requirements: No
Countries: Peru
Regions: Latin America
Comments: PAMS is dedicated to improving health care in Peru through education and medical missions. Physicians are needed to work in outpatient clinics on missions that generally last 1 or 2 weeks.
Paid or volunteer: Volunteer
Residents or medical students accepted: Residents and medical students
Last update: January 2008

Physicians for Peace

229 West Bute St, Suite 200
Norfolk, VA 23510
Phone: 757/625-7569
E-mail: info@physiciansforpeace.org
Web: www.physiciansforpeace.org

Minimum time: 4 days
Usual time: 2 weeks
Maximum time: 3 weeks
Who pays transportation: Organization
Who pays housing: Varies
Who pays food: Organization
Language requirements: No
Religious requirements: No
Countries: Worldwide
Regions: Africa, Asia/Pacific, Caribbean, Eastern Europe, Latin America, Middle East

Comments: Physicians for Peace sponsors medical education, training, and clinical care in developing countries. A new resident training program in Eritrea with George Washington University Medical Center has just opened.
Paid or volunteer: Volunteer
Residents or medical students accepted: Residents
Last update: January 2008

Pioneers

Warren Wagner
10123 William Casey Dr
Orlando, FL 32832
Phone: 800/755-7284, ext 148, or 407/382-6000
E-mail: wwagner@orlandoteam.com
Web: www.pioneers.org

Minimum time: 1 week
Usual time: 2 months to 2 years
Maximum time: Career
Who pays transportation: Volunteer
Who pays housing: Volunteer
Who pays food: Volunteer
Language requirements: Sometimes
Religious requirements: Christian
Countries: Worldwide
Regions: Africa, Asia/Pacific, Caribbean, Eastern Europe, Latin America, Middle East
Comments: No formal program with hospitals or clinics but they have missionaries in many countries who may be able to arrange medical work.
Paid or volunteer: Volunteer
Residents or medical students accepted: No
Last update: January 2008

Project Amazon (formerly PAZ International)

Kelly Klootwyk
PO Box 3253
Peoria, IL 61612
Phone: 309/263-2299
E-mail: dove@dpc.net
Web: www.projectamazon.org

Minimum time: 1 week
Usual time: 2 weeks
Maximum time: 3 weeks
Who pays transportation: Volunteer
Who pays housing: Volunteer
Who pays food: Volunteer
Language requirements: No
Religious requirements: Christian
Countries: Brazil
Regions: Latin America
Comments: Six Project Amazon medical boats provide care, medicine, and
    minor surgery to river communities. A Brazilian doctor must be present in
    order for an American doctor to treat patients. Must agree not to smoke or
    drink alcohol while on mission.
Paid or volunteer: Volunteer
Residents or medical students accepted: No
Last update: January 2008

Project Dawn

Dr Carmen Gannon
PO Box 60039
Savannah, GA 31420
Phone: 912/429-7272
E-mail: hornemc72@bellsouth.net

Minimum time: 1 week
Usual time: 1 to 3 weeks
Maximum time: 3 weeks
Who pays transportation: Volunteer
Who pays housing: Volunteer
Who pays food: Volunteer
Language requirements: No
Religious requirements: No
Countries: Guyana

Regions: Latin America
Comments: 3 to 4 trips per year to this English-speaking South American country. Doctors work in an established clinic in Georgetown.
Paid or volunteer: Volunteer
Residents or medical students accepted: Residents
Last update: January 2008

Project HOPE

Human Resources
255 Carter Lane
Millwood, VA 22646
Phone: 540837-9433
E-mail: recruitment@projecthope.org
Web: www.projecthope.org

Minimum time: None
Usual time: Varies
Maximum time: Career
Who pays transportation: Varies
Who pays housing: Varies
Who pays food: Varies
Language requirements: No
Religious requirements: No
Countries: Bosnia, China, Dominican Republic, Ecuador, Haiti, Honduras, Macedonia, Malawi, Mozambique, Nicaragua, Turkey. Visit Web site for a complete list.
Regions: Africa, Caribbean, Eastern Europe, Latin America
Comments: Health care professionals with teaching qualifications and experience preferred. Project HOPE has programs in more than 32 countries. Please visit our Web site for a current listing of volunteer, consultant, and intern opportunities. In a world of HOPE you make a world of difference.
Paid or volunteer: Paid and volunteer
Residents or medical students accepted: No
Last update: January 2008

Project Vietnam

Quynh Kieu, MD, FAAP
11100 Warner Ave #116
Fountain Valley, CA 92708
Phone: 714/641-0850
E-mail: qkieu@projectvietnam.net
Web: www.projectvietnam.net

Minimum time: 2 weeks
Usual time: 2 to 4 weeks
Maximum time: 8 weeks
Who pays transportation: Volunteer
Who pays housing: Volunteer
Who pays food: Volunteer
Language requirements: No
Religious requirements: No
Countries: Vietnam
Regions: Asia/Pacific
Comments: Since 1996 Project Vietnam has provided health care assistance
    to children at risk in needy rural areas and worked with local personnel to
    promote improved health care services. Medical and surgical group trips
    occur several times a year.
Paid or volunteer: Volunteer
Residents or medical students accepted: Residents and medical students
Last update: January 2008

Rafiki Foundation

Susy Harbick
19001 Huebner Rd #2
San Antonio, TX 78258
Phone: 210/244-2600, ext 615
E-mail: susyh@rafiki-foundation.org
Web: www.rafiki-foundation.org

Minimum time: 2 weeks
Usual time: 2 weeks
Maximum time: Lifetime
Who pays transportation: Volunteer
Who pays housing: Volunteer
Who pays food: Volunteer
Language requirements: English
Religious requirements: Christian
Countries: Ethiopia, Ghana, Kenya, Liberia, Malawi, Nigeria, Rwanda,
    Tanzania, Uganda, Zambia

Regions: Africa

Comments: Not-for-profit organization that is developing training villages in 10 countries in Africa. The goal is to turn helpless children into godly contributors in their countries.

Paid or volunteer: Volunteer

Residents or medical students accepted: Residents and medical students

Last update: January 2008

RedR UK (Placement Agency)

1 Great George St
London UK SW1P3AA
Phone: 207-7233-3116 (dial +44 0 before #)
Web: www.redr.org.uk

Minimum time: Varies

Usual time: Varies

Maximum time: Varies

Who pays transportation: Varies

Who pays housing: Varies

Who pays food: Varies

Language requirements: Sometimes

Religious requirements: Sometimes

Countries: Worldwide

Regions: Africa, Asia/Pacific, Caribbean, Eastern Europe, Latin America, Middle East

Comments: RedR is a charity helping to recruit health workers for other organizations doing humanitarian work in developing countries. Agencies seek assistance through their register of professionals and their *Health Exchange* magazine.

Paid or volunteer: Paid and volunteer

Residents or medical students accepted: No

Last update: January 2008

Red Sea Team International

PO Box 2047
Lexington, SC 29071-2047
E-mail: rsti@scrr.com
Web: www.rsti.org

Minimum time: Varies
Usual time: Varies
Maximum time: Varies
Who pays transportation: Volunteer
Who pays housing: Organization
Who pays food: Organization
Language requirements: Sometimes
Religious requirements: Christian
Countries: Djibouti, Mali, Pakistan
Regions: Africa, Asia/Pacific, Middle East
Comments: Physicians needed for longer-term placements in East Africa, South Asia, Middle East. Name will change in 2009.
Paid or volunteer: Volunteer
Residents or medical students accepted: No
Last update: January 2008

Remote Area Medical

Stan Brock
1834 Beech St
Knoxville, TN 37920
Phone: 865/579-1530
E-mail: ram@ramusa.org
Web: www.ramusa.org

Minimum time: 1 week
Usual time: 10 to 12 days
Maximum time: 3 weeks
Who pays transportation: Volunteer
Who pays housing: Varies
Who pays food: Varies
Language requirements: No
Religious requirements: No
Countries: Dominican Republic, Guatemala, Guyana, Haiti, Honduras, India, Kenya, Mexico, Nepal, Tanzania
Regions: Africa, Asia, Caribbean, Latin America
Comments: Doctors needed for long-term placement in Guyana. Food and housing usually provided by hosts.

Paid or volunteer: Volunteer
Residents or medical students accepted: No
Last update: January 2008

Roatan Volunteer Pediatric Clinic *(see Global Healing)*

RSVP (Reconstructive Surgeons' Volunteer Program) *(discontinued, see Volunteers in Plastic Surgery [VIPS])*

Saint Francis Hospital

Richard Newell, MD
Private Bag II
Katete Zambia
Phone: 26 06252210
E-mail: volunteer@saintfrancishospital.net or richard@saintfrancishospital.net
Web: www.saintfrancishospital.net

Minimum time: 3 months
Usual time: 6 months
Maximum time: 2 years
Who pays transportation: Volunteer
Who pays housing: Organization
Who pays food: Volunteer
Language requirements: No
Religious requirements: No
Countries: Zambia
Regions: Africa
Comments: 280-bed hospital with 2 operating rooms. Up to 30 pediatric admissions daily. Volunteers share workload with Zambian staff.
Paid or volunteer: Paid (long term) and volunteer
Residents or medical students accepted: Medical student electives
Last update: January 2008

Saint Jude Hospital

George Lee St Jour
PO Box 331, Vieux Fort
St Lucia West Indies
Phone: 758/454-6041
E-mail: stjourgl@hotmail.com

Minimum time: 1 month
Usual time: 1 month
Maximum time: Career
Who pays transportation: Varies
Who pays housing: Organization
Who pays food: Organization
Language requirements: No
Religious requirements: No
Countries: St Lucia
Regions: Caribbean
Comments: This site is available also through Health Volunteers Overseas (www.hvousa.org).
Paid or volunteer: Paid and volunteer
Residents or medical students accepted: Residents
Last update: January 2008

Serving in Mission (SIM USA)

Anthony Birdsong
PO Box 7900
Charlotte, NC 28273
Phone: 704/588-4300 or 800/521-6449
E-mail: info@sim.org
Web: www.sim.org (preliminary information form: www.simusa.org/getstarted)

Minimum time: 2 to 3 weeks
Usual time: 6 weeks
Maximum time: 2 years or longer
Who pays transportation: Volunteer
Who pays housing: Volunteer
Who pays food: Volunteer
Language requirements: No
Religious requirements: Christian, Evangelical
Countries: Angola, Bosnia, China, Ecuador, Ethiopia, Liberia, Malawi, Namibia, Niger, Nigeria, Zambia
Regions: Africa, Asia/Pacific, Latin America

Comments: This Evangelical Christian ministry needs physicians in family practice, internal medicine, pediatrics, obstetrics-gynecology, and general surgery for services projects in Africa, Asia, and South America.
Paid or volunteer: Volunteer
Residents or medical students accepted: Residents and medical students
Last update: January 2008

Siloé Project

Sue McKenzie (US), Jane MacRae (Haiti)
Centre PAZAPA, BP 92
Jacmel Haiti
Phone: 509/288-3673
E-mail: suemck1@chartermi.net (US) or pazapa99@hotmail.com (Haiti)
Web: www.siloe.org

Minimum time: 3 to 4 days
Usual time: 1 week
Maximum time: None
Who pays transportation: Volunteer
Who pays housing: Volunteer
Who pays food: Volunteer
Language requirements: Haitian Kreyol, French, English
Religious requirements: No
Countries: Haiti
Regions: Caribbean
Comments: Siloe supports Pazapa, a center for handicapped children in Jacmel, Haiti. We support the treatment, education, and development of children with disabilities. Orthopedic surgery, services for hearing/visually impaired and physical handicaps, and special education are provided.
Paid or volunteer: Volunteer
Residents or medical students accepted: No
Last update: January 2008

South American Missionary Society (SAMS)

Denise Cox
PO Box 399
Ambridge, PA 15003
Phone: 724/266-0669
E-mail: denisecox@SAMS-usa.org
Web: www.SAMS-usa.org

Minimum time: 2 weeks
Usual time: Varies
Maximum time: 3 years
Who pays transportation: Volunteer
Who pays housing: Volunteer
Who pays food: Volunteer
Language requirements: Spanish sometimes
Religious requirements: Christian
Countries: Bolivia, Honduras, Uganda
Regions: Africa, Latin America
Comments: Regional missionaries make requests for visits by specific kinds of
   medical practitioners. Bishops of the particular dioceses ultimately determine
   where the full-time medical staff will be placed. Very structured and closely
   knit with church officials.
Paid or volunteer: Volunteer
Residents or medical students accepted: Some sites may accept residents
Last update: January 2008

Sove Lavi (formerly Simeus)

Kimberley Simeus
1212 Wyndham Hill Lane
Southlake, TX 76092
Phone: 817/239-7298
E-mail: kimberleysimeus@yahoo.com
Web: www.sovelavi.org

Minimum time: 2 days
Usual time: 5 days
Maximum time: Indefinite
Who pays transportation: Volunteer
Who pays housing: Volunteer
Who pays food: Volunteer
Language requirements: No
Religious requirements: No
Countries: Haiti

Regions: Caribbean
Comments: Volunteers help staff a clinic 5 days a week to provide primary and preventive health care.
Paid or volunteer: Volunteer
Residents or medical students accepted: Residents and medical students
Last update: January 2008

Surgicorps International

2 Allegheny Center, Suite 530
Pittsburgh, PA 15212
Phone: 412/322-9309
E-mail: surgi.corps@yahoo.com
Web: www.surgicorps.org

Minimum time: 2 weeks
Usual time: 12 to 15 days
Maximum time: 2 weeks
Who pays transportation: Volunteer
Who pays housing: Volunteer
Who pays food: Volunteer
Language requirements: No
Religious requirements: No
Countries: Brazil, Guatemala, India, Kenya, Nepal, Nigeria, Paraguay, Peru, Philippines, Vietnam
Regions: Africa, Asia/Pacific, Latin America
Comments: 2 to 3 trips per year for reconstructive surgery, typically 20 people per group.
Paid or volunteer: Volunteer
Residents or medical students accepted: No
Last update: January 2008

Surmang Foundation

Dr Juliet Carpenter
13536 Gold Hill Rd
Boulder, CO 80302
Phone: 303/459-9030
E-mail: info@surmang.org or leeweingrad@surmang.org
Web: www.surmang.org

Minimum time: 1 month (accessible June–Sept only)
Usual time:
Maximum time: 4 months
Who pays transportation: Volunteer
Who pays housing: Organization
Who pays food: Organization
Language requirements: English. Mandarin Chinese and/or Khampa Tibetan a big plus.
Religious requirements: No
Countries: China
Regions: Asia/Pacific
Comments: The Surmang Foundation is a US 501c(3) philanthropy and European Union–registered foundation that works in a very remote part of East Tibet, Qinghai Province, China. Its core project is a primary care clinic that has treated more than 60,000 patients free (including medicines) in the past 10 years. Until the Surmang Foundation created a clinic in 1992, there was no medical care. The area has one of the highest maternal/infant mortality/morbidity rates in the world. Projects focus on health promotion, prevention, and outreach. In addition to pediatric needs, we are also interested in obstetricians-gynecologists, emergency medical technicians, and internal medicine specialists. Those with a master's degree in public health and epidemiologists needed. We are partnered with the Chinese government and the Soong Ching-ling Foundation. Altitude averages 4,000 m. No electricity or telephone. It is physically and culturally challenging.
Paid or volunteer: Volunteer
Residents or medical students accepted: No
Last update: January 2008

The Evangelical Alliance Mission (TEAM)

Irene Mellema
PO Box 969
Wheaton, IL 60189-0969
Phone: 800/343-3144, ext 248
E-mail: info@teamworld.org
Web: www.teamworld.org

Minimum time: 2 weeks
Usual time: 2 to 4 years
Maximum time: Career
Who pays transportation: Volunteer
Who pays housing: Volunteer
Who pays food: Volunteer
Language requirements: Sometimes
Religious requirements: Christian
Countries: Worldwide
Regions: Asia/Pacific, Middle East
Comments: Born-again Christians with recommendations from pastor and above-average health. TEAM provides language training. Some hospitals, clinics.
Paid or volunteer: Volunteer
Residents or medical students accepted: Residents and 4th-year medical students
Last update: January 2008

Trinity Health International (formerly Mercy International Health Services)

Patricia Williams
34605 Twelve Mile Rd
Farmington Hills, MI 48331-3221
Phone: 248/489-6100
E-mail: international@trinity-health.org
Web: www.trinityhealthinternational.org

Minimum time: 2 weeks
Usual time: 1 month
Maximum time: Indefinite
Who pays transportation: Organization
Who pays housing: Organization
Who pays food: Organization
Language requirements: No
Religious requirements: No
Countries: Bangladesh, Guyana, Marshall Islands, Nigeria
Regions: Africa, Asia/Pacific, Latin America
Comments: Stipend. They manage hospitals and provide staff and training.
Paid or volunteer: Volunteer
Residents or medical students accepted: No
Last update: January 2008

United Methodist Volunteers in Mission, SEJ

Rev Nick Elliott
315 West Ponce de Leon Ave, #750
Decatur, GA 30030
Phone: 404/377-7424
E-mail: sejinfo@umvim.org
Web: www.umvim.org

Minimum time: 10 days
Usual time: 2 months to 2 years
Maximum time: 2 years
Who pays transportation: Volunteer
Who pays housing: Volunteer or organization
Who pays food: Volunteer or organization
Language requirements: Sometimes
Religious requirements: Christian
Countries: Worldwide
Regions: Africa, Asia/Pacific, Caribbean, Eastern Europe, Latin America, Middle East
Comments: Churches, districts, and conferences sponsor volunteer medical teams for service around the world for periods averaging 1 to 2 weeks. Team leaders and their sponsors determine the destination, schedule, team size, and other aspects of their trip depending on needs.
Paid or volunteer: Volunteer
Residents or medical students accepted: Residents and medical students
Last update: January 2008

United Nations Volunteers

111 20th St NW
Washington, DC 20526
Phone: 800/424-8580, ext 2256
E-mail: unvcoordinator@peacecorps.gov
Web: www.unv.org

Minimum time: 1 year
Usual time: 2 years
Maximum time: Varies
Who pays transportation: Organization
Who pays housing: Organization
Who pays food: Volunteer
Language requirements: Sometimes
Religious requirements: No
Countries: Worldwide

Regions: Africa, Asia/Pacific, Caribbean, Eastern Europe, Latin America, Middle East

Comments: Provides stipend for up to 3 dependents, resettlement allowance, health/life insurance for its volunteers. 50% United Nations volunteers work in Africa; 21% in Asia and Pacific. Check Web site for specific volunteer listings.

Paid or volunteer: Paid and volunteer

Residents or medical students accepted: No

Last update: January 2008

United Planet

Cecile Chappey
11 Arlington St
Boston, MA 0 2116
Phone: 800/292-2316 or 617/267-7763
E-mail: quest@unitedplanet.org
Web: www.unitedplanet.org

Minimum time: 2 weeks

Usual time: 2 to 4 weeks

Maximum time: Several months

Who pays transportation: Volunteer

Who pays housing: Volunteer. A program fee covers homestay, local transportation, language lessons, weekend trips.

Who pays food: Volunteer

Language requirements: Spanish for Peru

Religious requirements: No

Countries: Ghana, Guatemala, Nepal, Peru, Romania, Tanzania

Regions: Africa, Asia/Pacific, Eastern Europe, Latin America

Comments: Direct medical care in clinics or hospitals except Romania (orphanage) and Tanzania (HIV/AIDS education).

Paid or volunteer: Volunteer

Residents or medical students accepted: Residents and medical students

Last update: January 2008

Uplift Internationale

PO Box 82
Wheat Ridge, CO 80034
Phone: 303/707-1361
E-mail: info@upliftinternationale.org
Web: www.upliftinternationale.org

Minimum time: 1 week
Usual time: 2 weeks
Maximum time: Varies
Who pays transportation: Volunteer
Who pays housing: Volunteer
Who pays food: Volunteer
Language requirements: No
Religious requirements: No
Countries: Philippines
Regions: Asia/Pacific
Comments: Operation TAGHOY (Philippine word for whistle) brings surgical
teams to public-funded hospitals in rural Philippines to repair facial deformities in indigent children.
Paid or volunteer: Volunteer
Residents or medical students accepted: Residents and medical students
Last update: January 2008

Vellore Christian Medical College Board (USA), Inc.

475 Riverside Dr, Room 243
New York, NY 29679
Phone: 800/615-8695 or 864/885-9023
E-mail: usaboard@vellorecmc.org
Web: www.vellorecmc.org

Minimum time: 7 to 10 days
Usual time: 2 to 6 weeks
Maximum time: 6 months
Who pays transportation: Volunteer
Who pays housing: Volunteer
Who pays food: Volunteer
Language requirements: No
Religious requirements: No
Countries: India
Regions: Asia/Pacific

Comments: Opportunities for physicians and other health care professionals interested in sharing their skills and exploring how health care is practiced in another culture and setting. Highly respected large teaching hospital in South India.

Paid or volunteer: Volunteer

Residents or medical students accepted: Medical students' 4th-year elective

Last update: January 2008

Volunteers in Medical Missions

Kathy Cater, Trip Coordinator
PO Box 756
Seneca, SC 29679
Phone: 864/885-9023 or 800/615-8695
E-mail: mission@vimm.org
Web: www.vimm.org

Minimum time: 1 week

Usual time: 2 weeks

Maximum time: 2 weeks

Who pays transportation: Volunteer

Who pays housing: Volunteer

Who pays food: Volunteer

Language requirements: No

Religious requirements: Christian

Countries: Belize, Bulgaria, China, Chile, Costa Rica, Dominican Republic, Ecuador, El Salvador, Guatemala, Haiti, Honduras, Hungary, India, Jamaica, Mexico, Moldova, Mongolia, Nicaragua, Nigeria, Panama, Peru, Philippines, Romania, Russia, Sudan, Tanzania, Thailand, Trinidad, Ukraine, Uruguay, Venezuela, Vietnam, Zambia, Zimbabwe

Regions: Africa, Asia/Pacific, Caribbean, Eastern Europe, Latin America

Comments: Eight clinics per year in underserved areas.

Paid or volunteer: Volunteer

Residents or medical students accepted: Residents

Last update: January 2008

Vietnam Assistance for the Handicapped

Mr Ca Van Tran
1421 Dolley Madison Blvd, Suite E
McLean, VA 22101
Phone: 703/847-9582
E-mail: vnah1@aol.com
Web: www.vnah-hev.org

Minimum time: Varies
Usual time: 2 weeks
Maximum time: Varies
Who pays transportation: Volunteer
Who pays housing: Varies
Who pays food: Varies
Language requirements: No
Religious requirements: No
Countries: Vietnam
Regions: Asia/Pacific
Comments: Develop programs for the disabled. They also work with a number
  of maternal and child health programs and health care institutions in Viet-
  nam and may be able to place volunteers there short term.
Paid or volunteer: Volunteer
Residents or medical students accepted: Residents and medical students
Last update: April 2008

Volunteers in Plastic Surgery (VIPS)

Mari Jo Quintana Maisonet
444 East Algonquin Rd
Arlington Heights, IL 60005
Phone: 847/228-3334
E-mail: surgicalmissions@plasticsurgery.org
Web: www.plasticsurgery.org

Minimum time: 3 days
Usual time: 10 days
Maximum time: 3 weeks
Who pays transportation: Varies
Who pays housing: Varies
Who pays food: Varies
Language requirements: Sometimes
Religious requirements: Sometimes
Countries: Worldwide
Regions: Africa, Asia/Pacific, Caribbean, Eastern Europe, Latin America,
  Middle East

Comments: VIPS serves as a coordinating body for organizations that go on overseas volunteer missions. Contact VIPS to receive a link to their Mission Trip Calendar.
Paid or volunteer: Volunteer
Residents or medical students accepted: No
Last update: January 2008

Volunteer Missionary Movement

Julie Pagenkopf
5980 W Loomis
Greendale, WI 53129
Phone: 414/423-8660
E-mail: jpagenkopf@vmmusa.org
Web: www.vmmusa.org

Minimum time: 2 years
Usual time: 2 to 3 years
Maximum time: Varies
Who pays transportation: Organization
Who pays housing: Organization
Who pays food: Organization
Language requirements: Spanish. We offer 8 weeks of training.
Religious requirements: Christian
Countries: El Salvador, Guatemala, Nicaragua
Regions: Latin America
Comments: Volunteers are placed in small clinics or visit rural villages. Application process. Volunteer asked to provide some fundraising.
Paid or volunteer: Volunteer
Residents or medical students accepted: Residents and medical students
Last update: January 2008

Volunteer Service Organization (VSO)

Lisa Ambaaye
44 Eccles St, Suite 100
Ottawa Ontario Canada K1R6S4
Phone: 613/234-1364 or 888/876-2911
E-mail: inquiry@vsocan.org
Web: www.vsocan.org

Minimum time: 1 year
Usual time: 1 to 2 years
Maximum time: 3 years
Who pays transportation: Organization
Who pays housing: Organization
Who pays food: Organization
Language requirements: Sometimes
Religious requirements: No
Countries: Malawi, Papua New Guinea, Sri Lanka, Tanzania, Uganda, Zambia
Regions: Africa, Asia/Pacific
Comments: Recruits, trains, and matches volunteers from North America with
overseas partners in developing countries.
Paid or volunteer: Volunteer
Residents or medical students accepted: No
Last update: January 2008

World Association for Children and Parents

Mary Moo
315 South Second St
Renton, WA 98057
Phone: 206/575-4550
E-mail: marym@wacap.org
Web: www.wacap.org

Minimum time: Varies
Usual time: Varies
Maximum time: Varies
Who pays transportation: Volunteer
Who pays housing: Varies
Who pays food: Varies
Language requirements: No
Religious requirements: No
Countries: Varies
Regions: Varies
Comments: Adoption agency that periodically needs pediatricians to examine
children and/or their records.

Paid or volunteer: Volunteer
Residents or medical students accepted: No
Last update: January 2008

World Medical Mission/Samaritan's Purse

PO Box 3000
Boone, NC 28607
Phone: 828/528-1980
E-mail: jmoore@samaritan.org
Web: www.samaritanpurse.org/wmm

Minimum time: 1 week to 1 month depending on location
Usual time: 1 month
Maximum time: 1 year
Who pays transportation: Volunteer
Who pays housing: Volunteer
Who pays food: Volunteer
Language requirements: No, except Cameroon (French) and Ecuador and
    Honduras (Spanish)
Religious requirements: Protestant
Countries: Afghanistan, Bangladesh, Cameroon, Ecuador, Egypt, Ethiopia,
    Gabon, Haiti, Honduras, Kenya, Mali, Nepal, Niger, Papua New Guinea,
    Rwanda, Togo, Zambia
Regions: Africa, Asia/Pacific, Caribbean, Latin America, Middle East
Comments: All opportunities are at Protestant evangelical mission hospitals.
    The motivation is to help open doors to the Gospel through quality health
    care. Statement of faith and practice, 2 professional and one pastor's reference
    required.
Paid or volunteer: Volunteer
Residents or medical students accepted: Residents
Last update: January 2008

World Mission Prayer League

Carmen Gronewold
232 Clifton Ave
Minneapolis, MN 55403-3497
Phone: 612/871-6843
E-mail: wmpl@wmpl.org
Web: www.wmpl.org

Minimum time: 6 weeks
Usual time: 4 years
Maximum time: Career
Who pays transportation: Varies
Who pays housing: Varies
Who pays food: Volunteer
Language requirements: Sometimes
Religious requirements: Christian
Countries: Bangladesh, Mongolia, Nepal, Pakistan, Romania
Regions: Asia/Pacific, Eastern Europe
Comments: Must be Christian/Lutheran for long-term service.
Paid or volunteer: Paid and volunteer
Residents or medical students accepted: Residents
Last update: January 2008

World Reach

Paul Whitmore
PO Box 26155
Birmingham, AL 35260
Phone: 205/979-2400
E-mail: info@world-reach.org or pwhitmore@world-reach.org
Web: www.world-reach.org

Minimum time: 8 days (Central America) to 2 weeks (Kenya)
Usual time: Varies
Maximum time: Varies
Who pays transportation: Volunteer
Who pays housing: Volunteer
Who pays food: Volunteer
Language requirements: No
Religious requirements: Christian
Countries: El Salvador, Honduras, Kenya
Regions: Africa, Latin America
Comments: Medical teams are recruited. Christian faith ministry.
Paid or volunteer: Volunteer
Residents or medical students accepted: Sometimes
Last update: January 2008

World Venture (formerly CB International)

Lucy Jaskey, Recruitment Department
1501 W Mineral Ave
Littleton, CO 80120
Phone: 800/487-4224, ext 2630
E-mail: serve@WorldVenture.com
Web: www.worldventure.com

Minimum time: 1 month
Usual time: 1 to 2 years
Maximum time: Career
Who pays transportation: Volunteer
Who pays housing: Volunteer
Who pays food: Volunteer
Language requirements: No
Religious requirements: Christian
Countries: Cote d'Ivoire, Guinea, Indonesia, Madagascar, Mongolia, Pakistan, Sudan, Uganda
Regions: Africa, Asia/Pacific
Comments: WorldVenture exists to assist churches and individuals in their vision for global ministry. WorldVenture provides training and assists volunteers in fund-raising for their expenses. Volunteer physicians join WorldVenture doctors and nurses at hospitals or clinics run by the organization or in partnership with other like-minded agencies.
Paid or volunteer: Volunteer
Residents or medical students accepted: Residents and 4th-year medical students
Last update: January 2008

World Vision

International Recruiter
PO Box 9716
Federal Way, WA 98063
Phone: 888/511-6548
E-mail: info@worldvision.org
Web: www.worldvision.org

Minimum time: 1 year
Usual time: 1 year
Maximum time: Career
Who pays transportation: Organization
Who pays housing: Organization
Who pays food: Organization
Language requirements: Sometimes
Religious requirements: Christian
Countries: Worldwide
Regions: Africa, Asia/Pacific, Caribbean, Eastern Europe, Latin America, Middle East
Comments: For most medical positions, we prefer those with a master's in public health.
Paid or volunteer: Paid
Residents or medical students accepted: No
Last update: January 2008

World Witness

John Hopkins
1 Cleveland St, Suite 220
Greenville, SC 29601-3696
Phone: 864/233-5226
E-mail: johnh@worldwitness.org
Web: www.worldwitness.org

Minimum time: 2 weeks
Usual time: Varies
Maximum time: Career
Who pays transportation: Varies
Who pays housing: Organization
Who pays food: Organization
Language requirements: Varies
Religious requirements: No
Countries: Pakistan
Regions: Asia/Pacific
Comments: Primary site for medical volunteers in Christian Hospital of Sahiwel, a 120-bed modern hospital and nursing school in Pakistan.
Paid or volunteer: Paid and volunteer
Residents or medical students accepted: Residents
Last update: January 2008

Index

A

Absorptive capacity, 129
Access
    to health services, 131
    to potable water
        rural, 132
        urban, 131
    to sanitation
        rural, 132
        urban, 132
Acronyms
    in international health, 97–123
    in nutrition, 130–131
Acta Tropica, 142
Acute mountain sickness, 60
Adequate nutritional status, 127
Administration, annotated bibliography on, 75–76
Adult literacy rate, 132
Advice, final, before going abroad to work, 40–41
Affected population, 129
Afghanistan, overseas opportunities in, 169, 177, 178, 205, 206–207, 247
Africa, overseas opportunities in, 154–155, 156, 157, 158–159, 160–161,
        164–165, 166, 167, 168, 169, 170–171, 172–173, 174–175, 176, 177,
        178–179, 180–181, 184–185, 188–189, 190, 196–197, 202, 203,
        204, 205, 206–207, 208–209, 210–211, 212, 213, 215, 216, 218–219,
        220–221, 222–223, 225, 226–227, 229, 230–231, 232–233, 234–235,
        236, 237, 239, 240–241, 243, 244–245, 246, 247, 248, 249, 250
African trypanosomiasis, 55
Alabama, University of, at Birmingham, Gorgas Memorial Institute, 148
Albania, overseas opportunities in, 179
Aloha Medical Mission, 153
Amazon.com, 34
Amazon Promise, 154
American Academy of Pediatrics
    Red Book Atlas of Pediatric Infectious Diseases (Baker), 81–82
    Red Book: Report of the Committee on Infectious Diseases, 24
    Section on International Child Health, 11, 12
American Baptist Board of International Ministries, 154–155
American College of Surgeons, 5
American Health Consultants, *Travel Medicine Advisor,* 53
American Institute of Philanthropy, 6
American Jewish World Service (AJWS), 10, 155
The American Journal of Tropical Medicine and Hygiene, 9, 142
American Medical Resources Foundation, 5

B

I

N

the GREAT CANADIAN JOKE BOOK

WARNING: Even if you are not easily offended, you will probably hate yourself for laughing at these jokes!

compiled by
Glen Warner

FOLK LORE PUBLISHING

The Publisher: Folklore Publishing
Website: www.folklorepublishing.com

Library and Archives Canada Cataloguing in Publication

Warner, Glen, 1947–
    Great Canadian joke book / by Glen Warner.
ISBN 978-1-894864-80-0
    1. National characteristics, Canadian—Humor. 2. Canada—
Humor. I. Title.
PN6231.C19W38 2008   818'.602   C2008-903932-7

Project Director: Faye Boer
Project Editor: Kathy van Denderen
Editorial Intern: Ashley Johnson
Cover Image: Courtesy by Dreamstime; © Webking | Dreamstime.com

We acknowledge the financial support of the Government of Canada
through the Book Publishing Industry Development Program (BPIDP)
for our publishing activities.

We acknowledge the support of the Alberta Foundation for the Arts for
our publishing program.

Canadian Patrimoine
Heritage canadien

PC: 1

Dedication

For my father, Frederick Warner (1916–98),
the funniest guy I've ever known. Miss ya, Dad.

Acknowledgements

First off, I'd like to thank all the people I've known over the years who went out of their way to tell me their favourite jokes, riddles and limericks. Even if I could remember all of your names, there are just too many of you to list here. I would have to include all the wild and crazy guys I went to high school and college with, as well as the many strange characters I met during my years of toil in the advertising and publishing businesses. You know who you are. While I cannot recall many of your names, at least I managed to remember your jokes, so give me credit for that.

Acknowledgement must also be given to my father, who told me many of the jokes included here, and from whom I think I inherited a funny bone or two that gave me the ability to remember almost every stupid joke, poem or riddle I've heard in my life.

I'd also like to thank my publisher, Faye Boer, for having the nerve to assemble all this nonsense between two covers, and my editor, Kathy van Denderen, for correcting my spelling, mopping up my sloppy syntax and for telling me, in no uncertain terms, where I'd crossed the line into the no man's land of bad taste. I must also raise a middle finger in jest to my old friend Barry Goodyear, on whom I "test marketed" most of these jokes before deciding which ones would be included.

Finally, much love and special thanks to my long-suffering wife Diane, who has endured my telling of every joke in this book a hundred times or more, and still manages to crack a forced smile and a guffaw or two, no matter how often she hears them.

A Note from the Author

Many years ago I began to collect jokes. All kinds of jokes. Everything from X-rated jokes to ethnic jokes, juvenile, sick jokes and toilet humour, to funny poems, limericks and riddles.

Whenever I heard a good one, I wrote it down in a little notebook. The collection grew from a single scribbler to many, each one containing hundreds of offbeat, tasteless and just plain silly jokes.

Living in Canada, I've naturally accumulated a lot of Canadian humour. My notebooks contain hundreds of jokes that poke fun at hosers, multiculturalism, Newfies, French Canadians, bilingualism, cowboys, Native people, crooked politicians, government-run health care, Mounties, hockey, Air Canada, the welfare state, the Toronto Maple Leafs, socialists, religious nutbars of all stripes, along with jokes about drinking beer, coping with shitloads of snow and the great Canadian obsession with political correctness.

Being a good Canadian, I am naturally compelled to share this treasure trove of politically incorrect humour with others. Although dozens of books by Canadian humorists have been published in recent years, most of them contain the kind of lily-white, squeaky-clean stories, jokes and lame limericks you could safely tell to your 80-year-old granny without causing her to blush. But who actually reads and laughs at that stuff?

None of them include the kind of jokes that you actually hear Canadians telling at parties, in bars or around office water coolers. That's where you hear the really great ones—the kind of jokes that are told in hushed voices because "someone" might be offended.

The simple truth is, the only really good jokes are the ones that make people feel uncomfortable. Squeamish, even. And let's face it, we all enjoy laughing at someone else's shortcomings. I mean, who hasn't told a Newfie joke or a dick joke, or better still, a Newfie dick joke?

This book is crammed with the kind of humour you'll hate yourself for laughing at. The kind of jokes that if told at your next office party will almost guarantee you a place in your company's sensitivity training program. There are jokes, riddles and limericks for all occasions that you'll enjoy telling to your more open-minded friends and relatives, leaving on their voicemail, or better still, text messaging them.

There are hundreds of pee-your-pants-funny jokes, stories, riddles, puns and limericks that poke fun at just about every province, region and minority group in Canada. I haven't left anyone or any group out. I like to think that I'm an equal-opportunity humorist; no one escapes unscathed.

Many of the jokes are about Canadian places that bring a smile at the mere mention of their names. Like Regina, for instance. (Funny for the thing it rhymes with.) Or Dildo, Newfoundland. (The name is a joke in itself.) And especially the infamous Toronto suburb of Scarborough, where waves of immigration, gangs, crime and gun violence provide endless material for local comics. (Example: "I went to a party in Scarborough last night and a guy stopped me at the door and asked me if I had a gun. I said, 'No.' And he said, 'Do you want one?'")

A few of the jokes do not relate to anything particularly Canadian at all, but I included them anyway because I thought they were just too funny to leave out. Please cut me some slack if you've heard a few of these before—off-colour jokes and limericks are the stock-in-trade of thousands of sickos who circulate their stuff on the Internet—it's hard to promise 100 percent "all-new" material.

So sit back, relax your hopelessly tight Canadian posterior portal, and laugh your way through this book. Memorize the jokes. Tell them to your friends. Lighten up! Try not to be so nice...so polite...so politically correct...so damn Canadian. Help me in my diabolical mission to lower community standards and destroy family values across this country!

Finally, one simple request. Each and every joke, riddle and limerick included here is a carefully crafted work of comic genius, so I beg you, please, please don't screw them up when you repeat them. Many thanks.

Have fun!
Glen Warner

Great Canadian Jokes

WARNING: *The jokes you are about to read may make you blush or look around to see who's watching, or you may think the book should have come in a brown paper bag, but they ARE guaranteed, in most cases, to make you laugh out loud!*

A street entertainer is performing his juggling act in Ottawa's Sparks Street Mall. He is spinning a loonie in the air and catching it in his teeth. All of a sudden the trick goes horribly wrong. The coin disappears into his mouth and gets lodged in his throat. He immediately starts choking and gasping for air as the horrified people in the crowd assemble around him and begin screaming for help.

Then, from out of nowhere, a middle-aged man in a grey suit appears and calmly walks up to the street performer and grabs him by the testicles. He proceeds to squeeze and twist them as hard as he can.

The crowd watches in stunned disbelief as the convulsing man begins to turn blue, writhing on the ground while the mystery man crushes his scrotum with a vice-like grip.

Then suddenly, the mystery man lets go of the hapless juggler, stands up, and administers a swift kick to his balls, whereupon the coin becomes dislodged and flies skyward, where it is snatched out of the air into the clasp of the mystery man's fist.

After taking a few deep breaths, the street performer jumps to his feet and thanks the man profusely for his quick, life-saving deed.

"How did you know what to do?" he asks. "Are you a doctor?"

"Hell no," says the mystery man. "I'm a tax auditor. I work for Canada Revenue."

A Grade 3 teacher in Winnipeg asks her class what they did on their summer holidays.

Little Mary stands up and says, "On my holidays, I got a bow-wow for my birthday."

The teacher tells her that she is a big girl now and that she should call her pet a "dog" and not a "bow-wow."

Little Billy stands up next and says, "I visited a farm on my holidays and I saw a moo-moo."

The teacher reprimands him as well and says that he is a big boy now and should call the animal by its proper name, "cow."

Dirty Wally, a tough little kid with a foul mouth, goes next. He says, "I read a book on my holidays about a bear that once lived in the Winnipeg zoo."

"What is the title?" asks the teacher.

Wally remembers what the teacher told the other kids and replies, "Winnie the Shit."

Three Newfies, Shamus, Rex and Clyde, are out in a boat fishing, drinking beer and getting very drunk. All of a sudden, Shamus, the drunkest of the three, stands up to take a pee. He loses his balance, falls overboard, and quickly disappears under the waves.

Rex dives in to save his friend and manages to bring a lifeless body to the surface, where Clyde helps him pull it into the boat.

"He ain't breathin'," says Clyde.

"Give 'im—whatchamacallit—mout to mout," says Rex.

Clyde locks his lips over Shamus' mouth and exhales. He then recoils in horror.

"Dammit!" he says. "I don't remember Shamus havin' such bad breath."

Rex examines the body closer and replies, "And I don't remember him wearin' that ratty old snowmobiler's suit, either."

There are three stages in married life in Canada:

For the first year of marriage it's, "To hell with watching the hockey game...let's just f**k!"

For the following year, it's, "Let's f**k, then watch the hockey game."

After that, it's, "Let's just watch the f**king hockey game."

A Texan arrives in Toronto for a business meeting at a downtown hotel. During his ride from the airport, his taxi driver takes him past Queen's Park.

"What's that?" asks the Texan.

"That's Queen's Park," says the taxi driver. "It's our provincial government headquarters; it's sort of like your state legislature. Those buildings are nearly 200 years old. And they're pretty big, too, eh?"

"That's nothing," says the Texan. "Back in Texas we have buildings twice that age and many of them are three or four times bigger, too."

A few blocks south, the taxi passes the Eaton Centre.

"What's that?" says the Texan.

Q. Where in Canada do you find a turtle with no legs?

A. Right where you left him.

"It's a huge indoor shopping mall," says the taxi driver. "It takes up an entire city block and it's filled with upscale stores and restaurants. There are two office towers and a big hotel attached to it. All together, it took over 20 years to build it."

"Aw, that's nothing!" says the Texan. "Back in Dallas, we've got malls three times bigger than that, and they've got movie theatres, high-end hotels and the biggest department stores in the world in 'em, too. What's more, we've got so much room in Texas that new malls like that one sprout up in the desert every month."

Farther south, the taxi passes First Canadian Place.

"What's that?" says the Texan.

"It's the biggest office complex in Toronto," says the taxi driver. "It took almost four years to build it. Nice, eh?"

"That's nothing!" sneers the Texan. "Down in Houston we have office towers that are twice that height, and we can build 'em in half that much time."

At this point, the taxi driver is getting really fed up with the Texan's boasting, so he devises a plan to shut him up once and for all. He makes a short detour and drives his cab past the CN Tower.

> New Democrats steal from the rich to buy votes from the poor.
>
> Conservatives have the reputation of stealing from the poor to buy votes from the rich.
>
> Liberals, on the other hand, steal from both rich and poor to buy votes in Québec.

"What's that?" asks the Texan.

"Damned if I know," says the taxi driver. "It wasn't there yesterday!"

Lucille, a French Canadian mother of a 17-year-old girl, is concerned that her daughter is having sex. Worried that the girl might become pregnant, she consults her family doctor.

The doctor explains to her that teenagers today are very rebellious, and any attempt to encourage her daughter not to have sex would probably backfire. He advises her to put her daughter on birth control pills as soon as possible, and to give her a supply of condoms right away.

Later that evening, as her daughter is preparing for a date, Lucille hands her a box of condoms. The girl bursts out laughing, hugs her mother and says, "Oh, Mamma! You don't have to worry about that! I'm dating my friend Celine!"

Three hosers are walking along a beach: one is from Newfoundland, one is from Québec, and one is from Ontario. They find a bottle in the sand, and when they uncork it, out pops a genie.

The genie says, "I will grant each of you one wish."

The Newfie says, "I'm a fisherman. All I want is for the cod to return to the Grand Banks."

The genie waves an arm, and in a flash, the waters around Newfoundland are once again swarming with fish.

The French Canadian says, "All I want is a big wall around Québec to keep all those Anglo bastards out...and the immigrants as well."

The genie waves an arm, and POOF!, there is a wall around Québec.

The hoser from Ontario steps up next and says to the genie, "Tell me more about this wall."

Q. Why is Kitsilano, BC, like granola?

A. Once you take away the fruits and the nuts, you're left with only flakes.

"Well," the genie replies, "it's about five metres high and one metre thick, and it completely surrounds Québec so that no one can get in or out. So what is your wish?"

The hoser thinks for a moment and says, "Fill it up with water."

A Sudbury miner comes home from work one day and finds that his wife has packed her suitcases and left them at the front door.

"Where are you going?" he asks her.

"I'm going to Toronto," she replies. "I've heard you can earn as much as $400 on the street there, and I figure that I might as well earn money for what I do with you for free."

"Give me a minute to pack my bags," says the husband. "I'm coming with you. I want to see how long you survive in Toronto on $800 a year!"

An elderly couple is driving along a snow-covered highway in rural Nova Scotia when they spot an injured skunk on the side of the road. They stop, and the old lady gets out and brings the skunk into the car.

"It's cold and shivering, what should I do with it?" she asks her husband.

"You could try to warm it up by putting it between your legs," replies her husband.

"What about the smell?" she asks.

The husband replies, "Hold its nose."

A Grade 3 teacher in Scarborough asks her class what they did at recess.

Little Sonja stands up and says, "I played in the sandbox."

"Okay, Sonja," says the teacher, "Now spell 'sand' for us." Sonja does and is rewarded with a candy.

Thomas stands up next and says he played in the sandbox with Sonja. "Okay, Thomas," says the teacher, "Spell 'box' for the class." Thomas does and is rewarded with a candy.

Little Abdul Singh, a recent immigrant to Canada, stands up next and says, "I tried to play with Sonja and Thomas in the sandbox, but they threw sand in my face and chased me away."

"That's blatant racial discrimination," says the teacher. "Abdul, spell 'blatant racial discrimination' and you'll get a candy, too."

A Newfie comes home from work early one day and finds his wife having sex with some guy on the livingroom sofa.

"Vera, what de hell are ya doin'?" he asks her.

His wife looks at the guy and says, "See, I told you he was kinda dumb."

As a hoser named Clifford is leaving church one Sunday morning, he stops to shake the preacher's hand.

"I just wanted tell you, that was a goddamned fine sermon you gave today," he says. "Bloody good!"

The preacher replies, "Well, thank you, young man, but I'd prefer that you didn't swear in my church."

Undeterred, Clifford continues: "Yup, I was so goddamned impressed with your sermon that I put 500 goddamned dollars on the friggin' offering plate!"

The preacher replies, "Hey, no shit?"

> Q. What's the best thing to do if a pit bull terrier starts humping your leg?
>
> A. Fake an orgasm.

Koslowsky, a Polish immigrant, goes to apply for his driver's licence shortly after his arriving in Canada. The examiner tests his eyesight by showing him a card with the letters C Z W I X N O S T A C Z printed on it.

"Can you read this?" the examiner asks.

"Read it?" says Koslowsky, "I know the guy."

Three recently married men were sitting in an Edmonton bar bragging about how they each told their brides what they expect of them in the way of household duties.

Terry married a woman from Korea, and he explains that when they first moved in together, he told his wife that she must do all the dishes and housework. He says that it took a couple of days, but by the third day she learned to follow his instructions. He came home to a clean house, and the dishes were all washed and put away.

James married a woman from Italy. He brags that when he first got married, he gave his wife orders that she was to do all the cleaning, wash all the dishes and do all the cooking. He told the other guys that on the first day he didn't see any results, but the next day things were going much better. By the third day, the house was clean, the dishes were done, and there was a fabulous dinner waiting on the table for him when he got home.

Frank married a Canadian girl. He boasts to the guys that when he first got married he, too, instructed his wife to keep the house clean and the dishes washed. He also told her to do the laundry and ironing twice a week and to keep the lawns mowed and the windows washed. And he explains that he really put his foot down and insisted that she prepare a hot meal for him every night.

Frank then says that on the first day he didn't see any improvement, the second day he didn't see anything, either, but by the third day most of the swelling had gone down, and he could see a little out of his left eye, just enough to fix himself something to eat, load the dishwasher and call a handyman.

A hoser from Welland, Ontario, decides to go fishing on the American side of the Niagara River. He drives across the Peace Bridge to Lewiston, New York, finds a public dock, drops his line in the water and proceeds to fill his bucket with fish.

Before long a game warden comes by and asks to see the hoser's fishing licence. He produces a card from his wallet.

"This is a Canadian fishing licence!" says the warden. "It's no good here. You need an American fishing licence."

"But I'm only catching Canadian fish," says the hoser. "Look in my bucket. What kind of fish do you see?"

"Why, those look like smallmouth bass," says the warden.

"That's right," says the hoser. "If they were American fish, they'd be largemouth bass."

Three Inuit guys are arguing about who has the coldest igloo.

Osuitok insists his igloo is the coldest, and tells the others to follow him into it to prove his point. Once inside, the other men watch as he throws a cup of water in the air. They are amazed to see that the ice freezes mid-air into a solid lump, and then falls to the ground with a thud.

But Kiawak claims his igloo is even colder, and asks the men to follow him over to his place, where he stands in the middle of a room and proceeds to take in several big breaths of air. When he finally exhales, the fog turns into a large hunk of ice, which falls to the ground with a thud. The other men nod approvingly.

Not to be outdone, Pauta asks the men follow him to his igloo, which he insists is the coldest of all. He takes them into his bedroom and

Q. What's a *pas de deux* in Québec?

A. It's a guy who is the father of twins.

pulls a large fur pelt off the bed to reveal a ball of brown ice. He picks up the lump of ice, takes out a match, and lights it. The ball of ice explodes in his hand and goes FFFAARRTTT!

A guy from New Brunswick tells his psychiatrist that he would like to become a Newfie.

The doctor says, "In order to become a full-fledged Newfie, you must have one-quarter of the frontal lobe of your brain surgically removed."

The guy is desperate to move to Newfoundland and to fit in, so he agrees to have one-quarter of his frontal lobe removed.

After the surgery, the guy awakens to find his psychiatrist standing over him. "I'm sorry to inform you," he says, "but the surgeon made a terrible mistake. He accidentally removed one-half of your frontal lobe instead of one-quarter of it. How do you feel?"

The guy replies, "Comme ci, comme ca."

A Toronto guy is walking along the boardwalk in the city's Beaches neighbourhood. He sees a bottle floating in Lake Ontario. When it drifts close to shore, he retrieves it, and when he unscrews the cap, a genie pops out.

"Thank you for releasing me from this bottle," says the genie. "I would like to reward you by granting you three wishes."

The Toronto guy thinks for a moment and replies, "Okay, I'd like the Toronto Maple Leafs to win the Stanley Cup this year, and I'd like the Toronto Blue Jays to win the next World Series. And then, for my third wish, I'd like the Toronto Raptors to win the NBA title."

The genie thinks about the request for a moment, and as she jumps back into her bottle she yells, "You've got to be kidding me! Geez, why did I have to wash up in Toronto?"

A Jewish guy, a Newfie and a French Canadian meet on the street outside of a popular Montréal brothel.

"I want you gentlemen to know that I am not a customer at this establishment," says the Jewish guy. "I'm the landlord. I'm just here to collect the rent."

"That's too bad," says the Newfie, "I'm just here to get laid."

The French guy looks sheepishly at the other two guys and says, "I'm here to pick up my wife."

A young woman is flying alone high above Lake Superior in a hot air balloon. Suddenly, she realizes that she is lost, so she lowers her altitude and cruises down towards a small boat she sees on the horizon.

"Hello," she shouts to the man in the boat. "I'm lost. I'm supposed to meet someone in Sault Ste. Marie in one hour. Can you tell me where I am?"

The man in the boat consults his portable GPS and replies, "You're approximately 25 feet above a ground elevation of 2155 feet above sea level. You are 38 degrees, 14.88 minutes north latitude and 100 degrees, 48.13 minutes west longitude."

The woman in the balloon rolls her eyes and says, "You must be a Conservative."

"Yes, I am," replies the guy. "How did you guess?"

"Well," says the balloonist, "I'm sure everything you told me is technically correct, but I have no idea what to do with the information you gave me. I'm still lost. You have not been much help to me at all."

The man smiles and says, "You must be a Liberal."

"Yes, I am!" says the balloonist. "How did you know?"

"It's obvious," says the man in the boat. "You don't know where you're going. You've risen to where you are because of a lot of hot air. You've made a promise that you have no idea how to keep, and you expect me to solve your problem. You're in exactly the same mess you were in before we met, but somehow, now it's all my fault."

A snooty Rosedale matron is being driven to her club by her chauffeur when her car gets a flat tire. The chauffeur gets out, jacks up the car and tries to remove the wheel.

After watching him struggle with it for several minutes, the matron leans out the window and says, "I say, would you like a screwdriver?"

"We might as well," replies the chauffeur, "'cause I'm sure not having any luck getting this god-damned wheel off."

A nun is sitting in a bathtub in her room at a convent in Québec. There is a knock on the door.

"Who is it?" she calls out.

"It's the blind man, can I come in?" is the reply.

Thinking there is nothing wrong with letting a blind man come into the room while she is bathing, the nun says, "Okay, you may enter."

The man walks in, stares at the naked nun and says, "Wow, nice rack! Now where do you want this blind?"

A Sarnia guy is concerned about his wife's failing health, so he takes her to the doctor. Her doctor examines her and then calls the husband into his office.

"Quite frankly, I can't decide whether your wife has Alzheimer's or AIDS," says the doctor.

"What should I do?" asks the husband.

"Here's an idea," says the doctor. "On your way home today, give her a list of groceries to pick up, and drop her off at Loblaws."

"Then, watch her carefully," the doctor adds. "If she gets lost, bring her in for more tests. But if she finds her way home and has the right groceries, whatever you do, don't have sex with her."

Two married guys are standing in line at an Air Canada ticket counter. One of the men notices that the ticket seller has enormous breasts. When he gets to the front of the line, he blurts out, "I'd like two pickets to Titsburgh. Oops! Sorry, I mean two tickets to Pittsburgh."

Embarrassed, he stands there red-faced while the clerk prepares the tickets.

His travel companion tries to console him. "Relax," he says, "we all make Freudian slips like that. Why, just this morning at breakfast, I turned to my wife and said, 'You fat, ugly bitch, you've made my life a goddamned nightmare!' And what I meant to say was, 'Sweetheart, please pass the sugar.'"

The Yuppie Survival Guide to Visiting Rural Alberta

Thank you for visiting our beautiful country-side. There are a few things you ought to know about life out here that will make a visit more pleasant for you city folk:

1. First off, you need to know that we have a lot of gravel roads. So no matter how slowly you drive, you're going to get dust on your BMW. We all have four-wheel drive vehicles out here because we need them. Now get it the hell out of the way.

2. Pull your pants up and turn your baseball cap around. You look like an idiot.

3. That slope-shouldered, dim-witted farm boy you are snickering at probably got more exer-cise before breakfast this morning than you will get all week at your gym.

4. Out here, we learn to hunt and fish when we are just nine years old. Yeah, sure, we've all seen Bambi die a hundred times. Get over it.

5. If that cell phone of yours rings when a flock of mallards is about to land near our duck blind, we will shoot it out of your hand. You might hope that you don't have it up to your ear at the time.

6. No, you won't find any "vegetarian" specials on our menus. Order steak, and order it rare. Or if you prefer, order the Chef's Salad and be prepared to pick off the two pounds of ham and turkey that comes in it.

7. No, you can't be served in French.

8. So what if you have a $60,000 car? We're not impressed. We have $250,000 combines that we only use two weeks out of the year.

9. Yup, our women hunt and fish and drive honkin' big pickup trucks. They like them. So you say you're a feminist? Well, I'll be damned! Isn't that cute!

10. Yeah, we eat trout, northern pike, walleye and perch. If you really want sushi and caviar, the only place you'll find them here is at the live bait shop.

11. That's what pigs and cows smell like. Get over it. Don't like it? Highways 1 and 16 go in two directions—get on one of them. The more people that leave, the better the hunting and fishing will be for the locals!

12. So you think it's weird that every person you see driving a pickup waves at you? It's called being friendly. Understand the concept?

13. Before you go back to the city with the impression that the people you've met out here are just a bunch of gun-totin' yahoos, remember one thing: All those guys you see driving pickup trucks and living in trailer parks near Fort McMurray are probably pulling down two or three times as much as you make in your high-falutin' big city office job. They'll make their pile and retire in 10 years. So who's crazy, eh?

A precocious little girl is sitting on Santa's knee in the toy department of the Bay. Santa asks her what she would like for Christmas.

"I'd like a Barbie doll and a G.I. Joe," says the girl.

"I thought Barbie comes with Ken," says Santa.

The kid replies, "No! Barbie comes with G.I. Joe. She just fakes it with Ken."

An American decides to write a book about famous churches across the United States and Canada. He begins his research in Florida and plans to work his way north and end his journey in Toronto.

On his first day, he is inside a church in Miami when he notices a golden telephone mounted on the wall with a sign under it that reads, "$10,000 per call."

He asks a priest what the telephone is used for. The priest explains that the golden telephone offers parishioners a direct line to heaven, and that for $10,000 anyone can talk to God. The American thanks the priest for the information and leaves the church.

The researcher's next stop is in Atlanta. He visits a large cathedral in the centre of the city and is surprised to see a similar golden telephone with a "$10,000 per call" sign under it. He asks a nun what it is for. She tells him the same story; that it offers a direct line to heaven and that for $10,000 anyone can use it to talk to God. He thanks her and continues on his journey.

The researcher then travels to Washington, Philadelphia, Boston and New York. In every church he visits, he sees more golden telephones with the now familiar "$10,000 per call" signs under them.

The American eventually crosses the border into Canada, where he heads for Toronto's huge St. Michael's Cathedral. Sure enough, he sees another golden telephone, but this time the sign under it reads "25 cents per call." He is baffled by this, so he decides to ask a priest about the price.

"Father," he says, "I've travelled all over the United States, and I've seen these golden telephones in almost every church I've visited. I'm told they offer parishioners a direct line to heaven, but in every state in the union, the price is $10,000 per call. Why is it so cheap here?"

The priest smiles and says, "You're in Canada now, my son. It's a local call."

A Canadian guy is in an American bar, drinking American beer. "Drinking your beer reminds me of having sex in a canoe," he says to the guys sitting around him.

"How's that?" one of the Americans asks.

The Canadian replies, "Because it's f**king close to water."

Three Calgary hookers, Lucille, Margaret and Louise, are comparing their experiences from the previous night.

"I picked up a cowboy last night," Lucille says.

"How did you know he was a cowboy?" asks Margaret.

"He kept his Stetson hat and his boots on the whole time we were having sex," replies Lucille.

"Typical cowboy," says Margaret.

"I had a lawyer last night," adds Margaret. "I knew he was a lawyer because he kept his briefcase beside the bed and checked his BlackBerry every few minutes while we were having sex."

"Yup, that sounds like a lawyer," says Lucille.

Louise says, "I had sex with a farmer last night."

"How did you know he was a farmer?" asks Margaret.

"First he complained that I was too dry," Louise replies. "Then he said I was too wet. And then he asked if he could pay me in the fall."

A recent immigrant from Palestine is showing his Canadian relatives pictures of his family and children who live back in the old country.

"This is my eldest—he's a martyr," he says, pointing to one of the photos. "And this is my youngest son—he's a martyr, too."

His brother sighs wistfully and says, "Ah, yes, they blow up fast, don't they?"

A young Native guy leaves his reserve in northern Québec and goes to Montréal to visit a brothel for the first time. He rings the doorbell, and when the madam answers, he says, "Me have lots of money but no experience with women."

The madam tells him he's too young to visit a prostitute and that he should go back to his reserve and get some experience before he visits a prostitute.

Two months later, the Native guy returns to the brothel and says to the madam, "Me now have lots of money and experience."

So he is sent upstairs to a room occupied by the oldest hooker in the joint. Before she takes off her clothes, the young Native guy tells her to stand up straight and to turn her back to him. He then picks up a coat rack and whacks her with it across her ass.

"Why the hell did you do that?" asks the hooker, rubbing her sore bum.

The Native guy replies, "In woods I learn early on—always first checkum for bees."

15 Things You'll Seldom Hear in Rural Saskatchewan

1. So who's this guy named Tommy Douglas that you keep talking about?

2. I think the bonspiel should be alcohol-free this year.

3. To hell with Tim Hortons, I feel like having a latte today at Starbucks.

4. Is the seafood you serve here fresh?

5. Perogies? What are they?

6. So if this is a buffalo, then what does a bison look like?

7. I think too many deer heads in a living room can detract from the decor, don't you?

8. Why do we need to stop for beer? I thought we were just going hunting.

9. Are you going to the Saskatoon Gay Pride Parade?

10. I think the Roughriders suck.

11. I would prefer to be served in French, please.

12. So tell me, which phone company are you with?

13. Did you remember to set your clock back one hour?

14. No thanks. No more beer for me. I'm snowmobiling home tonight.

15. I'm hoping the Edmonton Eskimos will go all the way this year!

On her wedding night, a middle-aged bride turns to her new husband and says, "Please be gentle, I'm still a virgin."

"How the hell can you still be a virgin?" asks the husband. "You've been married three times before."

"Well," says the wife, "my first husband was a gynecologist, and all he wanted to do was look at it. My second husband was a psychiatrist, and all he wanted to do was analyze it. Then there was my third husband. He was a clerk at the stamp counter at Canada Post, and all he wanted to do was... OOOH GOD! I do miss him sometimes!"

A little girl in New Brunswick goes with her father to the barbershop. She stands by the barber's chair licking a lollipop while her father gets his hair cut.

"Watch out," says the barber to the little girl. "You're going to get hair on your lollipop."

"I know," replies the little girl. "And I'm going to get boobs, too."

George and Dave have had sex with Sally. When Sally gets pregnant, there is no way of knowing which one of them knocked her up, so the two guys both chip in money to send her back to Newfoundland to have her baby.

Several months pass, and one day George hears from Sally and immediately phones Dave to tell him her news.

"I've got good news and bad news," says George.

"What's the good news?" asks Dave.

"She had twins!" says George.

"What's the bad news?" asks Dave.

George replies, "Mine died."

A Canadian lawyer and two accountant friends are in a sleazy Montréal strip joint. One of the accountants pulls out a $10 bill, licks it and sticks it on one cheek of a stripper's butt. Not to be outdone, the second accountant pulls out a $20 bill, licks it and sticks it on the stripper's other cheek.

The lawyer watches this and decides to go one better. He pulls out his ATM card, swipes it down the crack of the stripper's ass, grabs the 30 bucks and walks out the door.

The Canadian government recently sponsored a research study at the University of Toronto to find out why the head of a man's penis is generally bigger than the shaft.

After spending six months and $80,000 of taxpayers' money, researchers concluded that the head was bigger than the shaft in order to give more pleasure to the man during intercourse.

Not to be outdone, the Québec government sponsored a study on the same subject at McGill University in Montréal. After spending four months and $50,000, they concluded that the head was bigger in order to provide greater satisfaction to the woman during sex.

Meanwhile, in Newfoundland, students at Memorial University spent a whole evening and dropped almost $100 on beer to do a comparative study of their penises in a dormitory room. After drinking as many beers as they could each force down, the Newfies concluded that the head is bigger than the shaft to prevent the man's hand from slipping off and causing an injury if he accidentally hits himself in the forehead.

A Canada Post mailman is trudging through the snow carrying a huge sack of mail at Christmas time. As he is stuffing a stack of envelopes in one mailbox on his route, the door of the house opens and a beautiful young woman beckons him to come inside out of the cold.

After serving the mailman a warm drink, the woman invites him to stay for lunch. After a sumptuous meal, she disappears into her bedroom and returns wearing only a skimpy nightgown. She proceeds to lure the mailman into her bed, where they spend the rest of the afternoon.

As he prepares to leave, the mailman says, "You know, I've delivered the mail for almost 20 years, and I've never experienced anything like this before. Why did you decide to do all this for me?"

"Well, actually," the woman replies, "it was my husband's idea."

"Your husband's idea?" says the mailman incredulously.

"Yeah," replies the woman. "I was writing out our Christmas list, and when I asked him what we should get for the mailman, he said, 'Aw, f**k him.' But the lunch was my idea!"

Q. What's the best birth control method for people in their 40s?
A. Nudity.

A naive young hoser from a remote northern Saskatchewan farming community goes into a downtown Regina bar and orders a drink. He tells the bartender to send two drinks to the two attractive women he sees sitting at the other end of the bar.

"Take my advice," says the bartender. "Don't waste your money on those two, they're lesbians."

"No problem," says the young hoser. "Send the two lovely ladies each a drink on me."

A while later the hoser orders another drink and tells the bartender to send two more to the women at the end of the bar.

> Q. Why are French Canadians like cue balls?
>
> A. The harder you hit 'em, the more English they pick up.

"Okay," says the bartender. "But I'm telling you, you're wasting your time, they're both lesbians."

Finally, the hoser decides to make his move. He sits down next to the two women and strikes up a conversation. "I understand you ladies are both lesbians," he says.

"That's right," replies one of the dykes.

"You know," says the hoser, "I've led a sheltered life way out there on the farm. I'm not exactly sure what a lesbian is. Can you tell me?"

"Sure," says the other dyke. "We like big, big boobs and we just love having lots of sex when we get together with our friends."

"Jesus! That sounds great to me!" says the hoser. "Bartender, another round of drinks over here for us lesbians."

An old lady goes into a Calgary sex shop and says to the clerk, "Gg-good mo-mo-mo-morning! Ca-ca can you he-he-help me?"

"I'll try," says the clerk. "What can I do for you?"

"Dah-da-do you se-se-sell vi-vi-vibrators?" asks the woman.

"Yes, we do," says the clerk.

"Dah-da-do you have th-th-the one ca-ca-ca-called ma-ma-ma-Magic Thruster?" she asks.

"Yes, we have that one," says the clerk. "It comes in small, medium and large, and in a variety of colours."

Q. What do lesbians call women who have fat fingers?

A. Well hung.

"Dah-da-da does it vi-vi-vibrate?" asks the woman.

"Yes," says the clerk. "It has an adjustment, too. You can set it for slow speed, medium speed and fast."

"Th-th-th-that's the one," says the woman.

"Would you like me to wrap one up for you?" says the clerk.

"Nnnnn-no," says the woman. "Th-th-th-that wo-wo-wo-won't b-b-be necessary. I ju-ju-ju-just ha-ha-have one qu-qu-qu-question ab-ba-ba-bout it. Ha-ha-how da-da-da the he-he-hell do ya-ya-you ta-ta-ta-turn it off?"

On the first day back at school, a Grade 6 teacher in Barrie, Ontario, tells her class that she is a devoted fan of the Toronto Maple Leafs. All the kids are eager to seek the approval of their new teacher, so they agree with her and claim they, too, are Leaf fans. All except for one defiant little girl who shouts out, "I am a devoted Sens fan!"

"Why are you a Sens fan?" asks the teacher.

"I'm a Sens fan because my mother is a Sens fan, and my father is also a Sens fan," says the kid.

"So if I told you that your mother is an idiot, and your dad is a moron," says the teacher, "what would you be?"

The kid replies, "I'd be a Leafs fan."

A guy takes his dog into an Edmonton bar and sits him on a stool beside him. The guy orders a beer, and when the bartender brings it to him, he says, "I'll bet you the price of this beer that my dog Floyd here can talk."

"You're on!" says the bartender.

"Okay, watch this," the dog owner says.

He stares the dog in the eye, points at the ceiling and says, "What's that up there, boy?"

"Wroof! Wroof!" replies the dog.

"See," says the dog owner. "He called it a roof—this beer is on the house!"

"You've got to be joking," says the bartender. "You conned me. Pay up."

"No, wait," says the dog owner. "This time you ask him a question. Go on, ask Floyd anything you want."

"Okay," says the bartender, "but if he doesn't speak clearly, you're paying for the next beer, okay?"

The bartender stares the dog straight in the eye and says, "Who is the greatest hockey player of all time?"

Floyd thinks for a moment and then looks up to the heavens and lets out a loud, "HOW, HOW, HOWWWLLL" cry.

"See, he got it right again," says the dog owner. "He said, 'HOW,' and Gordie Howe was the greatest hockey player of all time. I win the bet! Gimme another free beer."

"That's it," says the bartender. "I've had enough. Both of you get the hell outta here, NOW!"

The bartender grabs the guy and the dog by the scruffs of their necks and tosses them out the door onto the sidewalk.

The dog owner is lying on his back in the gutter. Floyd gets up, shakes himself off, walks over to his master, licks his face and says, "Sorry about that. Was the correct answer Wayne Gretzky?"

> Q. When paleontologists in Drumheller discover the first gay dinosaur, what will they likely call it?
>
> A. A Megasaurass.

Agnes is having sex with her lover in her bedroom when suddenly she hears her husband come in the front door of the house.

"Quick," she says to her boyfriend, "hide in the bathroom."

The husband enters the bedroom and says, "Why are you lying naked in bed in the middle of the afternoon?"

"I've been waiting for you," replies Agnes.

"Okay," says the husband, "I've gotta pee first, but I'll be right back."

He opens the bathroom door and sees the boyfriend hiding in the shower. "Who the hell are you?" he asks.

> Q. What would Sir John A. Macdonald be doing if he were alive today?
>
> A. Clawing at the lid of his coffin.

"I'm the exterminator," replies the guy standing in the tub. "Your wife hired me to get rid of your terrible moth problem."

"But you're naked!" says the husband.

The boyfriend looks down at himself and acts surprised. Thinking fast, he replies, "They're hungry little bastards, aren't they?"

Hung Chow works in a Vancouver restaurant. One day he calls his boss and says, "I sick today, got terribo headache. No come in to work."

The boss says, "When I have a headache, I go to my wife and tell her that I must have sex with her three times in a row in rapid succession. Clears my head. Makes everything better. Then I can go to work. You should try it."

Two hours later Hung Chow calls back. "Boss, I did exactry what you say. Feer great now. Be back at work soon. By the way, you got nice house."

Top 10 Signs That Your Mennonite Teen Is Losing His Faith

10. You can't get him out of bed until 5:00 AM.

9. He starts to wear his big black hat backwards.

8. He says things like, "If thou loveth thine son, thou would buy him a radio so he could listeneth to his rap music."

7. Although his name is Jacob, his friends suddenly start calling him "Jake Daddy."

6. When doing his laundry, you discover that he has bought some very colourful socks.

5. He shows up at a barn-raising sporting a Mohawk haircut.

4. He starts to use expressions like, "Dost thou wanteth my attention? Then thou must speaketh to the hand, 'cause the beard ain't listenin'."

3. When he argues with you, he'll say things like, "Thou can kisseth my Mennonite arse."

2. When he agrees with you, he keeps repeating the phrase, "Thou shooteth no shit," over and over.

1. When cleaning his room, you find his stash of pictures of Mennonite women who are not wearing bonnets.

Dirty Wally gathers a group of kids together at the back of his Grade 5 classroom.

"Okay, you guys," he says. "Here's how it works. You start neckin', see, and then your little weenie gets big and hard. An' then—this is the best part—you put it inside her..."

"Yuck! That's GROSS!" shouts one of the boys.

"What's the matter?" asks Dirty Wally.

The kid replies, "I don't like cider."

Jill is making a big breakfast of Canadian back bacon and fried eggs for her husband, Gary. Suddenly, Gary bursts into the kitchen.

"Careful," he says, "CAREFUL! Put more butter in! Oh, my god! You're cooking too many pieces of bacon at once. TOO MANY! Turn them! TURN THEM NOW! More butter. Dammit! Get more butter! They're going to all run together! Careful. CAREFUL! I said be CAREFUL! You NEVER listen to me when you're cooking! Never! Turn them! Hurry up! Are you CRAZY? Have you lost your mind? Don't forget to put salt on the eggs. You know you always forget to salt them. Use the salt. USE THE SALT NOW! C'MON, MORE SALT!"

Jill stares at him in disbelief. "What the hell is wrong with you? You think I don't know how to fry some bacon and eggs?"

Gary calmly replies, "I just wanted to show you what it feels like when I'm driving with you in the car."

The coach of the Toronto Maple Leafs desperately needs to find talented new hockey players. He hears about a young Somalian player who has all the makings of a hockey superstar. The coach flies to Mogadishu to watch him play and is so impressed that he offers to bring him to Canada to play in the NHL.

A month later, the Somalian is in Canada playing his first game for the Toronto Maple Leafs. He is a huge success and scores five goals and wins the game for Toronto.

As soon as he comes off the ice, he phones his mother to tell her about his first day in the NHL. "It was fantastic," he tells her. "I scored five goals. We won the game. I'm a hockey hero. The Toronto fans love me, and my teammates love me. Everyone thinks I'm great!"

"That's fine for you, son," says his mother. "But let me tell you about our day. While you were out having fun, your father got shot in the street, your sister was raped and beaten, and your brother joined a gang of Somalian thugs."

"Gee, Mom," replies the hockey player, "I'm so sorry to hear that."

"Sorry?" says the mother. "It's all your goddamned fault that we moved to Toronto in the first place!"

A Russian, an American and a Canadian are out horseback riding in Alberta. As they wander across the prairie, the Russian suddenly stops his horse. He opens an expensive bottle of vodka, takes one sip, and then throws the bottle up in the air. From another pocket he pulls out a gun and blasts the bottle to smithereens.

The American looks at him and says, "Why did you do that? That was a perfectly good bottle of expensive vodka!"

The Russian says, "In my country, there's plenty of vodka, and bottles are cheap."

Not wanting to be outdone, a few minutes later the American pulls a mickey of Jack Daniels out of his pocket. He takes a sip, throws the bottle in the air, pulls out his gun and shoots it to pieces, too.

The Canadian can't believe what he's seeing. "What did you do that for?" he says to the American. "That was an expensive bottle of whiskey!"

The American replies, "In America there's plenty of whiskey, and bottles are cheap."

The three continue along the trail. Suddenly, the Canadian stops and pulls out a bottle of beer. He opens it, takes one sip, then another, and another. Then he chug-a-lugs the rest. He carefully puts the bottle back in his saddlebag, pulls out his gun, turns around and shoots the American.

The Russian watches in stunned disbelief and says, "Why the hell did you do that?"

The Canadian replies, "In Canada, we have plenty of Americans, but beer bottles are worth 10 cents each."

A Newfie woman complains to her doctor about her husband's flagging libido. The doctor suggests that they try Viagra, but the woman explains that her husband won't take any medications, not even aspirin.

"Just slip one pill in his coffee when he isn't looking," says the doctor, who then writes her a prescription.

Several days later, the Newfie woman goes back to see the doctor, who asks her how the Viagra worked.

"Jaysus, Mary and Joseph," says the woman. "Ya shoulda warned me! It was horrible what happened."

"Was the sex not good?" asks the doctor.

"Da sex was fantastic," replies the woman. "Best in years."

"So what went wrong?" asks the doctor.

"I dropped one o' them Viagras in his coffee just like you said," says the woman, "an' within seconds an enormous bulge appeared in his pants. He stared at me like a thing possessed, he did. And then with one sweep of his arm he cleared da table, sendin' the coffee cups flyin'. Then he reached over and tore off all me clothes and ravished me on da table right deres and den."

"The pill worked exactly as I told you it would," says the doctor. "So what was so awful?"

"Dey works too fast, me son," says the Newfie woman. "I don't tink I'll ever be able to show me face in Tim Hortons again."

A bigshot from a huge American corporation shows up one day at the company's Canadian branch office and tells the manager that he must cut back his staff to save money. "It's your choice," he says to the manager. "But either Jack or Barbara will have to be laid off."

> Q. How can you tell when a moth farts?
>
> A. It suddenly flies in a straight line.

"But Barbara is my best worker," says the manager. "And Jack has a wife and three kids. I don't know which one to fire."

The manager gives it some thought, and the next morning he confronts Barbara with his dilemma. "Barbara," he says, "I've got a problem. I've got to lay you or Jack off and I don't know what to do."

Barbara replies, "You better jack off...I've got a terrible headache."

A Chinese couple is lying in bed in their apartment above their restaurant in Vancouver's

Chinatown. The guy nudges his wife and says, "How bou' 69?"

His wife thinks about it for a moment and replies, "Why you want chicken and broccoli now?"

Way up in the Yukon, a famous old gunfighter is sitting in a saloon having a few drinks and giving tips to a young cowboy on how to draw his gun faster.

"The first thing ya gotta remember," says the old cowboy, "is to tie your holster down real low on your leg."

"Will that make me a better gunfighter?" asks the kid.

Q. Did you hear about the constipated mathematician?

A. He worked it out with a pencil.

"You bet it will," replies the cowboy. "Just try it."

So the young gunfighter ties his holster low on his leg, draws his gun and shoots the hat off the piano player.

"Wow! That's much better," the kid says. "Any more tips?"

"Sure," says the old gunfighter. "Cut a notch in your holster so that your finger can grab the trigger of your gun and you'll be able to shoot it faster."

"Will that make me a better gunfighter?" asks the kid.

"You betcher boots it will," replies the old man.

So the kid cuts a notch in his holster with his penknife, then draws his gun and shoots a gold button off the piano player's jacket.

"This is fantastic," says the young shooter. "Any more ideas?"

"Yeah, sure," says the cowboy. "Get some Vaseline and smear it all over your gun. Coat the barrel, the handle, everything."

"Will that make me a better gunfighter?" asks the kid.

"No, it won't," says the cowboy. "But when Sergeant Preston over there is finished playing that piano, he's gonna shove that gun of yours right square up your ass, and this way it won't hurt as much!"

> The Canadian prime minister, Charles Tupper
> Once took a young lady to supper.
> At half-past nine,
> They sat down to dine,
> And by a quarter to twelve it was up her.

In a Regina hospital, a pretty young nurse is having coffee with an elderly colleague. The women are talking about the unusual tattoo that one of their patients has on his penis.

The elderly nurse says, "When I gave Mr. Miller a sponge bath, I noticed that he has the word 'SWAN' tattooed down the length of his penis."

"That's funny," says the pretty young nurse, "when I gave him a sponge bath, he had the word

'SASKATCHEWAN' tattooed down the length of his penis."

It is rush hour in Toronto on a blustery winter morning. Commuters are pushing and shoving onto a crowded streetcar when suddenly the Pakistani driver holds up his arm and blocks a man's entry.

Q. How come very few Canadians participate in group sex?

A. Because there would be too many thank-you letters to write afterwards.

"I am jam-packed full," he says to the harried commuter.

"I don't care what your name is," replies the man. "I'm getting on this streetcar!"

Two Newfies, Clyde and Rex, are camping out in the bush. Rex tells Clyde that he needs to take a dump, and he disappears behind some shrubbery. A few minutes later he calls out to Clyde that he doesn't have anything to wipe his bum with.

"Have ye got five dollars on ya?" asks Clyde.

"I tink so," replies Rex.

"Well, use that, then," says Clyde.

A few minutes later Rex comes out of the bushes with his hands and fingers covered in shit.

"My God," says Clyde. "What de hell happened to ya?"

"This ain't the worst of it," says Rex, "I lost me two toonies and me loonie."

A depressed young woman is so unhappy and desperate that she decides to end her life by throwing herself into Vancouver harbour. As she stands on the edge of the pier and gets ready to jump, a young sailor passing by sees what she is about to do and tries to console her.

He tells her that she has a lot to live for and offers her a way to escape her humdrum life in Canada. "My ship sails for the Orient in the morning," he says. "I'll sneak you aboard as a stowaway. I'll take good care of you and bring you food every day."

And with a wink he adds, "I'll keep you happy, and you'll keep me happy."

The woman thinks she has nothing to lose and follows the sailor to his ship, where he hides her in a lifeboat. Then every night he brings her tea and sandwiches, and they have wild sex until dawn.

A week goes by, and one day during a routine inspection, the captain of the ship discovers the stowaway. "What are you doing here?" he asks her.

The young woman spills the beans: "I have an arrangement with one of the sailors," she says.

"He said he'd take me to the Orient, and he's feed-ing me and screwing me."

"He sure is," replies the captain. "This is the Van-couver-to-Nanaimo ferry."

A young French Canadian man gets elected to Parliament and moves to Ottawa and takes his place as a backbencher. Before long, he befriends another, older, French Canadian politician who is currently serving as the Minister of Public Works.

One night, the young politician attends a lavish party at the Minister's house. He is overwhelmed by the man's wealth and the size and opulence of his home. "My God," he says to the Minister, "You have only been in Ottawa for a few years. How did you accumulate so much wealth in such a short time?"

"Tomorrow I will show you," replies the Minister.

The next day the old man takes the young politi-cian for a drive along the Ottawa River. "See that bridge," he says. "More than half the cost of its construction went straight into my pocket."

Then an election is held, and the older French Canadian politician loses his seat. But the younger one wins his back for a second term, and by a strange turn of fate, he is appointed the new Min-ister of Public Works.

Two years pass, and one day the young Minister invites his old friend and mentor to dinner at his house. The old Minister of Public Works is staggered by the young man's newfound wealth—his mansion, servants, chauffeur-driven limousine—so he asks him how he accumulated so much wealth in such a short time.

"Let's go for a drive and I'll show you," he replies.

They get in the young politician's limousine and go for a drive along the banks of the Ottawa River.

"See that bridge over there?" says the young politician.

"No, I don't see a bridge over there," replies the older man.

"That's right," the young Minister says. "The entire cost of that bridge went into my pocket."

Three Canadians, a guy from Ontario, a guy from BC and a Newfie, are sitting in a bar talking about their wives. The guy from Ontario says, "My wife isn't real smart. She wears a bra every day even though she's completely flat chested."

The guy from BC adds, "My wife is kinda dumb too. She carries a laptop and a BlackBerry everywhere she goes, but she doesn't have a job or do any work."

Q. What do you call Scottish Catholic Native people?

A. Mi'kmaqs.

The Newfie says, "You tinks your wimmins are dumb. Mine is so stupid she keeps a whole bunch of condoms in her purse, and she don't even have a penis."

On Baffin Island, a baby polar bear goes up to his mother and says, "Mom, am I a real Canadian polar bear?"

The mother replies, "Yes, my dear, you most certainly are a real, pure-blooded Canadian polar bear. I'm a polar bear, your father is a polar bear, and we were both born here on Baffin Island, and you were born on Baffin Island, so that makes you a genuine Canadian polar bear, too."

"But are you absolutely sure that I'm a real Canadian polar bear?" asks the cub.

"Yes, I'm sure," says the mother. "But if you don't believe me, why don't you ask your father?"

So the little polar bear cub goes up to his father and asks, "Dad, am I a real Canadian polar bear?"

Q. What do you call a Canadian who becomes world famous as an actor, a scientist, a musician or an athlete?

A. An American.

"Yes, son, you certainly are," replies the father. "I'm a polar bear, your mother is a polar bear, our parents were polar bears, and all of us were born right here on Baffin Island...so there's no doubt about it, son, you are 100 percent pure Canadian polar bear. Why do you ask?"

"Well," replies the cub, "I was just wonderin'. If I'm a real Canadian polar bear, then how come I'm always f**king freezing?"

A customer goes up to a clerk in the produce department at a Loblaws grocery store in Toronto and asks if he can buy one-half of a head of lettuce.

The clerk tells him that the store only sells whole heads of lettuce but says he will check with the manager to see if an exception can be made. He goes into a back room and says to the man-ager, "There's some asshole out there who wants to buy one-half of a head of lettuce."

Q. What goes clip-clop, clip-clop, clip-clop, BANG! Clippity-clop, clippity-clop, clippity-clop?

A. A Mennonite drive-by shooting.

The clerk turns around and is shocked to see that the customer has followed him into the room and is standing right behind him. Thinking fast, he points to the customer and says, "And this gentle-man would like to buy the other half."

After the customer leaves, the manager says to the clerk, "Boy, that was close, you almost got into a lot of trouble there. But I must say, I was really impressed with the way you got yourself out of it. You think on your feet. We need more people like you around here. By the way, where are you from, son?"

"North Bay, Ontario, sir," replies the clerk.

"And why did you leave North Bay?" asks the manager.

"Oh, they're all just whores and hockey players up there," says the clerk.

"Really," says the manager. "My wife is from North Bay."

"Hey, no shit!" says the clerk. "Which team did she play for?"

Two trees, a birch and a beech, are growing side by side in the woods of northern British Columbia. A small sapling starts to grow up between them. One day the birch tree turns to the beech tree and says, "Is that a son of a beech or a son of a birch?"

The beech says that he's not sure.

The sapling grows bigger and bigger, and one afternoon a woodpecker lands on one of its branches. The birch tree asks the woodpecker if he can tell if the sapling is a son of a beech or a son of a birch.

Q. What's a hoser's idea of a perfect start of the day?

A. He's eating a big plate of eggs and back bacon. His son the hockey player has his picture on the Wheaties box in front of him. His girlfriend's semi-nude photo is in today's issue of the *Sun*, and his ex-wife's picture is on the back of the milk carton.

The woodpecker tastes the wood and replies, "It is neither a son of a beech nor a son of a birch, but it's the best piece of ash I've ever had my pecker in!"

A big shot Bay Street lawyer phones home to his Forest Hill mansion one morning, and a woman with a strange voice answers. "Are you the new maid?" he asks.

"Yes, I am," the woman replies.

"Would you call my wife to the phone, please?" says the lawyer.

> Q. Why did the referee call time-out at the leper hockey game?
> A. There was a face off at centre ice.

"She can't speak right now," says the maid. "She is up in the bedroom... she's uh...she's uh..."

"Come on, out with it, woman," says the lawyer. "I haven't got all day. What the hell is she doing?"

"She's having sex with the guy who lives next door," replies the maid.

The lawyer thinks for a moment and then says, "Okay. Here's what I want you to do. Sneak upstairs, go into my den and look in the bottom drawer of my desk. There you'll find my old Colt .45 handgun. Take the gun and go into the bedroom and shoot them both dead. It's okay, you won't take the rap for this. I'm a hotshot lawyer. I'll get you off scot-free, no doubt about it.

And I'll make sure that you are very well rewarded for your trouble."

The maid agrees to follow the instructions. A few minutes later, the lawyer hears several loud gunshots followed by dead silence. Then the maid comes back to the phone and says, "It's done. Now what should I do?"

Q. Why don't women ever need watches?

A. Because there is always a clock on the stove.

"Okay," says the lawyer. "Now I want you to go back upstairs and get the bodies and drag them outside and throw them in the swimming pool."

"What swimming pool?" replies the maid.

"Uh-oh," says the lawyer. "Is this 815-2232?"

A very pregnant Newfie woman is standing on a St. John's street watching a parade. A guy standing next to her points to her belly and says, "It's too bad he can't see the parade."

"Yes, it is," replies the Newfie woman. "But I took off my panties so at least he can hears da music."

An RCMP officer stops a hoser who is swerving back and forth as he drives down the Trans-Canada Highway in rural New Brunswick. He tells the guy that he'll have to take a Breathalyzer test.

"I can't do that," says the hoser. "I'm asthmatic. I'll have a wheezing fit if I try to blow into that thing."

"Okay," says the Mountie, "I'm taking you down to headquarters for a blood alcohol test."

"I can't do that, either," says the hoser. "I'm anemic. I'll pass out if you take any of my blood."

"Okay," says the Mountie, "get out of the car and walk in a straight line."

"Sorry, can't help you there, either," says the hoser.

"Why not?" asks the Mountie.

> Q. What do you call a Canadian who becomes world famous as an actor, a scientist, a musician or an athlete?
>
> A. An American.

The hoser looks the Mountie straight in the eye and says, "Because I'm drunk out of my mind, you jerk!"

On Veterans Day, an ace Canadian pilot is invited to talk about his experiences in World War II on a CBC news program.

"There I was alone in my fighter plane flying over Germany," says the pilot. "There was a bunch of fokkers flying over me, and another bunch of fokkers coming up from behind—"

The host of the show, concerned that the old man's language might upset his viewers, interrupts and says, "Excuse me, sir, but for the benefit of our audience, perhaps I should explain that a Fokker, spelled F-o-k-k-e-r, was a type of plane used by the Germans. Isn't that right, sir?"

"Oh, maybe," says the pilot. "But these fokkers were Messerschmitts!"

Two boys are playing ball hockey on a street in Toronto. Suddenly, from out of nowhere, one of the boys is attacked by a vicious pit bull terrier. The second boy runs to his friend's rescue and whacks the dog's bum with his hockey stick, making it run away.

A reporter from the *Toronto Star* happens to be driving by and witnesses the dog attack. He jumps out of his car and interviews the boy who chased the pit bull away. In his notebook he scribbles a headline for his story: Young Leafs Fan Saves Best Pal from Dog Attack.

The boy sees the headline and says, "But I'm not a Leafs fan!"

The reporter scratches out what he wrote and replaces the headline with: Brave Little Blue Jays Fan Rescues Friend.

The boy says, "That's not true, either. I'm not a Jays fan at all."

Q. How many French Canadians does it take to change a lightbulb?

A. Three. One to hold the ladder, one to screw in the bulb, and one to bribe the officials for the permit.

"My goodness," says the reporter, "I thought every Toronto kid was either a Leafs fan or a Blue Jays fan."

"I happen to be a devoted Montréal Canadiens fan," says the kid, proudly.

So the reporter scribbles yet another headline: Little French Bastard from Québec Severely Injures Much Loved Family Pet.

Q. What do Mennonites call a guy with his arm up a horse's ass?

A. A mechanic.

A Canadian guy and some American tourists are drinking in the bar at the top of Toronto's CN Tower. They are arguing about how the wind blows around tall buildings.

"Lookie here, now," says one of the drunkest Americans, "what you can't see are the circular winds. They blow down and around and up again," he says. "In fact, they're so strong at this height that if you jumped off this tower, you'd only fall a few feet and the winds would push you right back up again."

"Bullshit," says the Canadian, who is almost as drunk.

"I can prove that I'm right," says the American. "Come with me."

The Canadian follows the American up to the observation deck where the two men stagger over to the edge.

"Watch this," says the American, who climbs up on the railing, steadies himself for a few seconds, and then jumps off. To the amazement of the Canadian, the American guy remains suspended in the air.

"See, I didn't fall more than a few feet," he says, as he lands back on the platform. "Why don't you try it?"

"Okay," says the Canadian guy, who is really drunk by now. "Help me get up on the railing."

The Canadian climbs up, steadies himself, jumps, and plunges straight to the ground. The American guy looks down, shrugs, and goes back to the bar and rejoins his friends.

"Did he jump?" one of them asks.

"Yeah, he did," says the American guy.

His friend shakes his head and says, "You know, you're normally a nice guy, Superman, but when you've had a few drinks you can be a real asshole."

A Canadian guy is sitting in an American airport bar. At the other end of the bar he sees a gorgeous young woman wearing a flight attendant's uniform. After a few drinks, he decides to try to pick her up. But since the flight attendant is a cut above the usual women he meets in bars, he decides that he'll have to come up with an imaginative pick-up line.

He sits down beside her and says, "You love to fly and it shows!"

The woman ignores him. He thinks, okay, she doesn't identify with Delta's slogan, but maybe she works for American Airlines.

He leans over and says, "I'll bet 'you're something special in the air!'"

Still no response.

Then he thinks that maybe the woman works for a Canadian airline, so he turns to her again and with a sly wink says, "I'll bet 'it's better up there' with you."

She gives him another icy stare. He concludes that she doesn't work for WestJet, either.

Finally, the woman turns to the guy and snarls, "EXACTLY WHAT THE HELL DO YOU WANT?"

And then it dawns on him: She works for Air Canada!

Two young French Canadian girls are riding their bicycles down a street in the oldest part of Québec City. One says to the other, "I don't believe I've come this way before."

"Me neither," says the other one. "It must be the cobblestones."

A Vancouver guy phones his wife one day and says, "Pack your bags, I just won five million dollars in the provincial lottery."

"Wow," says his wife, "should I pack for skiing at Whistler or lolling on the beach in Hawaii?"

"I don't care where you go," says the husband, "just get the hell out!"

A French Canadian zoologist is on a lecture tour in the United States. One night, while giving his talk to a group of Sierra Club members made up mostly of little blue-haired old ladies, he makes the following statement: "The Canadian porcupine's prick is, on average, 10 to 12 inches long."

Hearing this, the little old ladies all begin to giggle. The zoologist peers at his notes to see if he has misread them and announces, "Oh, my goodness," he says, "I have made a terrible mistake in English. I meant to say that a porcupine's *quill* is 10 inches long. Hell, his prick is only about the size of your thumb."

Q. What do Inuit people get when they sit on the ice too long?

A. Polaroids.

A mother grizzly bear and her cub emerge from their cave in the Rocky Mountains after a long winter. The little cub's knees are wobbly, and he is bleary-eyed, dishevelled and stares at his mother with huge, dark circles under his eyes.

"Did you hibernate all winter like I told you?" she asks.

"Hibernate?" says the cub. "I thought you said masturbate."

A hoser is lying on a hammock in his backyard drinking a beer while his wife mows the lawn.

His neighbour leans over the fence and says, "That's disgusting. You let your wife do all the work while you just lie there and drink beer. You should be damn-well hung!"

Q. How do you spot the Newfie at Jerusalem's Wailing Wall?

A. He's the one with the harpoon.

"I am," replies the hoser. "That's why she mows the lawn for me."

An English Canadian woman is in the fragrance department of a Holt Renfrew store in Montréal when a French clerk comes up to her and offers to spray a perfume sample on her wrist.

"That smells lovely," says the customer while sniffing her wrist. "What's it called?"

"Viens a moi," replies the French clerk.

"What does that mean in English?" asks the customer.

"It means 'come to me,'" says the clerk.

"Gee, that's funny," says the woman. "It sure doesn't smell like come to me."

A drunk stumbles out of a Calgary bar and wanders along the banks of the Bow River. He sees a group of Baptists gathered in the river performing a baptismal ceremony. The drunk staggers into the water and walks up to the preacher.

The preacher says to him, "Son, are you ready to find Jesus?"

"Sure. What the hell, why not?" replies the drunk.

The preacher dunks the drunk's head under the water and pulls him back up. He asks, "Have you found Jesus?"

"No!" replies the drunk.

The preacher then dunks the man's head under for a longer time before pulling him up. Again, he asks him, "Now, brother, have you found Jesus?"

"Uh, no!" the drunk replies.

The preacher dunks the drunk for a third time, holding him under the water even longer still, and when he brings him back up, he says again, "Brother, have you found Jesus?"

"No, I haven't," replies the drunk. "But I have a question. About this guy Jesus...are you sure this is where he fell in?"

A nymphomaniac is walking out to the parking lot of her local Loblaws with a bag boy who is carrying her groceries. She leans over and slyly whispers in his ear, "I have an itchy pussy."

The bag boy shrugs and says, "Well, you'll have to point it out to me, lady, 'cause I can't tell one Japanese car from another."

Ralph, a city slicker from Vancouver, is visiting old friends in Alberta. They decide to take him to a rodeo, where the big attraction is a famous bronco named Bucky. Old Bucky is so fearsome that the rodeo organizers offer a prize of $5000 to anyone who can ride him for eight seconds.

> Q. What did the Alberta rancher do when he found he couldn't keep his hands off his new wife no matter how hard he tried?
>
> A. He fired them all.

All the local cowboys try to ride old Bucky but they fail miserably. Each one of them is thrown to the ground within a few seconds of mounting him. So then Ralph, the city guy, volunteers to give it a try.

Everyone laughs as the dude from Vancouver mounts the huge bronco. But to their amazement, Ralph holds on for five seconds, then 10 seconds, then a whole minute. Before long, he's got ol' Bucky prancing around the ring like a show horse.

Ralph wins the prize. He goes to the podium, and as the judge hands him his cheque, he says, "You claim you've never ridden a bronco before, and yet you tamed the wildest beast in the West. What's your secret?"

Ralph looks down on the crowd sheepishly and in a low voice says, "My wife is an epileptic."

A Newfie gets stopped by a game warden who asks to inspect the ice chest he is carrying. The game warden looks inside, sees that the chest is full of fish and says, "Do you have a licence to catch these fish?"

"No, sir," replies the Newfie. "An' I don't need one, either, 'cause these here fish are my pets."

The Newfie explains that he takes his fish down to the river every night for a swim, and when it's time to return home, he just whistles and they all jump back into the ice chest.

The game warden doesn't believe the story and asks for a demonstration. So the Newfie takes the fish down to the riverbank and dumps them into the river. The warden just stands there and stares at the water.

"Well?" says the warden.

"Well, what?" replies the Newfie.

"When are you going to call them back?" asks the warden.

"Call who back?" says the Newfie.

> There was an old maid from Vancouver,
>
> Who once captured a man by manoeuvre.
>
> She jumped on his knee,
> With a chortle of glee,
>
> And nothing on earth could remove her.

"The fish," replies the warden.

The Newfie shrugs and replies, "What fish?"

The owner of an Ontario lumber camp dislikes French Canadian workers so much that he devises what he thinks is a foolproof test that will ensure that all job applicants from Québec will fail. The test, he reasons, will prevent anyone from accusing him of bigotry for not hiring French Canadian workers. He can just claim that they all failed a simple test.

Weeks go by until a French guy appears at the camp looking for work. The lumber camp owner decides that this is a great opportunity to try out his test.

> Q. What's the only animal in Canada with an asshole in the middle of its back?
>
> A. An RCMP officer's horse.

He begins by giving the French guy a pad and pencil, and says to him, "Without using numbers, illustrate 'nine.'"

The French Canadian guy draws three trees.

"How does that make nine?" asks the owner.

"Tree, tree and tree," says the French guy, "dat make nine!"

"Okay," says the owner, "now, without using numbers, illustrate '99.'"

The French guy reaches over and smudges the drawings of the three trees he just made and says, "Dirty tree, dirty tree and dirty tree. Dats 99!"

By this time the owner of the lumber camp is getting really concerned that his test may not be so foolproof after all. Fearing that he may actually have to hire the guy, the owner tries one more time. "Okay," he says. "Without using numbers, indicate '100' on this same piece of paper."

The French guy looks at his tree drawing for a moment, and then reaches over and puts a little scribble at the bottom of each tree.

"How does that represent 100?" asks the owner.

"Well, look around you," says the French guy. "See how all de dogs in the camp always shit near de trees? Well, dirty tree and a turd, dirty tree and a turd, and dirty tree and a turd—dey all add up to 100. Can I start tomorrow?"

It's February 2006. Stephen Harper has just become prime minister of Canada, and he is in Washington visiting President George W. Bush at the White House for the first time. The two men are sitting alone in the Oval Office when Bush turns to Harper and says, "So Stevie-boy, tell me how you plan to control your minions."

"I'm not sure I know what you mean," replies Harper.

"Let me show you," says Bush, pressing a button on the intercom on his desk. "Cheney! Get your sorry ass in here now!" he shouts.

A few seconds later, Dick Cheney appears at the door.

"Dicko," says Bush. "Answer one question for me. Let's say your mother had a child. It's not your brother, and it's not your sister. Who is it?"

"Give me a few minutes, Mr. President," says Cheney. "I'll get right back to you."

"Right, but hop to it. Make it snappy," replies Bush. "I ain't got all day."

Q. What do you call a guy who drives a Hummer?

A. A gashole.

A few minutes later, Cheney returns, "I've figured out the answer to your question, Mr. President. If it's not my brother, and not my sister, then it must be me."

"Way to go, Dicko," says Bush. "That's exactly right. Now piss off, get back to work and try to find us a new Third World country that we can bomb the shit out of."

The president then turns to Harper and says, "See the way I handled that, Stevie? Ya gotta show these pricks who's in charge, keep 'em on their toes, and make 'em jump to your attention."

"I'll try to remember that when I get back to Ottawa," replies Harper.

A few days later, Harper is back in his office and decides it's time to throw his considerable weight around and shake up his troops.

He phones Stockwell Day and says, "Stockwell, drop everything and get in here right now!"

Day comes running into Harper's office and says, "Yes, Prime Minister?"

"Day," says Harper. "Here's a question for you that I need answered right away: If your mother has a kid, and it's not your brother, and it's not your sister, who is it?"

"I'll need some time to think about that and get back to you with an answer," replies Day. "But I'll get right to work on it."

"Okay," replies Harper, "but don't fart around, this is important."

Day leaves Harper and quickly heads to his office. On the way there, he bumps into the Minister of Finance, James Flaherty, in the hall.

"Jim," he says, "You've got to help me with a pressing question. If your mother has a kid, and it's not your brother or your sister, who is it?"

"That's obvious," replies Flaherty. "It's me!"

"Thanks, Jim," says Day. "You've been a great help."

Day runs back to the prime minister's office, bursts in the door and announces, "I've got the answer for you, sir."

"Okay," says Harper, "If it's not your brother, and not your sister, who is it?"

"It's Jim Flaherty," says Stockwell Day, proudly.

Q. What do you call a Jamaican hired to go around and collect the porta-potties on a Canadian construction site?

A. A black lavatory retriever.

"No, it's not, you dumb prick," replies Harper. "It's Dick Cheney!"

A little girl goes into a pet store in Winnipeg and says to the clerk, "Excuthe me misthes, I'd wike to buy a widdo wabbit."

The clerk thinks the way the kid talks is kind of cute, so she decides to have some fun and mimic her.

> Q. What's the difference between a seagull and a baby?
>
> Clue: A seagull flits along the shore.

"Would you wike to buy a widdo bwack wabbit?" asks the clerk. "Or would you wike to buy a soft, fuwwy widdo bwown wabbit? Or perhaps you'd wike a cute widdo white wabbit?"

The little kid shrugs and replies, "I don't weawy fink my pyfon gives a shit."

A group of tourists is in Toronto's zoo feeding the monkeys. One of the tourists notices that whenever he throws a peanut to one monkey, he always sticks it up his ass and then pulls it out before he eats it.

The tourist thinks this monkey's behaviour is disgusting, so he calls the zookeeper over and says, "You've got to do something about this monkey's revolting habits. He's making everyone in our group feel sick. Watch what happens when I throw him a peanut."

Once again, the tourist throws the monkey a peanut, he catches it, shoves it up his ass, then pulls it out and eats it.

"That's the most disgusting monkey I've ever seen," says the tourist. "I think I'm going to puke."

"Aw, give him a break," replies the zookeeper. "He's just being cautious. You see, the other day, someone threw him a peach, and he ate it, but then he couldn't pass the pit. So now he measures everything before he eats it."

A convention for people who are interested in psychic phenomena is underway in Edmonton. To determine how gullible his audience is, the master of ceremonies begins his presentation by asking for a show of hands in response to a series of questions.

"Would everyone who has heard a voice from the other side please raise their hands," he says.

Almost everyone in the room raises their hands.

"Would everyone who has seen a spirit or a ghost please raise their hands," he says.

About half the people in the room raise their hands.

"Okay, now," says the MC, "has anyone here actually spoken to a ghost?"

About 10 people raise their hands.

"Now," he says, "has anyone here ever had sex with a ghost?"

A new immigrant to Canada sitting at the back of the room timidly raises his hand.

Q. What's a "piece de resistance"?

A. A frigid French Canadian woman.

"That's incredible, sir," says the MC. "Would you come up here and tell us about your experience?"

The man reluctantly walks up to the stage and stands in front of the microphone.

"So," says the MC, "tell us what it's like to have sex with a ghost."

"Oh, my goodness me," replies the man. "I make terrible mistake. I thought you said goat!"

A sadist and a masochist are having sex. The masochist cries out, "PINCH ME, BITE ME, MAKE ME SUFFER!"

And the sadist replies, "No."

A resident of Scarborough goes into his local welfare office one morning to pick up his cheque.

As he takes it from the clerk, he says, "I want you to know that I am ashamed to be acceptin' handouts like this. It's an insult to me and my family, and I would much rather have an honest job."

"Well, I must say, your timing is amazing," replies the clerk. "Just this morning we received a request from a very wealthy gentleman who needs a chauffeur for his nymphomaniac daughter. The job requires the applicant to drive the young woman around town in her father's new BMW and to escort her on her numerous overseas vacations. It pays $100,000 a year and offers a generous clothing allowance and free room and board in their mansion."

"You're shittin' me, right?" says the welfare recipient.

"Yeah, of course I am," replies the clerk. "But you started it."

A hoser in rural BC is in court, accused of killing an endangered spotted owl. After the charges against him are read out, the judge asks the defendant to explain his actions in the woods.

"I was out hunting in the mountains," he says. "It was bucketing rain and I slipped on the trail and twisted my ankle. I dragged myself into a nearby cave and remained there in agony for five days. I had nothing to eat or drink with me, so in desperation, I must confess, I shot and ate the spotted owl."

The judge is sympathetic to the young man's harrowing tale and is about to let him off, when, out of curiosity, he asks the hoser, "What does a spotted owl taste like?"

The hoser replies, "A bit like a bald eagle."

Bertha is an enormous, fat woman. One day she steps out of the shower soaking wet, sits on the toilet, and gets her butt stuck to the seat. No matter how hard she tries, she can't get up. She eventually calls out to her husband for help, but when he tries to lift her, he finds he can't budge her off the seat either, so he calls a plumber.

Bertha reminds her husband that she's sitting on the toilet stark naked, and she needs to cover up. So before the plumber arrives, the husband runs to get a hat, which he places on her lap.

Three religious truths about Canadians:

1. Canadian Protestants don't recognize the Pope as their spiritual leader.
2. Canadian Jews don't recognize Jesus as the Messiah.
3. Canadian Baptists don't recognize each other at the titty bar or in the liquor store.

The plumber arrives and goes into the bathroom to assess the situation. He notes how far she has slipped down into the hole of the toilet seat. He carefully studies the hat on her lap. Then he turns to Bertha's husband and says, "I think I can help your wife, sir, but I'm pretty sure the guy in the hat is a goner."

In a Dartmouth trailer park, a single mother is upset about the foul language her two sons use. The woman's live-in boyfriend tells her that the best way to handle the problem is to apply physical violence whenever one of them curses.

"When one o' them little pricks says somethin' that pisses you off," he says, "jus' reach over and whack him a good one on the side o' the head," he tells her.

The next morning at breakfast, the young mother asks one of her boys what he wants to eat.

"Gimme some o' them f**king Cheerios," he replies.

The mother reaches across the table and smacks the kid so hard he falls off his chair. She then turns to her other boy and says, "And what would you like for your breakfast, dear?"

The kid replies, "Well, you can bet your boots I ain't havin' none o' them f**king Cheerios."

> There was a young fellow from Arnprior
>
> Who was a really magnificent farter.
>
> On the strength of one bean,
>
> He'd fart "God Save the Queen,"
>
> And a spirited rendition of "O Canada."

A Canadian guy travels to Hong Kong where he visits numerous brothels over the course of his stay. When he returns to his home in Vancouver, he wakes up one morning and finds his penis is covered with yellow and purple sores. He freaks out and makes an appointment with his doctor.

The doctor tells him that he's never seen anything like this before and orders some tests.

A few days later, the doctor calls the man and tells him that he has got Mongolian VD. He explains that it is very rare and almost unheard of in Canada.

"How do you treat it?" asks the man.

"It spreads very fast," replies the doctor. "The only solution is to cut off your penis."

"No way!" says the patient. "I want a second opinion."

The next day the man goes to a Chinese doctor, thinking that he'll have special knowledge of Asian venereal diseases. The Chinese doctor examines the sores and says, "Ah yes, Mongolian VD. Vely lare disease."

"Yeah," replies the patient. "I already know that. What are my choices? My other doctor wants to cut my dick off."

The Chinese doctor shakes his head and laughs. "Stupid Canadian docta," he says. "Always want to opelate to make mo' money. No need to opelate!"

"Thank God!" replies the patient.

"You no worry," says the doctor. "Wait two weeks. Pwick fall off by itself!"

How to Identify Where a Canadian Driver Is From

- One hand on steering wheel, one hand out window with middle finger extended upwards—got to be from Toronto.

- One hand on wheel, one hand on horn— from Montréal, of course.

- One hand on wheel, one hand pushing white substance up nose, handgun on lap—from the Toronto suburb of Scarborough. Where else?

- One hand holding latte, one hand on wheel while cradling cell phone in crook of neck—must be from Vancouver.

- One hand on wheel, hunting rifle across lap, other hand tossing a Tim Hortons bag out window—New Brunswick, or maybe rural Nova Scotia.

- Pickup truck, shotgun rack in rear window, beer cans littering floor, raccoon tail on antenna—rural Alberta, rural Manitoba, rural Saskatchewan, rural Ontario, rural BC, rural New Brunswick, rural Nova Scotia...could be any one.

- Both hands firmly gripping wheel, foot on accelerator pedal planted to floor, shattered window glass all over seat, cops in hot pursuit—definitely from Winnipeg, car theft capital of the world!

- Both hands gripping wheel, eyes shut, both feet on and off the brakes, shaking in terror—from rural Ontario, driving in Toronto for the first time.

- Two hands on wheel, shock of grey hair barely visible in rear window, driving at 40 kilometres per hour in the left lane of the Trans-Canada Highway with turn signals flashing—definitely from Victoria!

A businessman staying at an upscale Toronto hotel picks up a copy of NOW and decides to call one of the hookers who advertise in the paper's classifieds. He dials the number on the hotel room phone, and a woman with a sexy voice answers and asks how she may be of service.

"I want to see you dressed in leather," says the guy. "I want to strip you naked. I want you to beat me senseless with a whip. And then I want you to have wild sex with me in the doggie position all night long."

"That sounds like fun, sir," replies the woman. "But I'm kind of busy right now. However, if you just press '9,' you'll get an outside line..."

A 95-year-old woman is so depressed over the death of her husband that she decides to commit suicide. She gets out his old World War II Canadian army pistol, deciding that she will shoot herself in the heart. But not wanting to botch it and become a vegetable, she first calls her doctor and asks him to tell her exactly where her heart is located.

"Your heart is just below your left breast," says the doctor.

That night, the old lady was admitted to hospital with a gunshot wound to her left knee.

A young woman in Newfoundland hears a song on the radio called "Two Hugs and Six Kisses" and decides that she must have the CD. She calls a St. John's music store to inquire about it but accidentally dials the phone number of a local fish plant by mistake.

"Do you have 'Two Hugs and Six Kisses?'" she asks the Newfie guy who answers the phone.

Q. Why did the proctologist use two fingers?

A. He wanted a second opinion.

The Newfie laughs and says, "Hell no, but I gots me two balls an', oh, I'd say, about a good six inches."

"Is that a record?" asks the Newfie woman.

"Nah," replies the Newfie guy. "I tink it's about average."

A yuppie couple from downtown Toronto buys a farm in rural Ontario for use as a weekend retreat. One day they are walking along a country road near their place when they meet a neighbour, who is a pig farmer. They notice that he is accompanied by a huge pig that is missing one leg. A wooden peg leg is strapped onto the pig's body so he can walk.

"That's quite an unusual pig you've got there," says the yuppie guy, trying not to laugh.

"Don't make no smart-assed remarks about my pig, you hear," replies the farmer. "This here is the best goddamned pig in this whole friggin' country, he is. Why, if it wasn't for this pig, I wouldn't be alive today."

The farmer explains that one day while he was plowing his fields, his tractor rolled over on top of him. The huge pig heard his screams for help, broke out of his pen, dug under the tractor and dragged the farmer to safety.

"Another time," says the farmer, "me and the missus were in bed one night when the house caught on fire. Again, this pig here saw what was happening, broke out of his pen, crashed through the front door and woke us up. Saved our lives, he did. So don't you city slickers come up here and insult my pig."

"Hey, relax, man," says the yuppie woman. "We didn't mean to offend you. We just thought it was kind of funny to see a pig with a wooden leg."

The farmer frowns. "That's 'cause you city folk don't know nuttin' about livestock," he says. "Yessiree, when you've got a first-class pig like this, you don't eat him all at once."

A Canadian politician spends the night with a high-class Ottawa hooker. In the morning, he leaves $500 on the dresser.

"That's very generous, sir," says the hooker. "I usually only charge $100."

"But I spent the whole night with you," says the politician. "How do you make a living when you only charge $100 a night?"

"No problem," says the hooker. "I do a lot of blackmail on the side."

An Inuit hunter is driving his snowmobile across the tundra on a freezing cold afternoon. Suddenly, his snowmobile's engine begins to sputter, so he heads back to town and drives it straight to a repair shop.

The mechanic looks at the hunter and says, "Looks like you blew a seal."

"Nah," replies the Inuit guy, brushing the frost from his moustache, "I just had a sneezing fit."

Two Newfies are out hunting. One of them suddenly grabs his chest and collapses on the ground. The other guy pulls out his cell phone and dials 911.

"My friend is dead!" he screams at the operator. "What should I do?"

"Now, calm down, sir," replies the operator. "The first thing you must do is make sure that he is dead."

Suddenly, the operator hears a loud gunshot. The Newfie comes back on the phone and says, "Okay, now what?"

An American, a Scot and a Canadian are riding in a car that is involved in a horrific crash. The three young men are rushed to the same hospital, and when the doctors examine them, they all appear to be dead on arrival. But just as a doctor is about to tag and bag the American, the man miraculously awakens.

"What happened?" asks the doctor.

> Q. What's the difference between a stud and a premature ejaculator?
>
> A. One is good for seconds; the other is only good for seconds.

"All I remember is standing with a Scottish guy and a Canadian at the Gates of Heaven," says the American. "Saint Peter approached us and said that we were all too young to die and that if we each donated $100 to the church, we could return to earth. So I paid the $100, and the next thing I know, I woke up here."

"So what happened to the others?" asks the doctor.

The American says, "The last time I saw them, the Scot was haggling over the amount of his donation, and the Canadian was insisting that his government must pay for his."

Over lunch at a Chinese restaurant in Montréal, Irving and Manny are talking about the worldwide migration of their people.

"Do you think there are any Jews in China?" Manny asks Irving.

"Probably," replies Irving, noting that Jewish people have migrated to the four corners of the earth. "Some of them must have ended up in China," he says. "But I'm not sure. Let's ask the waiter."

> Q. How do you stop your kid from wetting the bed?
>
> A. Give him an electric blanket.

"Excuse me, Dong," says Manny. "Are there any Chinese Jews?"

"I no think so," replies Dong, "but I'll check with the chef, he no fo' sure."

A few minutes later, Dong returns and announces, "No sir, no Chinese Jews."

Irving and Manny are still skeptical and tell him that they think there simply must be Chinese Jews somewhere.

"I check with boss," says Dong. "He from Beijing. Velly educated man...travel all over China."

Dong returns a few minutes later and says, "No sirs, boss say absorutry no Chinese Jews. We have orange jews, grape jews, prune jews, tomato jews, but no Chinese jews."

Conservative politicians promise to look after Canadians from cradle to grave.

Liberal politicians go one step further and promise to look after Canadians from womb to tomb.

Not to be outdone, the NDP promises to look after Canadians from erection to resurrection.

Q. Why do cannibals love Jehovah's Witnesses?

A. Free delivery.

Canadian libertarians, on the other hand, don't care much about making Canadians feel secure. Instead, they propose that the government should remove the maple leaf from the Canadian flag and replace it with a picture of a condom. They reason that a condom is a more appropriate symbol for Canada is because (a) it allows for inflation; (b) it protects a bunch of pricks; and (c) it gives Canadians a false sense of security while they're being screwed.

So God sayeth unto the French Canadians, "I have Commandments for you that will improve your lives."

"What are Commandments?" ask the French Canadians.

"Rules to live by," replies God.

"Can you give us an example?" they ask.

Q. How do Newfies circumcise whales?

A. They send down foreskin divers.

"Thou Shalt Not Covet Thy Neighbour's Wife," replies God.

"Forget it," say the French. "We love boinking each other's wives. We're not interested."

So God goes to the Italian Canadians and says, "I have Commandments for you."

The Italians also ask for an example of a Commandment, and God replies, "Thou Shalt Not Steal."

"What, no thievin'? Are you crazy?" reply the Italians. "We're not interested."

So God takes his Commandments to the Jamaican Canadians and says, "I have Commandments for you."

When the Jamaicans ask for an example, God replies, "Thou Shalt Not Kill."

"Say what?" reply the Jamaicans. "Yer shittin' us, right? No way, man."

So God goes to the Canadian Jews and says, "I have Commandments for you."

"How much do they cost?" ask the Jews.

God says, "They're free."

The Jews reply, "Give us 10."

High above the Rocky Mountains, an eagle swoops down and swallows a little mouse. He then takes off. A few minutes later, the mouse pokes his head out of the eagle's ass. He looks down and says to the eagle, "How high up are we?"

"Oh, about 500 metres," says the eagle.

> Q. What do hosers call a guy with a snow-plow?
> A. Designated driver.

"No kidding!" replies the mouse. "You wouldn't shit me, would you?"

A hoser who lives in the wilds of northern Ontario shoots a deer, butchers it and serves it to his family for dinner one night. His kids are fussy eaters and won't eat anything unless they're told what it is, so the hoser makes them try to guess what's on their plates.

"Here's a hint," he says. "It's what your mother sometimes calls me."

"Oh my God!" screams one of the kids. "We're eating asshole!"

A guy on a flight from Edmonton to Winnipeg is sitting next to a shapely young woman who is reading a book titled, *A Comparative Physiological Study of the Male Sex Organ*. He strikes up a conversation with her, which eventually turns to the subject of her book.

"That looks interesting," he says.

"Yes, it is," the woman replies. "It's full of amazing facts and statistics. For instance, did you know that Native men have penises that are, on average, four inches longer than those of any other racial group in the world?"

Q. Why do French Canadian couples always do it doggie style?

A. So they can both watch the hockey game.

"No, I didn't," replies the man.

"And did you know that Jewish men have the world's thickest penises?" she adds.

"No," replies the man, "I didn't know that, either."

The conversation continues in this vein for the rest of the flight. As the plane is landing, the woman turns to the guy and says, "You know, we're talking about all this sexy stuff, and we haven't even introduced ourselves yet. My name is Sally, what's yours?"

He replies, "The name's Rosenbaum, Ma'am, Chief Running Bear Rosenbaum."

A drunken Newfie is stopped on a street one night by an old St. John's hooker.

"Would ya likes a blow job, me son?" she asks him.

"No, tanks," replies the Newfie. "I'd rather stay on welfare."

A woman goes into a Canadian Tire store to buy a fishing rod for her husband. She chooses one and takes it to a sales desk where a clerk is standing wearing dark sunglasses. "Excuse me," she says. "Can you tell me anything about this fishing rod?"

Q. What do you call kids who are born in brothels?

A. Brothel sprouts.

"Yes, I can," replies the clerk. "I'm completely blind, but if you drop it on the counter, I can tell you everything you need to know about it by the sound it makes."

She finds this hard to believe, but she drops the fishing rod anyway.

"That's a six-foot Shakespeare graphite rod with a Zebco 501 reel," says the clerk. "An excellent choice, and on sale this week for only $49."

"That's incredible!" says the woman. "You can tell all that just by the sound of it hitting the counter? I'll take it."

As the woman opens her purse, she accidentally drops her credit card on the floor.

"Oh, that sounds like a Visa card you dropped," says the clerk.

"Yes, it is," says the woman. Then, as she bends over to pick up the card, she accidentally lets out an enormous fart. At first, she is embarrassed, but then she realizes that there is no way the blind clerk could tell for sure who farted in the busy store.

The clerk rings up the sale and says, "That comes to a total of $64 plus tax."

"Wait a minute," says the woman. "Didn't you tell me that the fishing rod was on sale for $49? How did you get $64?"

"That's right, Ma'am," says the clerk. "The fishing rod is $49, but the duck call is another $10, and the live bait costs $5."

A Canadian guy suffers a massive heart attack and is rushed to a hospital emergency room. After conducting many tests, the doctor informs him that he needs a heart transplant. The doctor searches for a suitable donor on the Internet and finds two hearts that are compatible.

Q. What do you call a band of Iroquois on Prozac?

A. Former worriers.

"One belonged to a Canadian social worker," says the doctor, "and the other came from a lawyer. Which one do you want?"

"I'll take the lawyer's," says the guy, without hesitation.

"Don't you want to know more about the donors?" asks the doctor. "And why would you prefer a lawyer's heart over a social worker's?"

"It's a no-brainer," replies the patient. "All Canadian social workers are bleeding hearts, right? And lawyers never use theirs, so I'll have the lawyer's, please."

Mavis, an elderly Jewish woman, dies. After her funeral service, the pallbearers are carrying the casket down a corridor in the synagogue when they accidentally bump it into a railing on the stairs. They hear a loud moaning sound coming from inside the casket, and when they open it, they discover that Mavis is still alive.

> Q. What do you call a French Canadian guy who wears sandals?
> A. Philippe Philoppe.

She lives another 10 years, and then dies.

At her second funeral, which is held in the same synagogue, the pallbearers are once again carrying her casket down the same corridor. When they are nearing the spot where the casket got bumped the first time, Mavis' husband stops the procession. He turns to the pallbearers and whispers, "From here on, I want you all to proceed very, very carefully. And whatever you do, be sure to watch out for that damn railing!"

The Shortest Books Ever Published in Canada

Stephen Harper: My Wild and Crazy Years

The Canadian Book of Really Nasty Insults

Who's Who in Labrador

Famous Inuit Surfers

My Quest for World Dominance, by Jack Layton

Bob and Doug McKenzie's Guide to Fashion

Tasty Recipes for Poutine

David Suzuki's Directory of Jobs for Loggers

French Canadian War Heroes

Jean Chrétien: Portrait of Integrity

The Canadian Mennonite Telephone Directory

Fun Things to do in Hamilton, Ontario

The Newfie Book of Foreplay

The Canadian Wildlife Federation's Favourite Spotted Owl Recipes

The Fine Dining Guide to the Northwest Territories

The Canadian Bar Association's Guide to Lawyer Ethics

Fun Nights Out on the Town in Flin Flon

Conrad Black's Business Ethics Manual

The Mennonite Guide to Alternative Sex Practices

Famous Canadian Recipes for Ice

Danny Williams' Guide to Political Etiquette & Diplomacy

The Canadian Guide to Great American Beer

The French Canadian Guide to Hospitality

Arctic Water Polo

Jean Chrétien's Most Memorable Quotes

Soothing Nervous Polar Bears with Tickling Tricks

A hoser picks up a young woman in a remote northern Ontario bar. They get in his car and drive down a remote country road where they park and start necking. The woman suddenly pushes the guy away and says, "I should tell you before we go any further that I am a hooker, and I charge $50."

So they climb into the backseat. When the hoser finishes, he climbs back into the driver's seat and just sits there, staring out the window.

"Why aren't we going anywhere?" asks the hooker.

"I should tell you," the hoser says, "I'm a taxi driver, and the fare back to town is $60."

A blind man applies for a job as a quality control manager at a British Columbia lumber mill. During the interview, the mill owner asks him how he could possibly do the job with no ability to visually inspect and classify the lumber.

"I can do it by smell," replies the man. "My nose is so sensitive that I can distinguish over 20 different types of wood. With one sniff, I can even grade your lumber and purge the bad pieces from your inventory."

The mill owner decides to test the man, and he puts several pieces of wood in front of him. "Can you tell me what this is?" he says, holding up a two-by-four.

"That's a very good piece of western red cedar," says the blind man after sniffing it. "Probably cut somewhere in British Columbia."

"Correct!" says the mill owner. "Now what's this?"

Q. How many Canadians does it take to change a lightbulb?

A. None. Canadians don't change lightbulbs. We accept them the way they are.

The blind man sniffs the second piece for a second or two and says, "That's a bad piece of eastern white pine, probably cut somewhere in Québec."

"You're absolutely right!" says the interviewer, who is so impressed with the blind man's talent that he decides to play a trick on him. He leaves the room for a minute and returns with his secretary, a tough old broad with a loose reputation around town and a weird sense of humour. The mill owner instructs her to lift up her dress and stick her crotch in the blind man's face.

> Q. What's the French Canadian definition of a seven-course dinner?
>
> A. A six-pack and a plate of poutine.

"What's this?" asks the mill owner.

"I'm not sure," replies the blind man. "Can you turn it around for me?"

The old woman turns and shoves her ass in the blind man's face.

"Boy, this is a tough one...I think...yes, uh-huh, now I'm sure," he says. "That's an outhouse door off a Nova Scotia tuna boat."

A young and very attractive Newfie woman is driving through Nova Scotia when she is stopped by a Mountie for speeding.

The Mountie looks at her driver's licence and says, "Oh, so you're a Newfie, eh?"

He reaches down and begins to unzip his fly.

"OH, NO!" says the woman. "Not another Breathalyzer test!"

A Native guy named Quivering Beaver is guiding a group of American hunters through the Yukon wilderness. He suddenly drops to his knees and presses his ear to the ground.

"Caribou come!" he says.

"How do you know?" asks one of the hunters, who is amazed at the guy's tracking skills.

Q. What was the first thing the Newfie mother said when she found out that her daughter was pregnant?

A. "Are you sure it's yours?"

Quivering Beaver replies, "Stickum to my ear."

Darryl, a hoser from rural New Brunswick, fancies himself as a lady's man. One night, he gets drunk, picks up a woman named Debbie in a bar and takes her back to his trailer where he quickly manages to hustle her into bed.

Afterwards, he rolls over, lights a cigarette and stares at Debbie with a smug grin on his face. Debbie glares back and says, "You may think you're the hottest guy around here in a plaid shirt, but I'm here to tell you that you're a lousy lay."

Darryl replies, "Oh yeah, well, what makes you think you're such an expert after only 10 seconds?"

Janet, Sara and Kendra are three pregnant women who are sitting together in a Halifax obstetrician's waiting room.

"Did you know that this doctor claims he can predict the sex of a child by the position you were in while having intercourse?" says Janet.

"Yes," replies Sara. "I told him I was on top the night I conceived my baby, so he thinks I'll have a boy."

"Well," says Janet, "I told him I was on the bottom, so he's quite sure I'm going to have a girl."

"OH, NO!" shouts Kendra.

"What's the matter?" asks Janet.

"This is terrible," replies Kendra. "I think I'm going to have a puppy!"

A senile old man goes out one night to Toronto's red light district and tries to pick up a hooker. He walks up and down Isabella Street and eventually tries to strike up a conversation with a young hooker. The woman thinks he's crazy and gives him the brush-off.

"Get lost, you senile old bastard," she says. "You're ruining business for me."

"But I can pay," says the old man.

"You've got to be joking," says the hooker. "You're past it. You're finished!"

"What did you say?" asks the old man, leaning closer.

"I said, you're finished!" screams the hooker.

"Oh, okay," says the old man. "How much do I owe you?"

Once upon a time in the Kingdom of Heaven, God goes missing for six days. Eventually Michael, the archangel, finds him sitting on a cloud, resting on the seventh day. He asks, "Where have you been?"

God gives him a big smile and proudly points down through the clouds. "Look, Michael," he says, "look at what I've made."

Archangel Michael looks puzzled and replies, "What is it?"

Q. Why is Viagra like Canada's Wonderland?

A. You have to wait an hour for a three-minute ride.

"It's a planet," says God. "And look, I've put life on it. I've decided to call it 'Earth,' and I'm going to make sure that it is a place of great balance."

"Balance?" asks Michael. "What's balance?"

God explains: "See that land mass over there, that's northern Europe. It will be a place of great opportunity and wealth, while southern Europe will be poor." Pointing to Africa, God says, "Over there I've placed a continent full of black people, and over here on the other side I've made another one populated by white people. There are several countries that are going to be hot and arid, and they will be balanced off with an equal number that are cold and covered with ice."

Michael then points to a large landmass at the top of the planet ands says, "What is that one?"

"Ah," says God. "That is Canada, the most glorious place on Earth. It has beauti-

Q. How are Canadian politicians like diapers?

A. They should be changed often, and for the same reason.

ful mountains, pristine lakes and rivers, and abundant natural resources. The people who live in Canada are going to be modest, intelligent and humorous. They're going to be sociable, hard working and known throughout the planet as diplomats and peace keepers. I'm also going to make them fantastic hockey players who will be feared and admired by all who play against them."

Michael gasped in wonder at God's creation. "I can see that Canada will certainly be blessed," he says, "but what about balance? You said there will be balance."

"Oh, there will be balance all right," God replies. "Wait 'til you see the loud-mouthed, know-it-all bastards I've put next to them...."

In rural Saskatchewan, a Grade 5 teacher gives her class an assignment. The children are to go home and ask their parents to tell them a story with a moral at the end. The next day the kids present their stories to the class.

Q. What are the three biggest lies told by an Alberta cowboy?

A. (1) I won this belt buckle.

(2) The truck is paid for.

(3) I'm just helping this sheep over the fence.

Little Lisa goes first. "My father is a farmer, and this one time we were taking our eggs to market in a basket when we hit a bump in the road and all the eggs went flying around inside our truck and many of them got broken," she says.

"And what is the moral of your story?" asks the teacher.

"Never put all your eggs in one basket," replies Lisa.

Next, Myrna tells her story. "This one time my father had 12 eggs, but when they hatched, he only got 10 live chicks," she says.

"And the moral of your story?" asks the teacher.

"Don't count your chickens before they are hatched," replies Myrna.

Wally, a tough kid from the wrong side of town, goes next. "My old man told me this story about my Uncle Bill," he says. "Uncle Bill was soldier and a paratrooper in Afghanistan, and his plane once conked out over Taliban territory. He had to bail out and parachute to the ground. All he had was a bottle of Canadian whiskey, a machine gun and a machete. He drank the whiskey on the way down so that the bottle wouldn't break, and then he landed right in the middle of 100 Taliban soldiers. He killed about 70 of them with his machine gun before he ran out of bullets. Then he killed 20 more with his machete before the blade broke. And then he killed the last 10 with his bare hands."

Q. What has 75 balls and screws old ladies?

A. Bingo.

"My God!" says the horrified teacher. "That's terrible. So what's the moral of your story?"

"Well," says Wally, "I guess it's just like what my old man always says, 'Don't mess with Uncle Bill when he's drunk!'"

A high school geography teacher in St. John's asks her class, "What is the capital of Newfoundland?"

"I know, I know," says a kid in the front row. "It's 'N.'"

Michelle is a devout French Canadian Catholic woman who gets married and has eight children. Then suddenly one day, her husband dies.

She remarries, has five more children with her second husband, then he dies. Six months after he dies, Michelle drops dead, too.

At her funeral, the priest looks directly at the members of Michelle's family and says, "Thank God, at last they are together."

Michelle's mother, who is sitting in the front pew, says, "Excuse me, Father, but do you mean you're thankful that Michelle is now together in heaven with her first husband, or are you saying it's good that she is together forever with her second husband?"

The priest replies, "I'm talking about her legs."

The Trojan condom factory in the United States burns down. The president of the company phones their Canadian factory in a panic and tells the manager that without condoms, the United States faces a major birth control crisis. A national emergency, even.

Q. What do Native people call their outhouses?

A. Their pee-pee teepee.

He tells the Canadian to ship him one million condoms to the head office right away. "I want 'em all coloured red, white and blue, and I want 'em all to be eight inches long and two inches wide," he says.

The Canadian manager promises to get right on it and immediately calls his factory foreman and tells him to ship a million condoms to the U.S. right away. "They only want red, white and blue ones," he says, "and they all must be eight inches long and two inches wide."

"No problem," replies the foreman. "Anything else?"

"Yeah," says the manager. "Print on them: 'Made in Canada, Size: Small.'"

A bigshot Toronto executive gets drunk at his company's Christmas party. The next morning he wakes up with a terrible hangover and asks his wife to tell him exactly what happened the night before.

"Well," she says, "as usual, you made a complete ass of yourself in front of your boss."

"Piss on him," says the guy.

"You did, and he fired you," says the wife.

"Screw him, then," says the guy.

"I did," replies the wife. "You've been rehired with a raise."

An old couple in Saskatoon realizes one day that they are becoming increasingly forgetful. They decide that the best solution to the problem is to simply make a habit of writing down everything that they have to remember.

One night while they are watching TV, the old guy gets up to go into the kitchen.

"Would you bring me a dish of ice cream?" asks the wife.

"No problem," replies the husband.

"Do you need to write that down?" she asks.

"No, I'll remember," says the husband.

"Okay," says the wife, "then I'd like vanilla ice cream with some chocolate sauce and a cherry on the top. Can you remember all that, or would you like me to write it down for you?"

"No, I'll remember," says the husband, who then leaves the room muttering to himself over and over, "vanilla ice cream, chocolate sauce, cherry on top…"

Ten minutes later he returns to the living room and hands his wife a plate of sizzling Canadian back bacon with two fried eggs on the side.

"You senile old fart!" shouts the wife.

"What's the matter?" asks the husband.

The wife replies, "You forgot the damn toast."

Two Newfies, Clyde and Shamus, spend the whole day drinking and fishing, but they only manage to catch one fish. It's a big fish, and the two men get into a heated argument over who will take it home. Then Shamus comes up with an idea. "Let's have a contest," he says. "We'll take turns kicking each udder in da balls as hard as we can, and when one guy gives up, da udder one keeps da fish."

"Okay," says Clyde, who is quite a bit drunker than Shamus. "But who goes first?"

"It was my idea," says Shamus. "So I'll go first."

Shamus lets loose with a vicious kick to Clyde's scrotum, making him drop to the ground and clutch his balls in agony. A few minutes later Clyde manages to get up and steady himself enough to try to put the boots to Shamus.

Shamus looks at him and starts laughing. "Aw, to hell wit' it, Clyde," he says. "You can jus' keeps da fish."

A young Newfie woman goes to her gynecologist for a checkup. The doctor informs her that she has a fissure in her uterus. "If you ever have a baby," he tells her, "it will be nothing short of a miracle."

That night the woman's husband asks her how she got on at the doctor's.

"I tink me doctor has lost his mind," she says.

"How so?" asks the husband.

The wife replies, "He told me I have a fish in my uterus, and if I have a baby it will be a mackerel."

Q. What's the difference between American senators and Canadian senators?

A. An American politician has to win a seat to get in the Senate. A Canadian politician has to lose one.

10 Reasons Why it's More Fun to Live in Québec

1. If you're French, expectations of you are low—everyone just assumes that you're an asshole.

2. Racism is socially acceptable.

3. It's the only province where protesters think nothing of kidnapping their politicians just to make a point.

4. It's fun to make bets on which English-speaking neighbour will move out next.

5. Ottawa and all the other provinces constantly bribe you with billions and billions of dollars just so you'll stay in Canada.

6. The FLQ is on the move again, and they're as crazy as ever!

7. The hockey teams are all made up of dirty French guys.

8. The province has the oldest, nastiest hookers in Canada.

9. Non-smokers are the outcasts.

10. You can blame all your problems on the new immigrants or those "effing Anglo bastards."

An aging Mother Superior in a rural Québec convent asks one of her nuns to do a special favour for her. She explains that the bishop will be visiting the convent and that he is a very old man who will require some assistance with his daily ablutions.

The Mother Superior instructs the young nun how to draw the old bishop's bath for him, how to arrange his towels and how to assist him in and out of the tub. The nun is told to do whatever the bishop tells her, and that under no circumstances is she to look at his naked body.

When the bishop arrives, the young nun follows the instructions to the letter. The next day the Mother Superior calls her into the office.

"How did you get on with assisting the bishop last night?" she asks.

"It was wonderful," replies the nun with a big smile. "The bishop told me that I have been saved!"

"Oh, really?" says the Mother Superior. "How so?"

"Well, the bishop asked me to wash his back and chest for him," replies the nun. "And then he guided my hand down between his legs to where he said God keeps what he called the Key to Heaven."

"And what did he tell you to do with it?" asks the Mother Superior.

"He told me that if the Key to Heaven fits my lock, I would be assured eternal salvation," replies the nun. "So I let him insert it."

"Tell me more," says the Mother Superior.

"Well, at first I felt a lot of pain," continues the nun, "but the bishop told me that the road to salvation is always painful, so I let him continue."

"This is terrible!" says the Mother Superior. "I'm absolutely shocked and appalled that he would tell you that."

"Why?" asks the young nun.

> Q. What were the most erotic words ever spoken on Canadian television prior to 1960?
>
> A. "Gee, Ward, you were kind of hard on the Beaver last night!"

"Because the bishop told me that thing between his legs is Gabriel's horn," says the Mother Superior. "And I've been blowing it for over 20 years!"

A French Canadian, a guy from Ontario and a Newfie are sitting in a bar talking about foreplay and the things they do to drive their wives wild in bed.

The French Canadian says, "I start by covering my wife's body with rose petals. Then, one by one, I blow dem off her. Dis drives 'er wild with passion, and she cannot contain 'er desire for me."

The guy from Ontario says, "My wife loves it when I pour warm oil all over her body, and then

I give her a gentle massage from head to toe. She's crazy about that."

The Newfie listens to this and says, "I don't do none o' that crap. But when I'm all done wit me lovin's, I jus' rolls off me old lady, jumps out of bed and I wipes me dick on the drapes. Now that really drives her wild."

A reporter for *Maclean's* gets an assignment to search the world for people with unusual occupations. He is travelling in Egypt when he meets an old Arab man. When the reporter asks the man what his occupation is, the man says, "I'm a camel castrator."

> Q. What do you call a Nova Scotia farmer who owns both sheep and goats?
> A. Bisexual.

"A camel castrator?" says the reporter. "How do you do that?"

"It's very simple," says the Arab. "You just tie a brick to each end of a rope and then loop the rope over the camel's hump. Then, hard as you can, you whack the two bricks together on the camel's balls."

"Jesus!" shrieks the reporter. "Doesn't that hurt?"

"Oh, sure," replies the Arab. "Every once in a while...if you accidentally get your thumbs caught between the bricks."

Dong Long is a problem child in a Grade 3 class at a Vancouver public school. His teacher is frustrated because Dong Long is clearly the brightest kid in her class but he refuses to pay attention to her lessons, and he never does his homework.

Q. Why are hosers like pickup trucks?

A. Because they always pull out before they check to see if anyone else is coming.

When she asks him what his problem is, he says, "Me too smart for this class. Me smarter than all other kids. Me smarter than my sister who is in Grade 6. Me want to be in Grade 6, too."

The teacher takes Dong Long to the principal's office and explains the situation to him.

After much discussion, the principal tells Dong Long that he will give him a test, and if he fails to answer any of the questions, he will agree to stay in Grade 3 and behave. Dong Long agrees.

"What's three times three?" says the principal.

"Nine!" says Dong Long.

"What's six times six?" asks the principal.

"Thirty-six!" says the kid.

And so it goes with every question the principal thought a sixth grader should know. He turns to the teacher and says, "I think young Dong Long should go to Grade 6."

"Before we promote him, I have some questions," says the teacher. "May I ask him?"

The principal and Dong Long both agree.

"Dong Long," says the teacher, "what does a cow have four of that I have only two of?"

"Legs!" says the kid.

"What's in your pants that you have, but I don't have," says the teacher.

"Pockets!" says Dong Long.

"What goes in hard and pink then comes out soft and sticky," she asks.

The principal cannot believe his ears, but before he can interrupt, the kid shouts, "Bubblegum!"

"What does a man do standing up, a woman does sitting down and a dog does on three legs?" the teacher asks Dong Long.

The principal's eyes bulge, and before he can stop the kid, Dong Long shouts, "Shake hands!"

"Now I'm going to ask some 'Who Am I' questions, okay?" says the teacher. "First, you stick a big pole inside me. Then you tie me down, and I get wet before you do. Who am I?"

"You're a tent!" shouts Dong Long.

> Q. What's the one thing that keeps most hosers out of university?
>
> A. High school.

"Next question," says the teacher. "A finger goes in me. The best man always has me first. Who am I?"

The principal is getting hot under the collar and is squirming in his chair.

"You're a wedding ring!" exclaims Dong.

"I come in many sizes. When I'm not well, I drip. When you blow me, I feel good. Who am I?"

"You're a nose!" says Dong.

"I have a stiff shaft. My tip penetrates, and I come with a quiver," says the teacher. "Who am I?"

"You're an arrow!" says the kid.

Q. What's the difference between a genealogist and a gynecologist?

A. A genealogist looks up the family tree; a gynecologist looks up the family bush.

"Finally, Dong," says the teacher, "what word starts with 'f' and ends in 'k' and means a lot of heat and excitement?"

"Fire truck!" yells Dong.

The teacher says, "Dong Long, you've passed my test with flying colours. I think you should be promoted to Grade 6."

The principal breathes a sigh of relief and says, "Forget Grade 6, send Dong Long to Simon Fraser—no, make that Harvard. I got the last 10 questions wrong myself!"

Two Newfies, Shamus and Rex, are out in a boat drinking beer and fishing. Rex snags a brass urn on his line, and when he opens it, POOF!, out pops a genie. The genie is so grateful for being released from the urn that she grants him one wish.

Rex thinks for a moment and says, "I'd like da whole friggin' ocean to be turned into beer."

POOF! the ocean suddenly turns into beer.

"Well, what do you tink of that, Shamus?" Rex asks.

"I tink you're an arsehole!" replies Shamus. "Now we'll have to pee in our boat."

Two boys from Scarborough get busted for possession of drugs. When they go to court the next day, the judge decides to reprimand them.

"I cannot believe the number of young people who appear before me for drug possession," he says. "But because this is the first offence for both of you, I'm going to give you a break. If each of you can get 10 of your friends in your neighbourhood to sign a pledge vowing to give up drugs for life, I'll let you off with a warning."

The two kids agree to try to get the signatures.

A week later they are back in court before the same judge. "How did you make out with your pledges?" he asks them.

The first kid stands up and says, "Yessir, your Honour, I got me 10 signatures."

"Good for you," says the judge. "How did you persuade them to sign?"

"Well, sir," replies the kid, "I just drew a dot an' a circle on a piece of paper. Then I pointed to the dot and said, 'This here is the size o' your brain when you're on drugs.' Then I pointed at the circle and said, 'This is the size o' your brain when you're not on drugs,' and they all signed the pledge right away!"

"Very good," says the judge. "You may go."

Then the second kid stands up, and the judge asks him how many signatures he was able to get.

"One hunnert an' five," replies the kid proudly.

"That's fantastic," says the judge. "How were you able to get so many?"

Q. How do you tell if your husband is dead?

A. The sex is the same, but you get control of the remote.

"Well, your Honour, it was easy for me, too," says the kid. "I also drew a dot an' a circle on a piece of paper. Then I pointed to the dot an' said, 'This here dot is the size of your asshole before you go to prison...'"

Eric comes home after work and says to his wife, "I've got a great idea. Tonight let's change positions."

"Terrific," replies his wife. "You do the dishes, and I'll sit on the sofa and fart."

An executive in the Saskatoon office of a large corporation is told that he must relocate to a new position at the head office in Toronto. The executive tells his boss that he would rather quit than move to the big city.

"There's so much crime and so many senseless murders there," the executive explains. "I'm worried about moving my wife and kids to such a violent, scary place."

The boss tries to console the man by telling him that he once lived in Toronto and that it is a great city, with lots of restaurants, nightlife, museums and excellent transportation. "I lived there for over 10 years," he says, "and I never once felt threatened or had a problem with crime."

"What kind of work did you do there?" asks the executive.

"I worked for Molson," replies the boss.

"What did you do?" asks the executive.

> Q. Why do Canadian weathervanes have cocks on them?
>
> A. If they used pussies, the wind would blow right through them.

The boss replies, "I was a tail gunner on one of their beer trucks."

An old woman in Red Deer can't stop passing gas. She goes to her doctor and explains to him that although she farts all the time, her farts are silent and have no odour.

"In fact," she says, "you may not believe this, but I haven't stopped farting since I arrived here in your office."

The doctor gives the woman a prescription and tells her to come back in one week.

When she returns, she tells the doctor that her problem is much worse.

"I'm still farting all the time," she says. "They're still silent, but now they smell terrible."

"Relax," says the doctor. "You may not believe this, but I think we're making real progress."

"How so?" asks the old lady.

"Well, now that I've fixed your sense of smell," replies the doctor, "I can start to work on your hearing."

A hoser picks up a woman in a rural Manitoba bar. They get into the back of his van and proceed to have rough sex. In the heat of their passion, the woman starts yelling, "Whip me! Whip me!"

> Q. What's the difference between a hockey game and a high school reunion?
>
> Clue: At a hockey game, you see a lot of fast pucks.

The hoser doesn't have a whip in his van so he leans out of the window, breaks off his radio antenna and proceeds to beat her with it.

A few days later the woman is at her doctor's for a physical. He sees the welts from the antenna thrashing and asks, "Did you get these sores while having sex?"

"Yes, I did," replies the woman sheepishly.

"Migod," says the doctor. "This is the worst case of van aerial disease I've ever seen."

Omar goes to a psychic to try to get in touch with his deceased brother. The psychic goes into a trance and tells him that she has made contact. She then asks Omar to speak directly to his brother.

"Are you there, Arthur?" says Omar.

"Yeah, I'm here," comes Arthur's faint reply.

"What's it like on the other side?" asks Omar.

Q. What's the definition of safe sex in Newfoundland?

A. Branding the sheep that kick.

"It's not bad. Not bad at all," replies Arthur. "I get up in the morning, eat, have sex, then I take a nap. At noon, I have lunch, have some more sex, then take another nap. Then, in the evening, I have a big meal, get laid again, then go to sleep. Every day the routine is pretty much the same."

"That sounds wonderful," says Omar. "It must be great up there in heaven."

"Heaven?" replies Arthur. "Hell no. I came back as a prairie dog in Saskatchewan."

Garge, a Newfie fisherman, returns to St. John's after a long fishing trip. His friends on the dock notice that his appearance has changed dramatically while he was away. His body is twice as big and muscular as it once was, and his head appears to have shrunk in size.

"What happened to you?" the fishermen ask.

"Amazin' story," says Garge. "I snagged a mermaid in me net, and she granted me two wishes if I'd let her go free. So I told her I'd like to have a more muscular body. And she goes 'POOF' and all of a sudden, I've got big muscles. Then, for me second wish, I told her I'd like to have sex wit her, and she said that she couldn't, 'cause being a mermaid, she don't have the right parts. So then I said, 'How 'bout a little head?'"

A young Canadian mother finds an S&M magazine in her son's bedroom. She shows it to her husband and asks, "What should we do?"

"I'm not sure," replies the husband. "But whatever you do, don't spank him."

An architect, a doctor and a senior civil servant from the federal government are sitting in an Ottawa bar having a few drinks. The conversation turns to the subject of dogs, and as the drinks keep coming, the men soon find themselves in a heated argument over who owns the smartest dog. They decide to meet at a local park later that day with their dogs and have a contest to see which one is the most intelligent.

Q. What is a bigamist?

A. An Italian fog.

The doctor's dog goes first. The doctor dumps a pile of bones on the grass and says to his dog, "Okay, Diabetes, go to it!"

Diabetes runs over to the bones and within a few minutes assembles them in the form of a human skeleton. Everyone is impressed.

The architect's dog goes next. "Okay, Ruler," says the architect, "do your stuff!"

Ruler runs to the pile of bones and within seconds he constructs a model of Ottawa's Parliament buildings. The other men are amazed.

Then the government worker, who is drinking out of a flask and is quite pissed by now, brings out his dog and says, "Okay, Freeloader, give 'em hell!"

> Q. How do you tell if your wife is dead?
> A. The sex is the same, but the dishes pile up.

Freeloader slowly walks up to the pile of bones and, one by one, eats them all. He then humps the other two dogs and takes the rest of the afternoon off.

Billy and Bobby are arguing in the playground.

"My dad's better'n your dad," says Billy.

"Oh yeah," replies Bobby. "Well, my mom's better'n your mom!"

"You're probably right," says Billy. "My dad says the same thing."

Several old farts are sitting around the dinner table in their Victoria nursing home complaining about their ailments.

"My hands are so shaky that I can hardly hold my fork," says one old lady.

"My cataracts are so bad that I can't see to put my teeth in," says another.

"I can't turn my head 'cause I've got arthritis real bad in my neck," says one old guy.

"You think you've got problems," says another old woman, "my pills make me so dizzy that I can hardly stand up, even with my cane."

"Oh well," adds another old lady, "life here isn't so bad. Thank God we live in Canada where we're all still allowed to drive."

> Q. What are the three guiding concepts of Canadian federation that no politician will ever dare to tamper with?
>
> A. (1) The Natives must always appear to own it.
>   (2) The French must always appear to run it.
>   (3) The English must always appear ready and willing to pay for it.

Pasquale, a young Italian Canadian boy, is about to go out on his very first date with a nice Italian girl named Maria. Before he leaves the house, his father takes him aside and says, "Pasquale, there'sa justa one thinga you hava ta knowa about women. You justa remember: takea the hardest thinga you got, and put it ina the placea where she pees."

So that night, Pasquale takes his bocce ball over to Maria's house and puts it in her toilet.

Pasquale and Maria eventually decide to marry. On their wedding night they get naked and climb into bed together for the first time, but then discover that they have no idea about what to do next. So Pasquale phones his mother for advice.

"Justa hold her reala tight, give her lotsa kisses and let nature takea its course," his mother tells him.

Pasquale hangs up, hugs his bride and kisses her passionately, just like his mother told him, but still nothing happens. So he calls home again. This time his father answers.

> Q. What's the last thing that goes through a bug's mind when it hits your windshield?
>
> A. Its asshole.

"Jesa Christa Pasquale," he says. "Justa takea the biggest thinga you'va got and stick it ina the hairiest thinga she'sa got."

A few minutes later Pasquale phones his father again and says, "Okay, I'va shoveda my nose ina her armpit. Now what?"

A mountain lion is drinking from a stream in Banff National Park. A grizzly bear happens by and, seeing the lion in such a vulnerable position with his tail standing straight up in the air, walks up behind him and gives him a quick one in the rear.

The lion is enraged, and runs off in hot pursuit of the bear. The bear runs into a nearby campground, goes into a tent, puts on a Tilley hat, grabs a copy of the *Calgary Herald* and sits down in a chair and pretends to be reading.

The mountain lion runs into the campground, finds the bear hiding in the tent and says, "Did you happen to see a grizzly bear come by here?"

The bear replies, "You mean the one that buggered the mountain lion when he wasn't looking?"

The mountain lion says, "What! You mean it's in the newspapers already?"

A Newfie is necking with his girlfriend in his car.

"You wanna get in the backseat?" she says.

"No goddamn way," replies the Newfie. "I wanna stay up here with you."

Father Murphy has diarrhea real bad. Worse, it is his turn to hear confessions, and he is sitting in the confessional doubled over in pain. Fearing that he is about to have an accident, the old priest opens his door and summons the church janitor to take over for him while he runs to the can.

Q. What is an innuendo?

A. An Italian suppository.

"How will I know what penance to give out?" asks the janitor.

"No problem," replies the priest. "I've got a penance chart taped to the wall in my box. Just listen to the confessions and consult the chart."

The janitor agrees to help and enters the confession box.

The first confession was easy. "Forgive me, Father, for I have sinned," says a young male voice on the other side of the partition.

"What did you do?" asks the janitor.

"I had impure thoughts about my sister," says the voice.

The janitor looks at the chart, and finds "Impure Thoughts" and tells the young man to say three Hail Marys.

The second confession is more serious. A young man tells the janitor that he has touched his girlfriend's breasts. Again, the janitor consults the chart, finds an "Improper Touching" listing, and tells the man to say five Hail Marys.

The third confessioner is a young girl who says, "Forgive me, Father, for I have committed a terrible sin; I had sex with my boyfriend!"

The janitor thinks this must surely be a biggie and furiously scans the chart up and down, but nowhere can he find the penance for having sex out of wedlock. Desperate for an answer, he opens his door and runs over to a group of altar boys and says, "Hey guys, you gotta help me, what does Father Murphy give for sex?"

The altar boys all start giggling and then reply in unison, "Two Mars bars and a Coca Cola!"

A woman goes to see a top psychiatrist in downtown Vancouver. She says, "I think I'm a nymphomaniac, can you help me?"

The psychiatrist replies, "Yes, I think I can, but I charge $150 per hour."

The woman asks, "How much for all night?"

A hoser wakes up one morning and notices that he has numerous ugly sores up and down his right arm. He goes to the doctor who examines them and asks him what he does for a living.

"I work in the circus," the hoser says proudly. "I'm a veterinarian's assistant. I give enemas to constipated elephants."

The hoser looks down at his diseased arm and adds, "Sometimes my job requires me to shove my arm all the way up an elephant's rectum to clean out its colon."

"Well, that certainly explains the sores on your arm," says the doctor. "Tell me, have you ever considered another line of work?"

"What!" says the hoser. "Are you crazy? Give up show business?"

Linda tells her husband Victor that she would like to get breast implants.

"We can't afford them," says Victor. "Why don't you just try rubbing wads of toilet paper up and down between your boobs?"

"Do you think that will make them bigger?" replies Linda.

"Well," says Victor, "it seems to have worked on your ass."

A yuppie couple moves from the city to rural Ontario. One day they see a farmer hauling a load of manure past their house.

"What are you going to do with all that?" asks the woman.

"I'm going to put it on my strawberries," replies the farmer.

Q. What did the veterinarian say to the dog who kept licking his balls?

A. "Thanks."

"Oh, really?" says the woman. "We put whipped cream on ours."

A widow in Windsor puts a death notice in the local newspaper announcing that her husband died of gonorrhea.

At the funeral, her brother-in-law challenges her, saying, "Ol' Jack died of diarrhea, why did you put gonorrhea in the notice?"

"I did it out of respect," replies the widow. "I'd like him to be remembered as a great lover rather than the big shit that he was."

Two couples are on a golf course. One of the women steps up to her ball and whacks it straight down the fairway and into a sand trap.

"Dammit!" she yells. "And I just had a f**king lesson!"

The other woman leans over to her husband and whispers, "It might have been better if she'd taken a golf lesson."

A burly truck driver picks up two gay hitch-hikers on the Trans-Canada Highway.

As they ride along, one of the gays says, "Excuse me, but I have to fart."

He then leans over and emits a weak phhhtt sound.

A few minutes later, the second gay says, "I think I have to fart as well," and he, too lets out a weak phhhtt sound.

"Fer Chrissakes," says the truck driver. "You guys can't even fart like a man."

He then leans over on one cheek and lets an enormous ripper.

The two gays start giggling. "My goodness!" says one. "You're what we would call a real virgin."

A middle-aged guy in Halifax goes to the doctor and tells him that after 30 years of marriage to the same woman, he can't get an erection anymore. The doctor tells him to bring his wife with him for his next appointment.

A week later the guy returns with his wife. The doctor tells her to go into his examination room and to take off all of her clothes. She follows his instructions, and when the doctor enters the room, he walks around her and checks her over from all angles.

> Q. What's the definition of foreplay in rural New Brunswick?
> A. "Get in the truck, bitch."

He then returns to the husband and says, "You have nothing to worry about. There's nothing wrong with you."

"How can you be so certain?" asks the husband.

The doctor replies, "She doesn't give me a hard-on either."

"Do you and the wife ever do it doggie style?" says the bartender to a hoser.

"Naw," replies the hoser. "My old lady is more into what I would call 'doggie tricks.'"

"Hey," says the bartender, "that sounds kinda kinky."

"Not really," says the hoser. "You see, whenever I make a move on her, she just rolls over and plays dead."

A Newfie is on holiday in Florida, and he is having trouble meeting women on the beach. He asks an American friend for advice. He tells the Newfie that he has to try to look cool, and advises him to wear dark sunglasses and to buy the smallest Speedo swimsuit he can find. And if he really wants to get the attention of the ladies, his American friend advises him to stuff a banana into the Speedo. "It'll make you look like a real stud," he says.

The Newfie decides to try this and buys a tiny Speedo, stuffs a banana in it, and heads off for a day at the beach. Within an hour he's back at the hotel.

> Q. What has 10 legs and an I.Q. of 80?
>
> A. Five hosers watching a hockey game.

"It didn't work," he tells his friend. "It was embarrassing, humiliating even. They all pointed and laughed at me as I walked along the beach."

The American guy looks down and says. "You doofus! You're supposed to put the banana down the front."

Bernice is an 88-year-old Victoria woman who still has her driver's licence, even though she can barely see over the steering wheel. She is driving down Blanchard Street one day with her friend Edna, when suddenly, to Edna's horror, Bernice drives through a red light.

A few blocks later, Bernice drives through a second red light, and then a third one.

> Q. How many Torontonians does it take to change a lightbulb?
>
> A. None. Because the whole world revolves around Toronto, residents there need only hold a lightbulb up to a socket. It will screw in by itself.

Finally, Edna can't take it any more, and as they are approaching another intersection she screams, "Jesus Christ, Bernice! Don't you see that you've driven through three red lights?"

"Huh?" replies Bernice. "Am I driving?"

Surjit and Parminder are two Sikhs who emigrate from India to Canada with their families. Upon their arrival, the two old friends make a bet as to which one of them will most quickly adapt to the Canadian way of life within a year.

Twelve months later, the two men meet for lunch to compare notes.

"I'm proud to say that I now feel and think like a Canadian," says Surjit. "My family has completely integrated into Canadian society. I eat lunch every day here at Tim Hortons, my son plays hockey, my wife goes to the curling rink three times a week, and I barbeque all our meals on our back deck. How about you?"

Parminder replies, "Piss off, raghead."

Jill discovers that she is pregnant and is so excited about it that she decides to phone all of her friends one evening to tell them her news. It is nearly midnight when she makes the last call to her oldest friend Gina in Halifax.

Did you hear about the dyslexic pimp who bought a warehouse?

Or the dyslexic Satanist who sold his soul to Santa?

Or the dyslexic hoser who went into a bra?

"I can't believe that I have a person inside me right now," says Jill.

"So do I," replies Gina. "Can I call you back tomorrow?"

A senile old lady who lives in a Sudbury nursing home flips out one day. She goes into her room, takes off all her clothes, and ties a bed sheet around her neck like a cape. She then bursts out of her door into the corridor stark naked and yells, "SUPER PUSSY!"

She runs down the hall, stopping in front of everyone she meets to expose herself and yells, "SUPER PUSSY!"

Before the nurses can stop her, she goes up to an old guy sitting in his wheelchair, stands in front of him and again yells, "SUPER PUSSY!"

The old guy looks up, stares at the grizzled old lady's naked body, and replies, "I think I'll have the soup!"

Orznick has a terrible argument with his girl-friend. Feeling remorseful, he decides to try to patch things up by taking her a large bouquet of flowers.

When she opens her door and sees him standing there with the flowers she says, "Oh, that's great. You bring me a bunch of flowers, so I guess you expect me to spend the rest of the evening lying flat on my back with my legs up in the air."

"No," replies Orznick, "I thought you'd just put them in a vase."

A middle-aged guy and his new girlfriend are necking in the back row of a movie theatre in Saskatoon. Suddenly the guy's toupee slips off and falls on the woman's lap. As he is feeling around in the dark to find it, his hand accidentally slips up her leg and under her skirt.

"That's it, you've got it!" she whispers in his ear. "Oh my God, you've really got it!"

"No, I haven't," says the guy.

"Oh yes, I'm pretty sure you have," squeals the woman with delight.

"It can't be," says the guy. "I part my hair on the side."

A photographer sets up an old-fashioned wooden view camera on a Vancouver Island beach. He asks two pretty young British tourists named Bertha and Gillian if they will pose for him in their bikinis. They agree, and the photographer goes behind the camera and throws a black cloth over his head.

"Wot's he doing under there?" asks Gillian.

"I think he's trying to focus," replies Bertha.

"Really?" says Gillian. "Both of us?"

A bear is taking a dump in Banff National Park. As he squats down behind a bush, he sees a rabbit who is also taking a dump beside him.

"Do you have trouble with shit sticking to your fur?" the bear asks.

"No, I don't," the rabbit replies.

So the bear picks up the rabbit and wipes his butt with him.

A very rich Canadian bachelor is in love with three women and can't decide which one he should marry. So he decides to give each of them $100,000 to see how well they handle money.

Three months later, he asks each of them what they did with their $100,000.

The first woman proudly tells him that she invested her money in the Toronto Stock Exchange and that her portfolio had increased in value by 50 percent.

The second woman explains that she set up a trust fund with her money and that it will ultimately grow and provide an endless source of funding for one of the young bachelor's favourite charities.

Q. Why do deaf people need two hands to masturbate?

A. One hand to do it, and the other to sign the moans.

The third woman explains that she used her money as a down payment on a resort condominium on the young bachelor's favourite Caribbean island, where they could escape Canada's cold winters and vacation in luxury for the rest of their lives.

So, in the end, which one of the women did the rich young bachelor ask to marry him?

The one with the biggest boobs, of course!

An Alzheimer's patient walks up to a woman in a Victoria bar and says: "Tell me, do I come here often?"

Why Beer Is Better Than Religion

- You can prove that beer exists.

- No one has ever been hanged, tortured or burned at the stake over his or her brand of beer.

- No country has ever gone to war over beer.

- No one forces beer on minors who are unable to think for themselves.

- You don't have to wait 2000 years for a second beer.

- Once someone gets a beer, they usually don't go door to door trying to force it upon others.

- Few people ever get killed for not drinking beer.

- A six-pack of religion won't quench your thirst.

- Beer does not dictate how you may have sex or with whom.

- Once you've paid for your beer, you're not expected to keep making contributions to the brewery.

- You can change your brand of beer anytime and never worry about arguing with friends or family about your decision.

Why Religion Is Better Than Beer

- Religion won't give you a hangover.

- Too much religion won't cause vomiting.

- Yelling "Oh, God! Oh, God!" in church is more fun than saying it over and over at home while your head is in the toilet.

- You never have to worry about getting religion stains on your clothing.

- There's almost no chance of waking up naked in bed with an unattractive stranger after taking in too much religion.

A Newfie takes a large Thermos bottle into Tim Hortons. He asks the clerk how many cups of coffee it will hold.

"That looks like a six-cup Thermos," replies the clerk.

The Newfie guy says, "Okay, fill 'er up. I want three double-doubles, two black, and one with two sugars."

A Mother Superior in Québec calls her nuns together one day and announces, "We have a case of gonorrhea in the convent."

"Thank God!" says one of the nuns. "I'm really getting sick of that cheap Chardonnay."

A blind man with a guide dog is walking along West Georgia Street in Vancouver. He comes to an intersection and the dog stops, so the man stands still. As they wait for the light to change, the dog raises a hind leg and pees all over the blind man's pant leg and shoes. The blind man then reaches into his pocket and takes out a biscuit and gives it to the dog.

Just then a professional dog trainer happens to walk by and observes what the blind man did. "Excuse me, sir," the trainer says. "That dog just peed all over your clothes. If you reward him for that behaviour, he'll just keep doing it again and again."

"I know that," says the blind man. "I was just trying to find out which end is his head so I can kick him in the balls."

Hymie and Solly are walking down the street in Montréal one afternoon when they pass a Catholic church. A sign on the door reads "Special Sale— One Week Only: Convert to Catholicism and Receive $100 Cash!"

"Look, Hymie," says Solly. "We can each earn $100 just by changing our religion."

"Dammit," says Hymie, "surely you could never betray your proud Jewish heritage for a lousy $100."

"But $100 is a lot of money," says Solly as he goes into the church. "I'll be back in a minute."

Half an hour later, Solly returns.

"So Solly," says Hymie, "did you get your $100?"

"That's the problem with you Jews," replies Solly, "everything comes down to money, money, money."

Bertha, a grossly overweight middle-aged woman, is upset because she has not had a boyfriend or been on a date or even had sex for over 10 years. She decides to visit a therapist.

Her family doctor refers her to Dr. Chong, a well-known Vancouver sex therapist who specializes in female sexual disorders.

"Okay, take off all your crose," says Dr. Chong.

Bertha strips down as instructed and stands in front of the doctor completely naked.

"Now," say Dr. Chong, "get down on fwoor and craw reery, reery fass to odder side of room."

Bertha follows his instructions.

"Okay, now craw reery, reery fass back to me," says the doctor.

She does what the doctor orders.

Dr. Chong slowly shakes his head and says: "Your probrem vewy bad. You haf Ed Zachary disease. Worse case I ever see. That why you not haf dates or sex."

"Oh my God," replies Bertha, "what is Ed Zach-ary disease?"

"Ed Zachary disease velly serious," says Dr. Chong. "Occurs when your face rook ed zachary rike your butt."

A poor Saskatchewan farmer named Orville is lying on his deathbed. He beckons his wife, Sophie, to come to his side to talk to him as he desperately gasps his last breaths.

"You're an amazing woman, Sophie," says Orville. "You were at my side through those early years when we had no money and almost lost the farm when we couldn't make our mortgage payments."

Sophie sobs.

"You were there for me through those terrible droughts when I lost all my crops," he adds.

Sophie sobs some more.

"You were there when I fell into the thresher and lost both my legs," Orville adds. "And you were by my side again when the whole place almost got washed away in the flood back in '76."

Sophie starts sobbing uncontrollably.

"And now here you are again by my side as I lie on my deathbed," says Orville.

Sophie bursts into tears.

"You know, Sophie," says Orville, "I've been thinking..."

"Yes, my dear," sobs Sophie.

"I've been thinking about this a lot," gasps Orville, as he is about to expire. "Sophie, you're nothing but a goddamned jinx."

A Newfie couple with six kids moves to Toronto and moves in next door to a couple from Jamaica with four kids.

One day, while the two young mothers are watching their children playing in their backyards, the Newfie woman turns to the Jamaican and says, "You know it's amazing, I've got six kids and they all turned out white and homely as hell, but you've only got four kids and every one of them came out black and cute as hell. What's your secret?"

The Jamaican woman has never met a Newfie before and is mystified by the dumb question. So she decides to string her along. "Well," she says, "it all depends on the size of your husband's penis."

"How so?" asks the Newfie woman.

"Is your husband's dick at least 10 inches long?" asks the Jamaican.

"Oh, no!" replies the Newfie. "It's not nearly that big."

"Alright, that's okay," replies the Jamaican, "but is it at least two inches thick?"

"Geez, I don't think so," says the Newfie.

"Well, then, there's your problem, sister," says the Jamaican. "You're letting in too much light."

You Know You're a Hoser If...

- You think that a "sanitary belt" means drinking out of a clean glass.

- You've been married three times and you still have the same in-laws.

- You own four pairs of skates but only one pair of shoes.

- You have 10 recipes for cooking beaver tail, and three for baking bulrushes.

- You go to a dentist twice a year—once for each tooth.

- You enjoy driving in winter more than any other season because you like the way the roads appear to be much smoother when the potholes are filled with snow.

- You reject all beer with less than 6 percent alcohol content and claim that it is "only good for medicinal purposes" or "only suitable for children and the elderly."

- You know which leaves in a forest make the best toilet paper.

- You think the phrase "loading the dishwasher" means getting your old lady drunk.

- You have more appliances on your front lawn than you do in your kitchen.

- You observe that when a tornado rips through your house and destroys it, the insurance adjustor assesses the total cost of the damage at only $700.

- You think that when someone tells you that a woman is "out of your league," they just mean that she bowls on a different night.

A Nova Scotia fisherman is walking on the beach one day when he spies a bottle lying in the sand. He picks it up, wipes it off and, POOF!, a genie pops out and grants him one wish.

"I want to be rock hard and get plenty of ass for the rest of my life," the fisherman says.

The genie goes POOF! again…and turns the guy into a toilet.

Two Newfies, Garge and Willie, get roaring drunk and stagger into a St. John's brothel. The madam sees how pissed they both are and sends them upstairs to two rooms she keeps especially for drunks. Each room has a life-sized inflatable woman dummy on the bed.

The next morning the two men sober up in a nearby coffee shop and talk about their big night in the whorehouse.

"I tink the woman I was wit was dead," says Garge.

"Why do you say that?" asks Willie.

"She never moaned or groaned or nothin'," replies Garge. "She just lay there like a beached whale."

"I tink mine was a witch," replies Willie.

"Migod, what makes you tink that?" asks Garge.

"Well, I was on top doin' me lovin's," says Willie, "an' I wasn't gettin' much response, so I tought I'd trys out me new false teeth. So I bit one of her boobs, but I still got no response."

> Q. What's the difference between an ex-wife and a catfish?
>
> A. One is a scum-sucking bottom-feeder, and the other is a fish.

"But what makes you tink she was a witch?" asks Garge.

"'Cause when I bit her a second time, she farted real loud...and den she flew out de window."

Three old guys are sitting in their rocking chairs in a Victoria nursing home. One of them says, "Man, I'd give a $100 to have a good pee."

The guy next to him says, "Christ, I'd pay twice that if I could just work up a decent dump."

The third guy says, "Every morning at 7:00 AM I pee like a racehorse, and by 7:30, regular as clockwork, I lay a cable that a grizzly bear would be proud of."

The other two guys nod admiringly.

"The problem is," he adds, "I seldom wake up before 10 o'clock."

A little old lady in Winnipeg goes into her bank one day and asks to see the manager. She explains to the teller that she would like to deposit a very large amount of money and that she would only feel confident speaking directly to the manager.

> Great Canadian bumper sticker: Be fair. Be Canadian. Tolerate crime.

The teller telephones the manager and a few minutes later he appears and escorts the old lady into his office.

"How much would you like to deposit?" asks the bank manager.

"I've got $100,000 in cash, right here in my purse," says the old lady, who then proceeds to dump the money on the man's desk.

"Where did you get all this money?" asks the bank manager.

"I make bets," replies the old lady.

"Bets?" says the bank manager. "What kind of bets?"

"Well," says the old lady, "I'll give you an example. Suppose I bet you $10,000 that your testicles are square. Would you take my bet?"

"That's a dumb bet," says the bank manager. "You'll lose."

"So will you take my bet then?" asks the old lady.

"Sure," says the bank manager. "I'll bet you $10,000 that my testicles are not square."

"Are you willing to show them to me to prove it?" asks the old lady.

"Of course," replies the bank manager, thinking this is a great way to make a quick 10 grand and teach the old lady a lesson.

"Okay," says the old lady. "But since there is a large sum of money involved, I'd like to have my lawyer here with me as a witness. Is that okay with you?"

The bank manager agrees to meet with the old lady and her lawyer at 10:00 AM the next morning. And, as a precaution, when he goes home that night, he spends a long time in front of a mirror checking his testicles. He examines them from every angle to make sure that there is absolutely no way that anyone could claim that his balls are square. He is confident that it is impossible for him to lose the bet.

> Q. Why does a Canadian cross the road?
>
> A. To get to the middle.

The next morning at 10:00 AM sharp, the little old lady appears in the bank manager's office with her lawyer. She once again repeats her bet: "Ten thousand dollars says my bank manager's testicles are square!"

She then asks the manager to drop his pants. She examines his testicles closely and then asks if she can feel them. The bank manager agrees, and with a great sense of glee, the old lady reaches out and cradles both of his balls in the palm of her hand.

Watching this, the old lady's lawyer suddenly turns white and tears begin to run down his cheeks.

"What the hell is the matter with your lawyer?" asks the bank manager.

Q. How can Jewish people tell if their rabbi is dyslexic?

A. He begins every sentence of his sermon with the word "Yo."

"Oh, nothing really," says the old lady. "Except that I bet him $25,000 that at 10:00 AM this morning I'd have my bank manager's balls in the palm of my hand."

Did you hear about the Newfie whose wife had triplets?

Her husband got out his gun and went looking for the other two guys.

A guy goes to the Canadian Patent Office to register his latest invention.

"I'm here to register my revolutionary folding bottle," says the man. "I call it a fottle."

"That's a stupid name," says the clerk behind the counter.

"Well, then you won't like the name of the folding carton I've invented, either," says the inventor. "I call a farton."

"You can't use a name like that; it's not allowed in Canada," replies the clerk.

Q. How should you begin every ethnic joke you tell in Canada?

A. By looking over both shoulders.

"Oh yeah?" says the inventor. "Then I'll bet you're not going to like the name I've chosen for my folding bucket."

A guy at the back of a crowded elevator in Toronto's Royal York Hotel shouts out to a woman standing next to the control panel, "Ballroom, please!"

"Oh, I'm sorry, sir!" she shouts back, "I didn't know we were crowding you."

A hoser goes up to a young nurse-receptionist at a walk-in clinic in Flin Flon and says, "I've got a problem with my dick."

"I'm sorry, sir, but you can't use language like that in here," says the red-faced nurse. "If you want to see a doctor, please leave and then come back in and just tell me you have a problem with your nose or something."

The hoser leaves and comes back a few minutes later and says to the nurse, "I've got a problem with my nose."

"That's much better!" says the nurse with a big smile. "And what's wrong with it, sir?"

The hoser replies, "I can't get it hard any more, and I can't pee with it."

Two Canadian social workers are walking through Vancouver's notorious downtown east side. They stumble upon a woman lying on the pavement in a pool of blood. She calls out to them, "Help me! Help me! Someone beat me up and raped me and then stole all my money."

The social workers ignore the woman. As they walk past her, one says to the other, "You know, the guy who assaulted that woman really needs help."

> Did you hear about the gay midget who came out of his cupboard?

A Newfie dies in a house fire and his body is burned beyond recognition. His remains are taken to an outport morgue where the locals tell the coroner that they think the deceased is a guy named Gord, but they are not certain.

The coroner calls in two guys, Darryl and Garge, who are known to be Gord's best pals, to see if they can identify the body. They look at the charred remains and ask the coroner to turn the body over.

"Nope," says Garge after examining the corpse. "That ain't Gord."

"No, it sure ain't," adds Darryl.

"How do you know for sure?" asks the coroner.

"Ol' Gord has two assholes," says Garge. "This guy's only got one."

"Are you sure Gord has two rectums?" asks the coroner. "That would be very unusual."

"Yup," says Darryl. "Everyone 'round here knows about it, too."

> Q. What's the definition of a Canadian?
> A. An unarmed American with health care.

"That's right," says Garge. "Whenever the three of us went into town, people would say, 'Here comes ol' Gord with them two assholes!'"

A Calgary man gets royally pissed in a bar and decides to go to a massage parlour. He talks to a guy in the bar who tells him about a great massage parlour he visits that is located at 32 Northwest 17th Street. The drunk guy decides to try it, but by mistake, he tells the taxi driver to take him to 23 Northwest 71st Street, which turns out to be the office of a podiatrist.

He stumbles up to the reception desk, and the nurse says, "Go behind the curtain, lie down on the table and stick it out through the hole."

The drunk guy goes behind the curtain and, thinking that he's in a massage parlour, sticks his penis out through the curtain hole. When the nurse sees the organ protruding from the curtain she shrieks, "Jesus Christ! That's not a foot!"

"Oh," replies the drunk, "I didn't know you had a minimum."

A midget in New Brunswick tells her gynecologist that every time it snows she gets a terrible pain in her crotch. The doctor examines her and tells her that he cannot see anything abnormal. He then instructs her to come to his office the next time there is a major snowfall so that he can examine her while she is experiencing the pain.

A few days later a terrible snowstorm blankets the Maritimes, and when the woman is out walking in it, she suddenly experiences the same sharp pain in her crotch. She runs over to the doctor's office. He rushes her into his examination room and gives her a complete gynecological exam.

"I think I've found your problem," he says. "And I think I can fix it for you... there, that should do it...all done. Now stand up and tell me if that feels better."

> Q. What's the difference between a dog and a fox?
>
> A. About four beers.

The woman jumps down to the floor. "That feels great," she says. "What did you do?"

"Nothing to it," replies the doctor, "I just cut three inches off the tops of your galoshes."

Two guys are out walking their dogs in down-town Ottawa. They pass a restaurant and one says to the other, "Let's stop for a coffee."

"What will we do with our dogs?" says the other guy.

"No problem," says the first guy. "Just do what I do. Follow me."

So the first guy puts on a pair of dark sunglasses and takes his dog into the restaurant. A waiter stops him and says, "I'm sorry, sir, but you can't bring your dog in here. It's against the law."

"Excuse me," replies the guy, "can't you see that I am blind? This is a seeing-eye dog."

Q. What's a hoser's idea of foreplay?
A. Brushing his teeth.

"Since when did bulldogs become trained as seeing-eye dogs?" asks the waiter.

"Oh, they've been training them for us blind folk for years," replies the man. "They're great."

So the waiter reluctantly seats the guy with his dog.

The second dog owner watches all of this from outside of the restaurant and decides to try his luck as well. He puts on sunglasses and takes his dog in and is stopped by the same waiter, who says, "I'm sorry, sir, but no dogs are allowed in the restaurant."

"But I'm blind," says the man. "This is a seeing-eye dog."

"Wait a minute," replies the waiter. "You're not going to tell me that you're using a Chihuahua as a seeing-eye dog."

Thinking fast, the guy replies, "What? You mean they gave me a damn Chihuahua?"

A woman goes into a BMW dealership in Vancouver and wanders through the showroom looking at all the cars. When she sees one she likes, she bends down to open a door and accidentally lets out an enormous fart.

"Excuse me!" she says to the salesman.

The salesman laughs and replies, "If you farted just touching it, you're gonna shit your pants when you hear how much it costs."

> Q. What did one saggy boob say to the other saggy boob?
>
> A. If we don't get some support, people are going to think we're nuts.

A hoser tells his doctor that his wife is pregnant even though he hasn't had sex with her in over a year.

"How can this happen?" he asks his doctor.

"It's what we in the medical profession call a grudge pregnancy," replies the doctor.

"What's a grudge pregnancy?" asks the hoser.

"Simply put," says the doctor, "somebody's had it in for you."

"What part of a woman is a 'yet'?" Clyde asks his friend Rex.

"I don't know," replies Rex. "Why do you ask?"

"I read in the *Globe and Mail* that another woman got shot in Toronto," says Clyde, "and the doctors haven't been able to get the bullet out of her yet."

A middle-aged married guy is sitting at the roulette table in Casino Niagara when a hot-looking young hooker sits down beside him. They strike up a conversation, and when the hooker eventually propositions him, out of curiosity he asks her how much she charges.

"Two hundred dollars an hour," she replies proudly.

"Wow," says the guy. "I'd never spend that much to get laid."

"So," says the hooker, "how much would you spend?"

"Fifty bucks, tops," he replies.

"Well, so long," says the hooker. "You won't get much action in this town for $50."

Later that evening, the guy is strolling back to his hotel room with his wife when he passes the same hooker in the hall. She leans over and whispers in his ear, "See what I mean? That's what you get for $50 in Niagara Falls."

In Alberta, a woman's truck breaks down on a remote prairie road. A Native guy who happens to be passing by on a horse offers to give her a ride to the nearest gas station. The woman climbs on and sits behind him.

As they ride along, every few minutes the Native guy hollers "YAHOO!" at the top of his lungs. Eventually they reach the gas station, and the woman climbs down off the horse.

"Why is that guy so excited?" asks the gas station attendant.

"I dunno," replies the woman. "But it started when I reached around him and grabbed his saddle horn so I wouldn't fall off."

"Lady, I've got news for you," says the attendant. "That ain't no saddle horn you was holdin'. That Native guy was ridin' bareback!"

A Newfie working in a fish plant accidentally cuts off all his fingers with a saw. He is rushed to a hospital in St. John's, where the doctor looks at his injury and tells him there is a good chance that he may be able to re-attach the fingers.

"But I didn't bring 'em wit me," says the Newfie.

"Why not?" asks the doctor.

"Lord tunderin' Jaysus!" replies the Newfie. "How de hell was I supposed to pick 'em up?"

A middle-aged married couple is driving along the Trans-Canada Highway when a Mountie pulls them over. "You were doing 150 kilometres in a 100 zone," says the Mountie to the husband.

"I'm sorry, Officer, but I was just poking along doing the speed limit, and I had to speed up for a second to pass a truck," replies the guy.

The wife leans over and interrupts, "You're lying. You never went slower than 150 since we left home."

"SHADDUP, damn ya!" screams the husband.

"And I see you haven't got your seat belt buckled, sir," says the Mountie.

"I just undid it when you stopped me," replies the husband, "so I could get out my licence for you."

"Bullshit!" says the wife. "You never buckle it up."

The husband then turns to the wife and screams, "WILL YOU PLEASE SHUT YOUR BIG MOUTH AND LET ME HANDLE THIS MY WAY!"

"Is he always this abrasive with you?" the Mountie asks the wife.

"No, sir," she replies. "Only when he's really drunk."

A kid from one of Scarborough's toughest housing projects wins a scholarship at the University of Toronto.

On his first day on campus, he walks up to an elderly professor and says, "Hey man, can ya tell me where the library is at?"

The old professor looks down his nose at the young man and replies, "At the University of Toronto, young man, we never end a sentence with a preposition."

The kid thinks for a moment and replies, "Okay, where's the library at, asshole?"

A woman goes into Canadian Tire and tells the clerk that she is looking for a present for her nephew. "How much is that hockey stick?" she asks the young man.

"Eighty-nine dollars," replies the clerk.

Q. Why do women have smaller feet than men?

A. So they can stand closer to the sink.

"That's too much," says the woman. "How much is that baseball bat?"

"Forty-nine ninety-five," says the clerk.

"I'll take it," says the woman.

"Do you wanna ball for the bat?" asks the clerk.

"No," says the woman. "But I'll blow you for the hockey stick."

A homeless guy is going door to door begging for money in Toronto's posh Rosedale neighbourhood.

He knocks on the door of a snotty, young yuppie woman who tells him that she does not believe in giving people money for nothing. However, she says that she will gladly pay him $50 if he will do a small job for her.

"Take this can of paint," she says, "and go behind my house and paint my porch."

The guy agrees, takes the can of paint and goes around to the back of the house.

Two hours later he knocks on the front door and tells the woman that he has finished the job. She gives him the $50. As he turns to leave he says to her, "By the way, that's not a Porsche you've got back there, it's a Mercedes."

> Q. What's the creed of the Canadian Bar Association?
>
> A. A man is innocent until proven broke.

An RCMP constable stops a woman who is driving erratically along a highway. He smells alcohol on her breath so he tells her that she must take a Breathalyzer test. She blows into the machine and waits while the Mountie takes it back to his car for analysis.

A few minutes later he returns and says, "It looks like you've had a couple of stiff ones."

"Wow," replies the woman. "You mean your machine shows that, too?"

Two old Newfies, Hamish and Rex, are talking in a bar.

"So what's this newfangled ting the cops call a Breathalyzer?" asks Rex.

"I tink it's jus' a bag that tells you how much you've had to drink," says Hamish.

"Jaysus, Mary and Joseph," says Rex, "I married one o' those years ago."

Larry wants to get his much younger wife pregnant, so he goes to his doctor to have a sperm count test. The doctor gives him a specimen cup and tells him to take it home, fill it and return it the next day.

Larry shows up the next day with the specimen cup, still empty, and with the lid still on it.

"I've got a real problem," he says to his doctor. "I tried my right hand, and got nowhere. Then my left hand...nothing. My wife tried with her right hand...still nothing. Her left hand...no luck either. She even tried putting it in her mouth...still nothing.

"Then my teenaged daughter tried: right hand, left hand, her mouth...still nothing."

"Wait a minute," says the doctor. "You mean you asked your own daughter to..."

"Yeah," says Larry, "none of us could get the lid off the specimen cup!"

In rural Alberta, a midget with a terrible speech impediment wants to buy a horse. He sees an ad in the *Calgary Herald* for one and phones the owner and arranges an appointment to see it.

"Thath a nith lookin' north you've got there, mithter," says the midget when he sees the horse. "Isth it a male north or a female north?"

"It's a female," says the owner.

"Asth you can snee, I'm kinda snort," says the midget. "Can you liff me up so I can thsee her mouff?"

The guy lifts him up, and he looks in the horse's mouth.

"Thath a really nith mouff," says the midget. "Can you liff me up again so I can thsee her earsth?"

The owner grudgingly lifts the little person up so he can examine the horse's ears.

"Themsth really nith earsth," says the midget. "Can you liff me up one more time to thsee her eyesth?"

The owner is really getting peeved lifting this guy up and down, but he does it anyway in the hope that the midget will buy the horse.

"Nith goddamn eyesth," says the midget. "Now I needth to thsee her twat."

This time the owner lifts the midget up and forcefully shoves his head right into the horse's vagina. The little person struggles for several moments and eventually manages to pull his head out and wipe his brow. When he regains his composure, he says, "Perhapth you misthundersthood me, what I meanth was, I'd like to thsee her run."

A nurse goes up to an overworked doctor in a Toronto hospital and asks him what he is doing.

"I'm trying to write a prescription," says the doctor.

"With your thermometer?" replies the nurse.

"Dammit," says the doctor. "Some asshole has my pen!"

Two hosers are getting drunk in a bar. One of them suddenly throws up all over himself.

"My wife will kill me when she finds out I got so drunk that I puked on my best plaid shirt," he says.

> Q. What's scarier than a pit bull terrier with AIDS?
> A. The guy who gave it to him.

"I've got an idea," says his friend. "Just put $10 in your shirt pocket, and tell her someone threw up on you and gave you money for dry cleaning."

So the hoser puts a $10 bill in his pocket, leaves the bar and staggers home.

"What the hell happened to you?" says his wife, looking at the stain on his shirt.

"Some asshole puked on me," he says, "and then shoved 10 bucks in my pocket for the cost of cleaning my shirt."

"So how come you've got $20 in your pocket?" asks the wife.

"Oh yeah, I forgot," replies the hoser. "He peed in my pants, too."

Two old Vancouver hookers are having a drink after work and comparing notes.

Q. Why do so many Polish names end with "ski"?

A. Because Polish Canadians can't spell "toboggan."

"This guy comes up to me on Howe Street last night and asks me, 'How much?'" says one hooker. "So I tell him $100. He says he has only $40. I tell him that I can't do anything for that much. So then he stares me straight in the eye, reaches into his pants and pulls out the biggest one I have ever seen!"

"So what did you do?" asks the second hooker.

The first one replies, "I loaned him $60."

Two old guys are sitting on a bench in Victoria's Beacon Hill Park watching a bulldog licking his balls. One old guy turns to the other and says, "You know, all my life I've wished that I could do that."

The other guy replies, "Well, I think you better pet him first—he looks mean as hell."

A drunken hoser is staggering around downtown Red Deer late at night with a key in his hand. A Mountie stops him and asks him if he is okay.

"Some bastard stole my car," says the drunk.

"Where did you last see it?" asks the Mountie.

"At the end of this key," says the drunk, looking down at his hand.

The Mountie takes a closer look at the dishevelled man and says, "Are you aware that your fly is undone and that you are hanging out of your pants?"

"Goddamn it!" says the drunk, looking down at himself. "He's taken my girlfriend, too!"

A young boy with no arms or legs is sunbathing on a Prince Edward Island beach. An attractive young woman approaches and, feeling sorry for him, bends down and whispers, "Have you ever been hugged before, young man?"

"No, I haven't," replies the boy.

So she gives him a big hug and continues on her way.

A while later, a second woman walks by and she, too, feels sorry for the young man and bends down and says to him, "Have you ever been kissed before?"

"No, I haven't," says the boy, who by then is thinking that this is the best day of his life.

So she gives him a long, warm kiss on the mouth and walks on.

Later in the afternoon, yet another woman approaches and says, "Hey, kid, have you ever been screwed before?"

"Oh, God, no I haven't," says the boy.

"Well, you are now," says the woman. "The tide is coming in."

After a Saturday evening spent drinking beer, eating chili and watching the Stanley Cup playoffs, Rita and George fall into bed. Suddenly George lets an enormous fart and yells out, "One-nothing, bottom of the first period!"

Not to be outdone, Rita then lets one rip and yells, "Game tied, one-all!"

A few minutes later, she lets another huge, eye-watering ripper and shouts, "The score is now two to one, and I'm in the lead with only seconds to go in the first period!"

Desperate to tie the score again, George curls into the fetal position and strains as hard as he can in an effort to squeeze out just one more big juicy one. But instead he soils the sheets on his side of the bed.

"What the hell was that?" asks Rita.

"Siren call marking the end of the first period!" yells George. "The teams must now switch sides!"

A Mountie stops a hoser who is swerving back and forth as he drives his pickup down a country road.

"I notice, sir, that your eyes are bloodshot," says the Mountie. "Have you been drinking at the bar back in town?"

Q. What do they call re-runs of Don Messer's *Jubilee* in Newfoundland?

A. Documentaries.

The hoser replies, "I notice that your eyes are glazed. Have you been eating at the Tim Hortons back in town?"

A doctor in Newfoundland gives a naive young woman her first gynecological examination.

When the doctor finishes examining her, he says, "You have acute vaginitis."

The Newfie girl replies, "Thank you."

A group of tough kids from a Scarborough housing project is taken on a school bus trip to visit a farm for a day. When one of the kids returns home, his father asks him what he enjoyed most about the outing.

"The thing I liked best was the f**kers," says the kid.

"What do you mean?" the horrified father asks.

"Oh," replies the kid, "the farmer called them 'effers, but we knew what he meant."

A drunk stumbles into a Catholic church in Old Montréal, sits down in a confession box and passes out. The priest hears him come in but doesn't hear him say anything, so he knocks on the wall.

The drunk wakes up and says, "I can't help you. There's no paper in this one, either."

A Mother Superior and two nuns from a convent in Niagara Falls, Ontario, go on a shopping trip across the border in Buffalo, New York. When they drive back to Canada and approach the Canada Customs kiosk at the border, the nun who is driving the car expresses concern about having to pay duty on their purchases.

Q. Where was the toothbrush invented?

A. Newfoundland. If it had been invented anywhere else it would have been called a teethbrush.

The Mother Superior says, "Don't worry about it, just show the customs official your cross."

So when the nun pulls up to the customs agent, she rolls down her window and says, "Don't you give me a hard time, you bastard. I'm not taking any crap from you. So you can just piss off right now, you asshole!"

Did you hear about the Chinese couple named Wong who emigrated to Canada and nine months later Mrs. Wong gave birth to a black baby?

The father named the kid Sum Ting Wong.

"Okay, class," says the Grade 6 teacher at a posh Rosedale private school. "Which body part increases 10 times its normal size when stimulated?"

A precocious little girl named Courtney stands up and says, "You shouldn't be asking 11-year-olds a question like that. I'm going to tell my parents what you said, and they'll get you fired."

Then little Nigel stands up. "The body part that increases by 10 times when stimulated is the pupil of the eye," he says.

"Very good, Nigel," replies the teacher.

Later that day after class, the teacher takes Courtney aside and says, "I have three things to say to you. First, you have a dirty mind. Second, you didn't do your homework. And third, one day you are going to be very, very disappointed."

Why a Hoser Prefers Beer to Women

- He knows that he can enjoy a beer every day of the month.

- He likes that he can enjoy a beer with all of his friends.

- He likes the way a beer is always wet.

- He takes comfort in the knowledge that he's always the first one to "open" a beer.

- Beer doesn't have a mother.

- If he changes beers, he won't have to pay alimony.

- When he goes into a bar, he knows he can always pick up a beer.

- If he pours a beer properly, he knows he's always guaranteed to get good head.

- When his beer goes flat, he can just throw it away.

- His beer doesn't get jealous if he grabs another one.

- Beer looks the same in the morning.

- He knows that he can't catch anything but a hangover from beer.

An old couple in Saskatoon is watching a faith healer on TV. The televangelist tells his viewers to put one hand on their television and the other hand on the part of their body that they want healed. So the old lady gets up, walks over to the TV and puts her left hand on it, and her right hand on her arthritic knee.

Then her husband gets up, walks over and puts one hand on the TV and the other on his crotch.

The old lady says, "Fer Chrissakes, Bert, he only said he can cure our ailments, not raise the dead."

A Mountie stops a driver in Newfoundland. He asks, "Have you got any I.D.?"

The Newfie replies, "'bout what?"

An Irish immigrant enters a toastmasters contest in his local Toronto bar. He wins first prize for reciting the most original toast of the evening. He says, "Here's to spending the rest of me life between the legs of me lovely wife."

He sobers up and goes home and tells his wife about his win, but to avoid offending her, he changes the wording slightly to "Here's to spending the rest of me life sitting in church beside me wife."

A few days later, his wife bumps into one of the guys her husband hangs out with at the bar. "Did you know that your husband won the toastmasters contest by reciting a verse dedicated to you?" asks the man.

"Yes," replies the wife. "Funny thing though, he's only been there twice—one time he fell asleep, and the other time I had to pull him by the ears to make him come."

A Chinese guy goes into a Vancouver Foreign Exchange office with 1000 Hong Kong dollars and walks out with 150 Canadian dollars.

A week later he goes back to the same office to exchange another 1000 Hong Kong dollars, but this time he only receives 135 Canadian dollars.

> Q. Why did God make farts smell?
>
> A. So deaf people could enjoy them, too.

"How come wrast week you give me $150, and today you onry give me $135?" he asks the clerk.

"Fluctuations," says the clerk.

The Chinese guy storms out in a huff, then turns and shouts at the clerk, "Well, fluck you Canadians, too!"

A middle-aged woman in Victoria can no longer look after her elderly mother, so she has the old lady committed to a nursing home for a trial period. She drops her mother off one afternoon and promises to come back the next day to check on her.

The next morning the nurses bathe the old lady, give her breakfast and sit her in a chair in front of a window overlooking the ocean. After a while they notice that she has slumped over to one side of her chair, so a nurse rushes over and straightens her up. A few minutes later the nurses notice that she is tilting the other way, so another nurse dashes to her assistance and gets her sitting up straight again. This goes on all morning.

Q. How do you know when you have bad gas?

A. When you fart in the bathtub, your bubbles sink.

That afternoon the daughter returns to see how her mother is settling in.

"How do you like it here?" she asks her mother. "Are they treating you well?"

"Oh fine," replies the old lady. "Except for some strange reason they won't let me fart!"

An 85-year-old guy in Kelowna goes to his doctor for a physical.

Two days later the doctor sees the old guy walking down the street with a gorgeous young girl on his arm.

"Just doin' what you told me," says the old man. "Get a hot momma and be cheerful. That's what you said."

"No," replies the doctor. "What I said was, 'you've got a heart murmur, be careful.'"

Two gay guys are standing on the dock waiting for the ferry to the Toronto Islands.

"Oh look, Kyle, here comes the ferry boat!" one of them says.

Kyle says, "Wow, I know we were well organized, but I didn't know we had our own navy."

A Newfie comes home and tells his wife that he's bought them a condominium.

"Great!" she replies. "Now I can throw away me diagram!"

A Newfie has hemorrhoids, so his doctor gives him four suppositories and tells him to come back in a couple of days.

> Q. Why did they raise the drinking age in Newfoundland to 32?
>
> A. They wanted to keep alcohol out of the schools.

The Newfie doesn't know what to do with the suppositories, so he melts them down and drinks them.

A few days later, he goes back to the doctor and tells him that the pain has worsened.

The doctor gives him four more suppositories and tells him to come back in a couple of days. The Newfie takes them home and drinks them.

When the Newfie reports back to the doctor that he's still in pain, the doctor says, "I've given you eight suppositories, what the hell are you doing with them?"

The Newfie replies, "What d'ya think I'm doin' with 'em, Doc, shovin' 'em up me arse?"

An Air Canada plane is about to crash, when suddenly a female passenger stands up and starts screaming, "If I am going to die, I want to die feeling like a woman!"

She starts peeling off all of her clothes and yells, "C'mon, are any of you guys man enough to make me feel like a woman?"

Q. How does a Newfie fisherman tell one end of a worm from the other?

A. He puts it in a bowl of flour and waits for it to fart.

So one guy stands up, strips off his shirt and says, "Here, iron this."

A Grade 3 teacher in New Brunswick is giving her students a word exercise. She calls out different letters of the alphabet and asks the students to give her a word that begins with each letter. As each letter is called, Dirty Wally raises his hand. Wally is a foul-mouthed kid more mature than his years would suggest, and the teacher knows he will try to think up a swear word for each letter she calls out so she ignores him.

Finally, the teacher comes to the letter "u." She can't think of any swear words that begin with "u," so she reluctantly allows Wally to participate. "Okay, Wally," she says, "give me a word beginning with the letter 'u.'"

"Urinate!" shouts Wally.

"All right, Wally," says the teacher. "That's very funny, but I'm sure you don't even know what that word means. Give me a sentence using the word 'urinate.'"

"That's easy," replies Wally. "Urinate—but if your boobs were a little bigger, you'd be a 10."

Q. What's the best thing about Alzheimer's disease?

A. You can hide your own Easter eggs.

Q. What's another fun thing about Alzheimer's?

A. You get to sleep with a new woman every night.

Little Nancy wakes up one morning to find that her cat has died. The dead cat is lying on its back with its legs sticking straight up in the air.

She asks her father, "Daddy, why did Muffet die with her legs up in the air like that?"

Her father consoles her by telling her that the cat died in that position to make it easier for Jesus to come down to earth and carry Muffet by its legs up to heaven.

Nancy accepts this explanation and heads off to school.

That night, Nancy runs to the door to greet her father. "Daddy, Daddy, I'm so glad you're home. Mom nearly died this afternoon...it was terrible."

Q. Why do men fart more often than women?

A. Because women don't keep quiet long enough to build up the necessary pressure.

"Migod!" says the father. "What happened?"

"When I came home from school," says Nancy, "I found her lying on the floor with her legs up in the air, just like Muffet. And then I heard her shout 'Oh Jesus, I'm coming!' If it hadn't been for the mailman holding her down, I think she would have been a goner, Daddy."

An old guy goes to the doctor and complains that he has lost his hearing in one ear.

The doctor looks in the guy's ear and says, "Here's your problem, you've got a suppository stuck in your ear."

"Great!" replies the old man. "Now I know where I put my hearing aid."

Newfie Dictionary of Computer Terminology

LOG ON—Makin' da wood stove hotter.

LOG OFF—Don't add no more wood.

DOWNLOAD—Gettin' da firewood offa da truck.

MEGA HERTZ—How you feel after unloadin' da firewood.

HARD DRIVE—Gettin' home in da winter time.

INTERNET—Where da fish get caught.

NETSCAPE—When yer fish gets outta yer net.

PROMPT—What da mail ain't in da winter time.

WINDOWS—What to shut when it's cold.

SCREEN—What to shut when it's black fly season.

BYTE—What dem freakin' flys do.

BIT—What dem freakin' flys did.

CHIP—What ya eat in fronta da TV.

MICRO CHIP—What's left in da bottom of da chip bag.

SEARCH ENGINE—What ya do when yer pickup truck dies.

MODEM—What ya did last fall to da hay fields.

SOFTWARE—Dem shitty plastic knives an' forks dey gives ya at da Horton.

CURSOR—Someone who swears.

COMPUTER WENT DOWN ON ME—No idea. Sounds like sumptin' disgustin'.

Clyde, a Newfie who has lived in a remote out-port all of his life, decides to make a once-in-a-life-time visit to St. John's.

While in the big city, he wanders into a depart-ment store where, for the first time in his life, he sees a full-length mirror.

"Lord tunderin' Jaysus!" he mutters to himself. "That's amazin'. Where da hell did they get a big full-sized picture of me brudder Garge?"

He buys the mirror and instructs the clerk to wrap it carefully for the long journey back to his outport village.

When he gets home, he tells his wife his amaz-ing story. "Imagine that," he says. "A full-size pic-ture of me brudder Garge sittin' there in a big store in St. John's."

The wife unwraps the mirror and stares into it intently for a few minutes. She then looks at Clyde and frowns. "You asshole!" she shouts. "You've bought a picture of an old whore."

A hoser goes to court to have his name changed.

"What's your name," asks the judge.

"Joe Shithead," the hoser says.

"What do you want your name changed to?" asks the judge.

"Bill," says the hoser.

"Why do you want to change your name to Bill?" asks the judge.

The hoser says, "Because I'm tired of people coming up to me and saying, 'Hello, Joe, what do you know?'"

Oswald is invited to dinner to meet his girlfriend's parents for the first time.

Shortly after they sit down to dinner, Oswald accidentally lets an enormous fart. The girlfriend's father hears it and looks down and says, "Rufus, get out from under the table!"

Oswald is relieved that the old man thinks that the dog farted and not him. But a few minutes later, as he leans across the table to pass a serving dish, he accidentally lets out another eye-watering ripper. The father looks down and says, "Rufus, get out from under the table!"

Again, Oswald is relieved that the dog is blamed for the loud fart and the stench that now permeates the room. But then, over coffee, Oswald reaches over to pass the sugar to his girlfriend, and he accidentally lets tear another loud, wet fart.

Q. How is a woman like a hurricane?

A. When they come, they are loud and wet, and when they leave, they take your house and car.

"Rufus," screams the father, "fer Chrissakes get out from under the table before this jerk shits all over you!"

A guy is standing in front of the gorilla enclosure at the Toronto Zoo. He notices that one of the gorillas is mimicking every movement he makes. When the guy wipes his brow, the gorilla wipes his brow. When the guy scratches his balls, the gorilla scratches his.

So, just for fun, the guy starts to make faces at the gorilla. He thumbs his nose at him, and the gorilla thumbs his nose back. He sticks his thumbs in his ears and waves his fingers at the gorilla, and the gorilla responds with the same gesture.

Then the guy makes a terrible mistake. He places his index finger on his right cheek and pulls downward, exposing his eyeball to the gorilla.

Q. What's a shih tzu?

A. A zoo with a really poor collection of animals.

The gorilla becomes enraged. He goes hysterical and jumps up and down and throws himself against the bars in his cage. Then he grabs the cage door and tugs it so hard that the hinges break off. The gorilla then jumps into the crowd and proceeds to beat the crap out of the guy who made the faces.

Eventually, a zookeeper arrives on the scene and forces the gorilla back into his cage. Then he asks the guy what happened.

"I was just making faces at the gorilla, and he was mimicking everything I did," replies the guy. "Then I exposed my eyeball to him and he went berserk."

"Oh," says the zookeeper, "you should never make that face to a gorilla. That means 'f**k off' in gorilla talk."

Three rules all men should follow to survive old age:
1. Never pass an unoccupied bathroom.
2. Never waste a good erection.
3. Never trust a fart.

The guy goes home to nurse his wounds and plot his revenge.

A few days later he returns to the zoo. This time he brings two knives with him and a cucumber, which he stuffs down the front of his pants. He goes up to the gorilla and hands him one of the knives. Then he starts making faces at him as he had done before. The gorilla mimics his every movement. Then suddenly, the guy undoes his fly, pulls out the cucumber and slices it up with the knife.

The gorilla watches intently, then raises one hand to his cheek, pulls it down and exposes his eyeball.

A frog calls a psychic hotline. The psychic tells him, "You will soon meet a beautiful young girl who will want to know everything about you."

"Wow, that's great," says the frog. "But tell me, where will I meet her? In the forest? On the beach? On the street? At a party?"

The psychic says, "No, in biology class."

A guy wearing a bright pink suit bumps into an old friend on the street in downtown Vancouver. "What's up with the pink suit?" his friend asks.

The guy in the suit looks embarrassed and says, "Terrible misunderstanding. I told my wife to go to Cox's and buy me a seersucker suit."

"So what happened?" says the friend.

The guy in the suit shrugs and says, "She went to Sears."

A newlywed Canadian couple return home after their honeymoon. The groom decides to let his new bride know who's the boss right from the start of their marriage, so he takes off his pants and throws them at her.

"Put those on," he says.

"I can't wear your pants," replies the bride.

"That's right," says the groom, "and don't you ever forget that."

The bride then takes off her panties and throws them at the groom. "Try those on," she says.

"I can't get into your panties," he replies.

"That's right," she says, "and you never will again if you don't promise to change your attitude."

Sarah, a Mennonite woman, is riding in her horse-drawn carriage through the streets of Kitchener, Ontario, when she is stopped by a cop who informs her that her carriage has a broken reflector.

"I'll get my husband, Jacob, to fix it," she tells the cop.

Then the cop notices that one of the reins on her carriage is looped around the horse's balls. "That's clearly animal abuse," says the cop.

Q. Did you hear about the airliner that crashed into a St. John's graveyard?

A. So far the Newfoundland Search and Rescue team has recovered 3000 bodies.

"I'll get my husband to fix that, too," Sarah assures the cop.

That evening, Sarah tells her husband that she was stopped by a cop and that he must fix the broken reflector.

"No problem," says Jacob.

"Oh yeah," adds Sarah, "the cop also said to be sure to disconnect the emergency brake as well."

A Newfie woman can't get her old car to start, so she calls a local mechanic to come over and take a look at it. The mechanic fiddles under the hood for a few minutes and eventually he gets the engine to turn over and spring to life.

> Q. What's the longest and hardest thing a Greek bride will get on her wedding day?
>
> A. Her new name.

"What's the problem?" says the woman.

"Crap in the carburetor," says the mechanic.

The Newfie woman frowns and says, "How often do I have to do that?"

Dirty Wally is standing on a street corner with a loaf of bread in one hand and has his other hand in his pocket.

A priest walks by and says, "Hello, Wally, I see you have the staff of life in your hand."

"That's right," Wally says.

"And what have you got in your other hand?" says the priest.

Wally replies, "A loaf of bread."

A Vancouver yuppie buys a brand new BMW. He picks it up from the dealer and drives it straight home to show it off to his wife. He parks the car in front of his house, and as he opens the door to get out, a taxi zooms by and shears off both the door and the guy's arm.

The yuppie jumps out of the car and starts yelling, "OH MY GOD! MY BMW IS WRECKED! MY BMW IS WRECKED!"

The taxi driver runs up to him and says, "Get a grip man—you're in shock. Your arm is torn off and you're losing a lot of blood."

Q. What's a hoser's idea of foreplay?

A. An elbow jabbed in the ribs of his old lady, followed by, "Hey, you awake?"

The yuppie looks down and sees that his arm is missing and yells, "OH MY GOD! MY ROLEX WATCH IS GONE! MY ROLEX WATCH IS GONE!"

An old couple is sitting on the sofa watching TV when suddenly the old lady turns to her husband and says, "Let's go upstairs and have sex."

The old guy thinks about it for a minute and replies, "I don't think I can do both."

A newlywed Mennonite couple goes to a Niagara Falls hotel for their honeymoon. The husband walks up to the front desk clerk and asks for a good room.

"Do you want the bridal?" asks the clerk.

"Nah," replies the groom, "I'll just hold her ears until she gets used to it."

A Mountie stops a guy driving through Brandon and says, "Sir, did you know that your wife fell out of your car three blocks back?"

"Thank God," the husband replies, "I thought I'd gone deaf."

A drunken Newfie decides to go ice fishing. He staggers out on the ice and begins drilling a hole. Suddenly he hears a loud voice booming overhead: "THERE ARE NO FISH DOWN THERE!"

"Lord tunderin' Jaysus, God is telling me where not ta fish! I better goes somewheres else," says the Newfie to himself.

So he moves his equipment to another spot on the ice and begins drilling a second hole. Again he hears the same voice, "THERE ARE NO FISH DOWN THERE, EITHER!"

The drunken Newfie looks up to the heavens and says, "Who are you? God?"

"NO, DOOFUS," replies the voice. "I'M THE ARENA MANAGER!"

10 Things You Won't Hear in Rural Alberta

1. No way. Not a chance. We don't keep any firearms in our house.

2. We never allow kids or dogs to ride in the back of our pickup—it's just not safe.

3. Actually, we're vegetarians.

4. No thanks, no beer for me. I think I'll just have a Perrier.

5. You know, I don't think duct tape will fix that.

6. Hey, man, how about trimmin' some of that fat off my steak.

7. Honey, don't forget to mail the cheque to the World Wildlife Fund.

8. No, I never touched her. Nope, not me. Hell, she's only 16.

9. Do you really think my gut is too big?

10. Nosiree, just the one beer is plenty enough for me. After all, I'm driving.

Three Vancouver women are having lunch together. One says, "I'm a YUPPIE, you know, Young Urban Professional."

The second woman says, "My husband and I are DINKS. Double Income No Kids."

The third woman, who is a bit older than the others, says, "I'm a WIFE. You know, Wash, Iron, F**k, Etc."

Prior to their wedding, a Muslim couple living in Canada visits their mullah for counselling. They are very religious people and do not want to violate strict Islamic rules for conduct on the day of their wedding, nor on their wedding night, either.

"We know it's an Islamic tradition for men to dance with men and women to dance with women," says the groom. "But we live in Canada now and we want to dance with each other on our wedding day. May we have your permission?"

"Absolutely not!" says the mullah. "Islamic law states that it is immoral for men to dance with women."

"What about after we're married?" asks the bride. "Can we dance together then?"

"No!" says the mullah. "It is absolutely forbidden."

"Okay," says the groom, "what about sex?"

"Of course," says the mullah, "after you're married, sex is allowed."

"What about different positions?" says the groom.

"No problem," says the mullah.

"Woman on top?" asks the groom.

"Sure," says the mullah.

"What about doggie style?" asks the groom.

"Yes, doggie style is fine," replies the mullah.

"Can we do group sex with all four of my other wives participating as well?" asks the groom.

> Q. How do you get 50 little old Canadian ladies to yell, "Aw, shit!"?
>
> A. Get another old lady to yell "BINGO!"

"Not a problem," says the mullah.

"And can we spice things up a bit when we're all together?" asks the groom. "Are we allowed to use some hot oil, or maybe play with vibrators, dildos, whips, chains, leather harnesses while we watch porno videos?"

"You may, indeed," says the mullah. "Go for it."

"Can we have sex standing up?" asks the groom.

"Absolutely not!" says the mullah.

"Why not?" asks the groom.

"Because," says the mullah, "that could lead to dancing."

Albert and Zelda are patients in an Edmonton mental hospital. One day they are walking by the hospital's swimming pool when Albert snaps. He jumps into the deep end, sinks to the bottom and remains motionless.

Zelda jumps in and saves him.

When the head psychiatrist hears of Zelda's heroic act, he orders her to be discharged, since he now thinks that she is mentally stable.

He calls her into his office to tell her the news. "I have good news and bad news," he says. "The good news is that because you responded rationally in a crisis and saved the life of another patient, I believe you're well on the road to recovery and should be discharged."

"What's the bad news?" asks Zelda.

"The bad news is that Albert hanged himself in his bathroom with the belt of his robe right after you saved him," says the psychiatrist. "I am sorry to inform you that he is dead."

"He didn't hang himself," replies Zelda. "I hung him there to dry. Now when can I go home?"

> Q. What's the difference between white nursery rhymes and black nursery rhymes?
>
> A. White nursery rhymes begin with "Once upon a time..." Black nursery rhymes begin with "You little mothers ain't gonna believe dis shit..."

Harold and Ralph are walking their dogs in Toronto's High Park. Harold tells Ralph that he has taught his dog to count. Ralph is skeptical, but Harold says he can prove it.

"Watch this," Harold says, pointing to his dog. "Woofy, go down to Grenadier Pond and count the ducks."

Woofy disappears down the path and returns a few minutes later and barks three times.

"That means there are three ducks on the pond," says Harold proudly. "Go check if you like."

Ralph goes down to the pond to check and comes back and confirms that there are, indeed, three ducks on the pond.

"Let's see if he can do it again," says Ralph.

So Harold sends Woofy down another path to the pond, and when he returns he barks five times. When Ralph investigates, to his amazement he finds that there are in fact five ducks swimming on the pond.

> Q. How does an old gay guy keep his youth?
>
> A. By giving him lots of cash and expensive gifts.

"Make him do it one more time," says Ralph. "I still think he's faking it."

So Woofy is sent down another trail to a different part of the pond, but this time when he returns, he runs up to Harold and starts humping his shinbone, then he picks up a stick and starts running in circles, shaking it in the air.

"I think your dog has flipped out," says Ralph.

"Not at all," replies Harold. "He's just telling me that there are more f**king ducks down there than you can shake a stick at."

A drunk staggers into a toilet stall at the back of a Winnipeg bar. A few minutes later, a loud scream is heard from inside the men's room. The bartender runs in to investigate.

"Everything all right in there, sir?" the bartender yells through the bathroom door.

"No, I'm not all right," says the drunk. "I'm in agony. This is terrible."

"What happened?" asks the bartender.

"I was just sitting here on the toilet," says the drunk. "And when I reached over to flush it, something came up from below and squeezed my balls."

> Q. What's the difference between a fat woman and an old maid?
>
> A. One is trying to diet, and the other is dying to try it.

The bartender opens the door and says, "Look again, you drunken idiot, you're not on a toilet, you're sitting on our mop bucket."

A sex therapist in Fredericton is giving a hoser a word association test.

The therapist says, "What do you think of when I say the word 'chair'?"

"Sex!" replies the hoser.

The therapist asks, "How about the word 'car'?"

"Sex!" says the patient.

The therapist then asks, "What do you think of when I say the word 'tree'?"

"Sex!" replies the hoser.

"And what about the word 'vagina'?" asks the therapist.

"Saskatchewan!" replies the patient.

It's graduation day at a high school in one of the poorest 'hoods in Scarborough.

The principal is addressing the graduating class in the school auditorium, and explaining that everyone in the senior year is eligible to graduate—except one kid named Leroy. Leroy is the school's star basketball player, the class clown, and the worst behaved kid in the school. By no small coincidence, he is also very popular with the other students.

Q. What do you call a horny Inuit guy?

A. He's a frigid midget with a rigid digit.

When the students hear that Leroy won't graduate, they get agitated and start yelling and screaming at the principal. Then they all start stomping their feet and chanting, "GIVE LEROY ANOTHER CHANCE! GIVE LEROY ANOTHER CHANCE!"

The principal, sensing that the situation could turn ugly and that he could have a major incident on his hands, calls Leroy up to the podium.

"So, Leroy," he says, "here's what we're going to do. I'll give you another chance to graduate with the rest of the kids if you can correctly answer a few questions that will prove to me that you actually learned something during your time at this school. Okay?"

Leroy nods in agreement.

"Leroy, what's four times eight?" says the principal.

A hush falls over the auditorium. Leroy thinks for several seconds and then replies, "34!"

The principal says, "No, I'm sorry Leroy, that's not correct, I'm afraid—"

Suddenly all the kids in the audience jump to their feet and begin screaming: "GIVE LEROY ANOTHER CHANCE! GIVE LEROY ANOTHER CHANCE!"

The principal calms everyone down and tells them to go back to their seats and says, "Okay, Leroy, we'll give it another try. Leroy, what's 12 plus 15?"

Leroy thinks for a moment and then shouts, "28!"

Before the principal can utter a word, all the students are on their feet again, chanting: "GIVE LEROY ANOTHER CHANCE! GIVE LEROY ANOTHER CHANCE!"

Q. What causes you to fart?

A. Farts occur when a turd in your bowels is honking for the right of way.

Once again, the principal calms everyone down, and they all return to their seats. Fearing the situation could turn into a full-blown riot, he calls Leroy over again and says, "All right, Leroy, this is positively your last chance to graduate. I'll ask you one more question, and if you don't get it right, that is it. Okay, Leroy, what's five plus five?"

Again, a hush falls over the auditorium as Leroy thinks about his answer. Suddenly, he blurts out "10!"

And the students all jump out of their seats again and scream, "GIVE LEROY ANOTHER CHANCE! GIVE LEROY ANOTHER CHANCE!"

A senile old guy is sitting in his doctor's office. The doctor explains that he needs to do some tests. "I'll require a blood sample, a urine sample, and a stool sample," says the doctor.

Q. What's the German word for Vaseline?

A. Vienerslide.

"How am I going to do all that?" asks the old man.

His wife yells from the waiting room, "Just give him a pair of your underpants!"

A hoser working on a construction site phones his wife in a panic and says, "I've had a terrible accident—I've sawed off my finger!"

"The whole finger?" asks the wife.

"No," says the hoser, "the one next to it."

Dave and Fred are playing golf in Banff. Suddenly, Dave whacks his ball into the woods and finds it in a patch of pretty yellow buttercups. Trying to get his ball back in play, he ends up thrashing almost every buttercup in the patch.

All of a sudden…POOF! In a flash and puff of smoke, a little old woman appears. She says, "I'm Mother Nature! Do you know how long it took me to make those buttercups? Just for doing what you have done, I'll see that you won't have any butter for your popcorn for the rest of your life. What's more, you won't have any butter for your toast for the rest of your life. And as a matter of fact, I'm so angry with you that I'll make sure you'll never have any butter for anything for the rest of your life!"

Then POOF!…she disappears. After Dave recovers from the shock, he hollers to his friend, "Fred, where are you?"

Fred yells back, "I'm over here looking for my ball in the pussy willows."

Dave shouts back, "Fer Chrissakes, Fred, don't swing your golf club. Whatever you do, don't swing your golf club!"

A guy with a terrible stutter marries an epileptic woman. They are in a hotel room on their wedding night and just as they are about to get into bed, the bride has an epileptic fit. The groom panics and dials 911.

"C-ca-ca-come quick," he says. "Sh-sh-she's havin' a t-t-terrible f-f-fit!"

The 911 emergency team arrives and sees the woman lying naked on the bed rocking back and forth and flailing her arms and legs in the air. They ask the guy what he would like them to do.

"Ta-ta-ta-take th-th-this rope and ti-ti-ti-tie her arms to the head b-b-bo-board!" screams the guy.

"Now ta-ta-take th-th-this other rope and ti-ti-ti-tie her legs to the f-f-f-foot b-b-bo-board."

The 911 team follow his instructions and tie the woman down. Then the husband takes off all of his clothes and mounts her.

"O-k-k-kay now," he says, "C-cu-cu-cut her loose!"

A Toronto woman says to her doctor, "Kiss me!"

"I can't," replies the doctor. "It's against all the rules of professional conduct."

"Aw, c'mon, doctor," says the woman, "kiss me!"

"I can't," replies the doctor. "The Ontario College of Physicians has strict rules against—"

"Aw, just one little kiss," says the woman.

"Look, lady," replies the doctor, "I shouldn't even be screwing you."

Two Newfies, Clyde and Shamus, are out fishing in a rented boat. They are having a great day, hauling in one fish after another. It's getting late, so Clyde turns to Shamus and says, "This spot is fantastic. We should mark 'er so we can find it again."

"That's a good idea, Clyde," says Shamus. "I've got just the ting here to do it."

Shamus pulls a small can of paint and a brush out of his tackle box and proceeds to paint a large black "X" on the side of the boat.

"That won't work," says Clyde.

"I don't see why not," replies Shamus.

"Tink about it," says Clyde. "We might not get the same boat next time."

A therapist in a Canadian mental hospital is working with a sex offender by drawing little pictures on a blackboard and asking the patient to make word associations.

"What does this remind you of?" the therapist asks, pointing to a drawing he made of a tree.

"Sex!" replies the patient.

"And this?" asks the therapist as he draws a picture of a maple leaf.

> Q. How come blind people seldom take up skydiving?
>
> A. Because it scares the shit out of their dogs.

"Sex!" replies the patient.

And so it goes. The therapist draws pictures of a flower, a horse, a house, and when he asks the patient what each remind him of, he replies, "Sex, sex, sex!"

Finally the therapist puts down his chalk and says to the man, "It's hopeless, you're obsessed with sex."

"I'm obsessed with sex?" replies the patient. "You're the one who's drawing all the dirty pictures!"

A Jewish guy in Montréal picks up a hooker and negotiates her price down to just $20. The next morning he discovers that he has crabs. So that night he drives around the same neighbourhood until he finds the hooker who gave them to him.

Q. How do you spot the Canadian guy in a crowd when you're travelling abroad?

A. He looks exactly the same as all the Americans, except he's only carrying one camera.

"Hey, bitch," he yells when he sees her, "you gave me crabs."

The hooker replies, "So what do you expect for $20, lobster?"

A doctor says to a patient, "I've got good news and bad news. The good news is that your penis is going to grow four inches longer and it will expand by two inches in circumference."

"What's the bad news?" replies the patient.

The doctor says, "It's malignant."

In downtown Montréal, the parents of a three-year-old are concerned because their son has never uttered a single word in either French or English in his young life. They eventually take the boy to a pediatrician who tells them not to worry. "This is normal," he says. "He'll speak when he is ready."

The kid remains speechless until he is five years old. Then one evening at dinner, the kid turns to his mother and says, "Fer Chrissakes, Ma, this damn poutine you've given me tastes like shit."

The parents stare at him in stunned disbelief. "Why haven't you said anything before?" the mother asks.

The kid replies, "Up until now, everything's been fine."

An old woman gets on an elevator in a Toronto highrise apartment building and starts to ride down. The elevator stops, the door opens and a very attractive and elegantly dressed young woman gets on, and the scent of expensive perfume fills the air. She glares at the old lady and says, "Captivation by Hermes, $200 an ounce at Holt Renfrew."

The elevator door opens again a few floors down and a second well-dressed woman gets on and she, too, smells of expensive perfume. This woman also looks down at the old lady and says, "Chanel No. 5, $150 an ounce at the Bay."

The old lady reaches her floor, and as she steps off the elevator, she glares at the two young women, bends over, lets out an enormous fart and says, "Cabbage, 79 cents a pound at Loblaws."

A young girl with a speech impediment is having a medical exam. The doctor places the stethoscope on her chest and says, "Big breaths."

"Yeth!" the girl replies. "And I'm only sixth-theen!"

An 89-year-old lady in Swift Current tells her doctor that she wants an HIV test. The doctor asks her why she thinks she needs it, considering her advanced age.

> Q. What happens when a lawyer takes Viagra?
>
> A. His head swells up, and he grows fatter and taller.

She says, "I heard the nice man on the CBC say that everyone should be tested after having annual sex."

A groom is standing at the altar with a big, stupid grin on his face. His best man turns to him and says, "I know you're happy to be getting married, but why are you grinning from ear to ear?"

"Last night I got the best blow job I've ever had in my entire life," says the groom. "And in a few minutes I will marry the lovely woman who gave it to me."

At the back of the church, where the bride is preparing to walk down the aisle, the maid of honour notices that she, too, has a big smile on her face. "I know you're happy to be a bride, but what's so amusing?" she asks.

The bride leans over and whispers, "Last night I gave the last hummer I'll ever have to give in my entire life."

A Canadian guy and an American are talking in a bar. "You know what we say in America?" says the Yank. "We say that, sure, Canada is a nice country, but once you take away the clean air, the friendly people and the strong beer, what have you got?"

The Canadian replies, "America!"

Edna and Earl are a couple of hosers living in rural Ontario. They are sitting in their backyard one evening having a few drinks.

"I've noticed that your ass is getting really, really big," says Earl. "Why, I bet it's bigger than our barbeque here. Yup. I'd say your arse is at least five or ten inches bigger than this here ol' grill."

Later that night in bed, Earl gets a little horny and starts making moves on old Edna.

"Forget it," she says, pushing him away. "There's no way I'm gonna fire up this big-ass grill for just one tiny little sausage!"

A guy in a posh Toronto hotel bar is admiring a woman sitting next to him wearing the tightest pants he has ever seen.

"How do you get into those pants?" he asks her.

"Well," replies the woman, "you could start by buying me a drink."

A guy bumps into his ex-wife one day in downtown Regina and after a brief conversation he says, "Why don't we go back to my place and tear one off the way we used to?"

"Over my dead body!" the ex replies.

He says, "Like I said, just the way we used to."

A hoser marries an identical twin, and within six months he goes to court seeking a divorce.

"What's your problem?" asks the judge.

"My wife's twin sister is always staying over at our house," the hoser says, "and since she and my wife look so much alike I often wind up having sex with her by mistake."

"There must be some difference between them," says the judge.

"You bet there is," says the hoser. "That's why I want the divorce."

An English guy meets a French Canadian woman in a Montréal bar. They get quite drunk and begin talking about sex. The guy eventually asks her, "How many men have you slept with?"

> Q. What's worse than a male chauvinist pig?
>
> A. A woman who won't do what she's told.

"Zat ees my business," she replies.

"Sorry," says the guy, "I didn't know you made a living from it."

An old couple in Nova Scotia is sitting on the front porch in their rocking chairs.

After a long silence, the old guy turns to his wife and says, "Ma, I think I've got an erection."

After an even longer silence, the old lady says, "So what do you think you're going to do with it, Pa?"

There's another long silence. Eventually the old man replies, "I dunno."

The old guy sits quietly for a while longer and then turns to his wife and says, "You know, I've been thinkin'..."

"Ya, Pa?" says the wife, hopefully.

"Yeah," says the old man. "I've got an idea."

"What is it, Pa?" says the wife in eager anticipation.

"I'm thinkin'," says the old man, "now that I've got the wrinkles out, it might be a good idea to go upstairs and wash it."

A hoser with a terrible stutter goes to his doctor and says, "You g-g-gotta h-h-help me t-t-to ge-ge-get rid of th-th-this d–d-dreadful im-im-imp-pedi-ment!"

The doctor gives the guy a complete physical, and when he notices that he has an enormously oversized penis, he says, "Look, there's your problem, your penis is too big. We'll just cut that sucker off, and I guarantee that your stutter will go away."

"A-a-are you s-s-sure?" says the patient.

"I'm absolutely certain," replies the doctor.

So the hoser has the operation, and it is a huge success. The doctor cuts the hoser's penis off and his stutter goes away. Soon after, the hoser is back out in bars meeting women every night, but he can't get laid because he only has a tiny stump. Before long, he goes back to see the same doctor.

"I want you to re-attach my dick," he says.

The doctor replies, "Y-y-you can j-j-just g-g-go t-t-to h-h-hell."

A restaurant owner in Vancouver hires an efficiency expert for advice on how to streamline his business. The consultant comes in and follows the employees around with a stopwatch for several days and then leaves to prepare his report.

Meanwhile, the restaurant owner is anxious to get feedback from his employees on how their interviews went with the consultant. He begins with his headwaiter.

"He has some really good ideas," says the waiter. "For instance, you see these two spoons that I have in my breast pocket? The consultant told each waiter to always carry two spoons in their breast pocket like this. This way, whenever a customer asks for another bread roll, we don't have to run to the kitchen for a pair of tongs. We can just use these two spoons to pick up the roll from the tray and put it on the customer's plate."

Q. Do you know what happens at a birthday party for a bulimic?

A. The cake jumps out of the girl.

"I see," says the restaurant owner. "It's much more sanitary, too. You never have to touch the food with your hands."

"That's right," says the waiter. "And the consultant said that each waiter could save as much as 20 minutes per shift."

"Amazing," says the restaurant owner. "And what else did he recommend?"

"You see this string tied to my belt?" replies the waiter, pointing to a piece of string with one end tied to his belt and the other end tucked into the fly of his pants. "The consultant is very concerned about the amount of time the waiters spend in the bathroom washing their hands and clowning around wasting time at the sink.

"So he told each of us to tie a piece of string to our penis. This way, whenever a waiter needs to take a pee, he just has to undo his zipper, pull out his dick with the string, and aim it without actually touching it.

"We don't need to waste time washing our hands after we pee, because we haven't actually touched ourselves. The consultant says we can each save 18 minutes in every shift if all the waiters use the string method of peeing."

Q. What is 10 metres long and smells of urine?

A. The conga line in a nursing home.

"One question," says the restaurant manager. "Once you've pulled it out with the string, how do you put it back in?"

"Well," said the waiter, "the efficiency guy wasn't clear on that. But here's what I do...you see these two spoons in my breast pocket..."

Two guys are sitting in their retirement home in Victoria talking about old age.

"I'm 93 years old, and I ache from head to toe," says one.

"Oh yeah?" says the other. "Well, I'm 97 years old, and I feel like a newborn baby."

"How so?" asks the first guy.

"I've got no hair and no teeth," he replies, "and I think I just peed my pants."

In a Vancouver bistro, Sandra and Sherry are talking about their boyfriends. Sandra says, "I believe I've found the secret of true happiness."

"What is it?" says Sherry.

"My secret is that I now have two boyfriends," says Sandra. "The first one is unbelievably handsome, smart, sensitive, considerate, caring, attentive and reliable."

Q. What goes VROOM, SCREECH, VROOM, SCREECH?

A. A Newfie driving through a flashing red light.

"So why do you need a second one?" asks Sherry.

Sandra replies, "The second one is straight."

"Is it true," the young Newfie girl asked her mother, "that babies come out of the same place where boys put their thingies in?"

"Yes, that's right," replies her mother, realizing that the time may have come to explain the facts of life to her daughter.

"Okay, then," says the daughter, "I have another question. When I have a baby, won't it knock my teeth out?"

The Pope goes on his holidays. He flies from Rome to Canada and rents a beach house on Vancouver Island where he hopes he can relax incognito. One day he goes for a walk and accidentally ends up on one of the island's nude beaches. The sight of dozens of beautiful, naked women is too much for His Holiness, who suddenly realizes that he has a huge erection.

"Aw Jesa Christ!" the Pope mutters to himself. "Ima da heada da whola Catholica church anda hera I ama walkina arounda witha hardona da siza da state of Florida."

So the Pope runs behind some bushes and relieves himself.

A few weeks later, back at the Vatican, the Pope accepts a long-distance telephone call from a strange guy with a rural Canadian accent. "Your Holiness," the voice says, "I saw you abusin' yourself on a Vancouver Island beach. I took some pictures of you with my Nikon digital camera that I would like to sell to you."

"How mucha you want?" asks the Pope.

"Ten thousand dollars," says the voice. "For that, I'll send you the camera and the memory card with all the photos. And if you don't pay up, I'm sellin' these disgustin' pictures of you to the highest bidder."

The Pope agrees to pay the man, and a few days later he receives the camera and the memory card with the incriminating photos. He destroys the memory card, but because the camera is a Nikon, he decides to keep it on a shelf in his office.

Several months later, a group of Canadian dignitaries is given an audience with the Pope. One of the visitors notices the camera and asks him if he is a photographer. "No," replies the Pope, "I justa recently boughta that camera."

According to a recent Canadian survey, 95 percent of women who use personal vibrators during their pregnancy will give birth to children who stutter.

"It's a nice one," says the Canadian official. "How much did you pay for it?"

"It'sa longa story," replies the Pope. "But it enda upa costa mea 10,000 Canadian dollars."

"Wow!" says the Canadian guy. "Ten thousand dollars! Someone must have seen you coming!"

A hoser calls up a plumber and says, "I've gotta leak in my sink."

The plumber replies, "Don't worry about it, I do it all the time."

A Canadian businessman calls all four of his employees together one day and tells them that business is bad and that he will have to let one of them go.

The company's only black employee says, "It can't be me, 'cause I'm the only visible minority you've got on staff."

The female employee says, "You can't fire me, because I'm the only woman, and I'll go to the Canadian Human Rights Commission and lodge a complaint, and I'm sure I'll get re-instated."

The oldest guy on staff says, "If you fire me, I'll get a lawyer and sue you for age discrimination."

Then all eyes turn to the remaining employee, a young white guy sitting quietly in the corner. He looks sheepishly at the others and says, "I think I might be gay!"

An impotent guy goes to a top urologist in Toronto for a consultation. The doctor examines him and tells him that he has severely damaged the muscle tissue in his penis and that the only hope for him to ever get an erection again is to try radical, new experimental surgery. He explains that the surgery involves grafting muscles from an elephant's trunk into his penis.

"It'll not only give you terrific boners," says the doctor, "but it will also make your penis six times longer."

The guy decides to have the surgery.

A few weeks after the operation, the guy takes his girlfriend out in the hope that he will be able to try out his new, revitalized organ. They are sitting in a restaurant having dinner when all of a sudden the guy gets a huge erection. His penis gets so big that he has to undo his fly to relieve the discomfort.

But then, to his horror, his penis suddenly rises out of his pants, reaches up to the table, grabs a dinner roll, and disappears with it back into his pants.

"Wow, that's fantastic!" says the girlfriend. "Can you make it take another one?"

Q. Did you hear about the new woman-run Canadian courier service called UPMS?

A. They deliver your parcel whenever the hell they feel like it, and you'd better not complain if it's late.

"Oh, probably," replies the guy, grimacing in pain. "But I'm not sure I can stand having another dinner roll shoved up my ass."

A Jewish widow in Montréal has her husband cremated and takes the urn home with her. She empties it on the kitchen table and proceeds to talk to her departed husband as she runs her fingers through his ashes.

"Irving," she says, "remember how you promised me a condo on Miami Beach? Well, I want you to know that I bought one with your insurance money.

"And Irving, remember how you promised me a BMW sports car? You should know that I finally bought myself one of those, too, with your insurance money," she adds, while pushing Irving's ashes together in one large pile.

"Oh, and Irving, how about that mink coat you promised me but never got around to buying for me? Well, I bought a gorgeous full-length one with your insurance money. And you should know that I also bought a diamond ring, some new furniture, a plasma TV, and I've booked that trip to Europe that we planned but never actually got around to taking…all with your insurance money.

"Oh, yes, and one more thing, Irving. Remember that blow job I promised you, but never gave you? Well, get ready, 'cause here it comes!"

Nike is introducing a new running shoe in the Canadian market that is designed specifically for lesbians. It's called the Dykie. Each shoe has a really long tongue and it only takes one finger to get it off.

A vagrant goes into a Calgary bar and tells the bartender that he has no money, but that he will go on stage and fart out the tune of "Canadian Sunset" in exchange for a free beer. The bartender thinks his customers might find this entertaining, so he agrees to take him up on his offer.

The vagrant mounts the stage and announces that he will fart out the chorus of "Canadian Sunset," and the crowd cheers enthusiastically as he drops his pants and bends over. But instead of farting, the guy accidentally takes a dump on the stage. The crowd is grossed out by this spectacle and starts yelling and booing. Many of the people get up and leave in disgust.

> Q. Why is the local liquor store the most important store in rural New Brunswick?
>
> A. Because the worst thing that can happen to someone in New Brunswick is to wake up sober one morning and realize, "Holy shit, I live in rural New Brunswick!"

"What the hell!" says the bartender. "You said you were going to fart out a song, not crap on my stage."

"Gimme a break," says the vagrant. "Even Celine Dion has to clear her throat before she sings."

A 72-year-old Toronto man rushes to the hospital when he hears that his 21-year-old wife has been taken to the maternity ward. A nurse greets him with the news that his wife has just given birth to twins.

"That just proves what I've always said," says the old man. "Even though there's snow on the roof, there's still fire in the furnace."

"If that's true," replies the nurse, "Then I think you'd better change your filter—'cause both your kids came out black."

Esmeralda, a young music scholar, is touring the Royal Conservatory of Music in Toronto. As she is walking down a corridor, she hears someone playing a piano in one of the studios. She observes that the music is expertly played by a very gifted musician.

She approaches the pianist and says, "I have two degrees in classical music, yet I cannot identify a single tune you've played." The pianist, a young man named Devon, explains that the compositions are his own and that he has not enjoyed much success with them.

Q. Why do women call the thing they have every month a "period"?

A. Because "mad cow disease" was already taken.

The two strike up a conversation and discover that they are both from the same 'hood in Scarborough. Devon expresses his frustration in not being able to get his type of music accepted in Canadian society. "They expect me to just be a rapper or some shit like that," he says. "There's no place in this country for guys who play classy stuff like mine."

Devon continues playing. Esmeralda listens intently and cannot believe that such an extraordinary talent has gone unrecognized for so long. "Those last two melodies were exceptional," she says. "By the way, what do you call them?"

Devon replies, "That first one I call, 'I Love You So Goddamn Much I Could Shit.' And the one I'm playin' now I call, 'It's Midnight in Malvern and I'm Really Pissed Off 'Cause I Ain't Got No More Weed'..."

"Oh, my God!" says Esmeralda. "Now I understand where you've gone wrong...your titles are too long!"

Devon then goes for an audition to work as a piano player in an upscale Toronto bar. The owner is bowled over by his virtuosity at the keyboard. "But how come I've never heard any of this music before?" he asks Devon.

Devon explains that he composes all of his own music and that he has not enjoyed much success with it. "That first one I played for you is one o' my favourites," he says. "I call it, 'If I Could Only Come Again, I'd Come All Over You.' An' this tune is called, 'She'll Be Comin' Like a Fountain When She Comes'..."

"Christ almighty!" says the owner, "Are you crazy? This is a respectable bar. We have a nice, well-heeled clientele. I can't let you offend my customers with language like that."

Devon admits that his song titles have caused problems for him in the past, so he promises the bar owner that if he gives him a chance he will just play his music and never mention the names of his songs to the customers. The bar owner agrees and hires him on a trial basis.

Devon is a huge hit with the customers. Everyone loves his music, and he is careful with his language and never tells anyone the titles of his songs.

Then one night it happens. He's playing his music, having a few drinks, smoking a little weed and feeling pretty good when a middle-aged woman comes up to him and casually says, "Say, young man, do you know your fly is undone and your dick is hanging out?"

Without thinking, Devon replies, "Do I know it? Christ, lady, I wrote it!"

Old Hector finds out that he has cancer and only has six months to live. He is walking down the street one day with his son when he bumps into an old friend.

When the friend asks Hector how he is, he replies, "Not good. I've just found out that I have AIDS and only have six months to live."

After the friend departs, the son asks his father why he told one of his oldest friends that he has AIDS when he really has cancer.

"One simple reason," replies Hector. "When I'm gone, I don't want him banging your mother."

A Canadian doctor has a terrible argument with his wife. "You're a shitty mother, a crummy wife and a lousy lay!" he screams as he leaves the house one morning.

That evening, when he enters the house, he finds his wife having sex with some guy on the sofa.

"What the hell do you think you're doing!" he yells.

She replies, "Getting a second opinion."

How Canada Got its Name

Way back in the mists of time, long before Confederation, members of the British Parliament decided to name the new land they'd recently plundered Cold North Dominion, or CND for short.

When the British governor of the new territory first presented the name to a group of early settlers, the conversation went as follows:

"C, eh?" said one of the settlers.

"N, eh?" said another.

"D, eh?" said a third.

"Yes!" said the governor. "I like that spelling even better: C-A-N-A-D-A. And it's much easier to pronounce this way, too."

Did you hear about the young Canadian woman who was so uptight and paranoid that she put a condom on her vibrator?

Three old guys are sitting on a park bench in Victoria. "Old age is a terrible thing," one guy says. "My hands shake so bad that this morning when I was shaving, I cut my face to ratshit."

The second guy says, "I know what you mean. The other day I was working in my garden, and my hand was shaking so much that I accidentally cut the heads off all my flowers."

The third guy laughs and says, "That's nothing. My hands are so shaky that this morning I was standing at the toilet trying to take a pee and I came three times."

A Newfie family is watching TV. The wife leans over to her husband and says, "Let's S-E-N-D the K-I-D-S out B-A-C-K to P-L-A-Y so we can f**k!"

A middle-aged woman in Kelowna is getting her first golf lesson. The golf pro says to her, "Just grasp the club like you would your husband's penis."

The woman does what the pro says and hits the ball a short distance down the fairway. The pro watches and says, "Okay, that's a good start. But next time, take the club out of your mouth, grasp it with your hands, and we'll try for distance."

A severely constipated hoser is sitting on the toilet in a public washroom. He's grunting and groaning and pushing as hard as he can, but the turtle won't even poke its head out.

Suddenly, he hears footsteps—someone walking, then running into the stall next to him. The runner slams the door shut and lets loose a stunning array of dreadful farting and shitting noises.

The constipated guy says, "I'd give 100 dollars if I could do what you just did."

"No, you wouldn't," replies the other guy. "I didn't get my pants down in time."

Sister Bernadette lives in a convent in downtown Montréal that is located near a liquor store. One day she goes in and purchases a bottle of Canadian Club.

"I'm sorry," says the clerk, "but I'm a good Catholic. I can't sell whiskey to a nun."

"It's not for me," says Bernadette. "It's for my Mother Superior. The rye helps to relieve her dreadful constipation."

So the clerk sells Bernadette the whiskey. But later that day when he's walking home, he sees her staggering down the street.

"You're drunk!" the clerk says. "That's disgusting. I thought you told me that the whiskey was for the Mother Superior's constipation?"

"It is," replies Bernadette. "When she sees how loaded I am, she's gonna shit herself."

A farmer from rural Ontario takes his pet goose with him when he goes to visit Toronto.

He decides go out one night to see a movie, but he doesn't want to leave the goose alone in his hotel room, so he takes it with him to the movie theatre. He is stopped at the door by an usher who tells him that no pets are allowed. So the farmer steps outside, hides the goose down the front of his pants, and re-enters the theatre.

Halfway through the movie, the goose starts squirming around, so the farmer undoes his fly so the goose can stick his head out for some air. A few minutes later, the woman sitting beside him turns to her friend and whispers, "The guy sitting next to me has got his penis out."

"Try to ignore it," replies the friend.

"I can't," says the woman. "It's eating my popcorn."

Two midgets in Vancouver pick up a couple of hookers. The men take them to a sleazy hotel and rent adjoining rooms.

One can't get an erection, so he spends the whole night lying in bed listening to his friend in the next room. All night long he hears him huffing and puffing and yelling out, "One, two, three, ugh! One, two, three, ugh!"

The next day, the two men meet up.

"I had a terrible night," says the first midget. "I couldn't get it up."

"I had even worse luck," says the other one, "I couldn't get up on the bed."

Bell Canada hires a Newfie and an Italian guy on the same day. They are sent out to work with a crew installing telephone poles along the Trans-Canada Highway in Ontario. At the end of the day, the foreman asks the Newfie how many poles he put in.

"Three," replies the Newfie.

"Three?" says the foreman. "The Italian guy put in 18!"

"Yeah," says the Newfie, "But look how far his stick outta da ground."

A priest and a rabbi are riding in a car in downtown Montréal. Suddenly their car is involved in a terrible accident. As they climb out of the wreckage, the priest crosses himself, and to his amazement, he looks over and sees his rabbi friend crossing himself as well.

"My God!" says the priest. "You're crossing yourself! You've finally seen the light!"

"Crossing myself? Oh hell, no, that's not what I was doing," says the rabbi. "I was just taking inventory. You know, spectacles, testicles, wallet and watch!"

A 95-year-old guy goes into Shoppers Drug Mart for Viagra. After the pharmacist counts out the pills, the old guy asks him to cut each one into four pieces.

"It won't do you much good if you take it in such small doses," warns the druggist.

"Oh hell, I don't want it for sex," says the old guy. "I just want to be sure I can make it stick out far enough so that I don't pee on my shoes any more."

A guy walks into a Cape Breton bar with an octopus under his arm. He announces to everyone, "Ten dollars says that no one here has a musical instrument that this octopus can't play."

A musician in the bar's band gives his guitar to the octopus. The octopus takes it and effortlessly plays the opening bars of "O Canada." The owner of the octopus pockets an easy $10.

Another musician in the band comes forward with his harmonica. The octopus takes it and plays a spirited version of "Snowbird." Another easy 10 bucks.

Then the bartender, an elderly Scottish man, disappears out back and returns a few minutes later with a set of bagpipes. "If that octopus can play this instrument, I'll give you $50," he says.

The octopus takes a long look at the bagpipe. He lifts it up and turns it over and inspects the instrument from every angle.

"What's the matter?" says his owner, "Can you play it or not?"

"Play it?" says the octopus. "Once I figure out how to get these stupid plaid pyjamas off it, I'm gonna screw it."

A trucker is stopped at a red light on a street in St. John's. A Newfie woman pulls up behind him, jumps out of her car, runs up to him, knocks on his window and says, "Hi, I'm Wilma, I just thought I'd tell you that you're losing some of your load."

The trucker ignores her and drives on.

At the next red light, the same woman pulls up behind the trucker, jumps out of her car again, runs up to the driver, knocks on the window and says, "Hi, remember me? I'm Wilma, I thought you should know that you're still losing some of your load."

This time the driver shakes his fist at the woman and drives off.

At yet another red light, the truck driver looks in his mirror and sees the woman is still behind him, and to his amazement, he watches as she gets out of her car a third time, runs up to him and says, "Hi, remember me? I'm Wilma, and you're still losing some of your load."

At the next traffic light the trucker sees that the woman is still right behind him. He is getting pretty fed up with her nonsense, so this time he gets out of his vehicle, runs back to Wilma's car and motions her to roll down her window.

He says, "Hi, I'm Ralph. I've taken enough of this crap from you, Wilma. In case you haven't noticed, it's winter in Newfoundland, and I'm driving a salt truck."

A flasher goes up to a woman sitting on the Toronto subway, opens his coat and exposes himself in front of her.

"Did you see my gorgeous pink Hummer with its beautiful hardtop?" says the flasher after he closes his coat.

"No," replies the woman. "I just saw a little Volkswagen with two flat tires."

A dentist in Moncton is about to pull out a patient's tooth. "Do you want a needle to numb the pain?" he asks the man.

"I'm afraid of needles," replies the patient. "I don't want one."

"How 'bout some gas to put you under?" asks the dentist.

"No way," says the guy. "I'm allergic to gas."

The dentist then hands the patient a pill and says, "Try one of these."

"What is it?" says the guy.

"Viagra," says the dentist.

"What good will Viagra do?" asks the patient. "Will it ease the pain?"

"No, it won't," replies the dentist. "But at least it will give you something to hold onto while I yank this tooth."

An American couple from Montana decide to go to Canada for a vacation. They drive north across the border, stop at the dinosaur park in Drumheller, then continue their journey northeast.

After driving for a couple of days, they realize they are lost. They eventually end up on the outskirts of a large community, and as soon as they spot a pedestrian, they pull over to ask directions.

"Hey man, we're kinda lost," says the American. "Can you tell us where we are?"

"Yup," says the guy. "You're in Saskatoon, Saskatchewan,"

The American turns to his wife and says, "Boy, we're really in trouble now, the locals don't even speak English."

A French Canadian, a Pakistani, a Jamaican and a hoser from rural Ontario are walking along a beach together. The Jamaican guy finds an urn in the sand, picks it up, uncaps it, and out pops a genie.

"Thank you for releasing me from my prison," says the genie. "To show my appreciation, I would like to grant each of you one wish."

The Jamaican goes first. "I wish that all my brothers and sisters in the world could be reunited in Africa, where we could all live together in peace and harmony with nature."

"So be it," says the genie.

The French Canadian is next. "For my wish, I want all the French-speaking people in the world to return to our beloved mother country of France, where we will live together in isolation from the inferior cultures and races on the planet."

"Your wish is granted," says the genie.

The Pakistani is next. "I want all the Pakistanis in the world to be reunited with their fellow Muslims back in Pakistan, where we, too, will live together in peace and prosper."

"So be it," says the genie.

Then the hoser speaks up. "Before I ask for my wish," he says, "let me see if I've got this straight. All the blacks are going back to Africa, the French Canadians are all going to move to France, and the Muslims are all returning to Pakistan. Is that what I'm hearing?"

"That's right," replies the genie.

"Well, in that case," says the hoser, "I'd just like a nice, cold Molson Canadian."